How to Run Successful Projects II
The Silver Bullet

Here's what people have said about the first edition of 'How To Run Successful Projects' ...

"As soon as the book arrived I spent some time reading and browsing. It is a great, possibly the best, all round writing on the subject. It seems like one's life as well as work could be much improved by this publication. I expect it will be a constant companion during much of the work carried out by my company."
David J Hall of David J Hall Software Ltd.

"A practical, enlightened approach to the black art of Project Management. Fergus O'Connell's book forces you to focus on the essentials of your project, the issues that will make or break it. Plus, if it doesn't bring a smile to your face in the process, then you are probably already dead and nobody has bothered to tell you."
Dermot Bolger, Test and Support Manager, Telecom Ireland Software.

"An excellent background to project management, with a lot of practical suggestions from someone who clearly loves his work, and thinks carefully about it. It is a good introduction to the areas which any new project manager will need to cover, and it makes a great read for someone starting a project. The problem with many descriptions of project management is that, in order to be structured and systematic, they end up being as readable as a washing machine manual. But this one is more fun."
Computing Magazine.

"While the book is plainly aimed at the manager of software projects, the author is at pains to emphasize that the issues of project management are human and generic. On the software front, more than in most spheres of activity, the raw material is human hearts and minds, and O'Connell stays refreshingly close to what motivates people. Project managers at all levels will find a good deal to provoke rumination in this slim and readable volume. The underlying issues are human and books such as 'How To Run Successful Projects' can give you ideas to inspire your approach to the people on your project."
Irish Computer.

Here's what people have said about the approach described in 'How To Run Successful Projects'
...

"Our localization division is constantly faced with the challenge of new projects and demanding deadlines. The ETP approach has delivered the goods for us again and again. I have personally found that ETP works equally well for life goals. It is no exaggeration to say that this goal oriented, project based method has changed my life."
Tony Mulqueen, Localization Manager, ISOCOR.

"From the early days of IT Software, ETP has undertaken a series of assignments — all of which have either been successfully completed or are proceeding satisfactorily on target. Our experience of working with the 'Eyes on the Prize' methods has been a great success. We would recommend that you use the ETP method for guaranteed results."
Eugene Smyth, Commercial Director, Telecom Ireland Software.

Here's what people have said about the course based on 'How To Run Successful Projects' ...

"If you do only one Project Management course in your career it should be this one."
Paul O'Dea, Director, Credo Group Ltd.

"Great workshop, proving again that common sense is anything but common."
Dan Murphy, Irish Trade Board.

"Ten Steps Plan. No bullshit, no fancy window dressing, just a Plan for Success."
Allan Young, Project Manager, Scottish Equitable plc, Scotland

How to Run Successful Projects II
The Silver Bullet

Fergus O'Connell

Prentice Hall
London   New York   Toronto   Sydney   Tokyo   Singapore
Madrid   Mexico City   Munich

First published 1994 by
Prentice Hall International (UK) Limited
This edition published 1996 by
Prentice Hall Europe
Campus 400, Maylands Avenue
Hemel Hempstead
Hertfordshire, HP2 7EZ
A division of
Simon & Schuster International Group

Printed and bound in Great Britain by
T J Press (Padstow) Ltd

Library of Congress cataloging-in-publication data
is available from the publisher

British Library cataloguing in publication data

A catalogue record for this book is available from
the British Library.

ISBN: 0-13-239856-7

2 3 4 5   00 99 98 97

This book is dedicated to my friend, Jim Fallon, whose tragic death robbed the world of a truly good person

Contents

Preface to the second edition

If you are in the business of writing books, then one of the things you spend a lot of your time doing is in looking for the opening line. There are many reasons for this, but perhaps the most selfish one is that, unless you are very prolific, you don't get to do opening lines very often. In my own case it is three years since I did my last one, and goodness knows when it will be before I get to do another.

Tom DeMarco and Timothy Lister found their first line in the 1987 classic, PeopleWare [Ref. 20]. 'Somewhere today,' their memorable opening runs, 'a project is failing'. And today, nine years later, despite everyone's best efforts, projects are still failing. The French General Ducrot put things more colourfully after the defeat of the French forces at the Battle of Sedan, when he said *'Nous sommes dans un pot de chambre, et nous y serons emmerdee'*. And today, even as I write or as you read, somebody is waking up to find that they are indeed in a *pot de chambre*, and that they are very much *emmerdee*.

It doesn't have to be like this. That was the message of the first edition of this book, and it is more than ever the message now.

I had thought that I was finished with *How To Run Successful Projects*, that there was not much more that needed to be said, but the intervening years have proved me wrong.

By far the most significant thing that I have learned is that what *I* knew in 1992 to be true, others can now independently confirm: That is that the Ten Step Method is the *solution* to the software industry's biggest problem - that of software projects not coming in on time, within budget or delivering what was required. I knew this three years ago when I wrote the first edition, but I didn't think the world was quite ready for a claim like that then. Now, I can come out of the closet and make the claim unashamedly and secure in the knowledge that it can be backed up by people who have actually used it. Of course, in a sense, this should come as no surprise because of the origin of the Ten Steps. Since the Ten Steps were derived from understanding why some projects succeed and others fail, the fact that they work for software projects merely confirms what I have thought for years - that despite all the propaganda to the contrary - software projects are no different from any other kinds of projects.

I have learned something else: The Ten Steps don't just guarantee a successful project. They are also the *minimum* that has to be done for a successful project. Mathematicians would call the Ten Steps a necessary and sufficient condition for a successful project - you have to do what the Ten Steps require, but having done this much, this is all you have to do. To put it differently, the Ten Steps tell you when you have done enough project management. Your days of waking in the middle of the night and wondering if you are doing enough, are over once you start applying the Ten Steps.

This property of the Ten Steps opens up the wonderful vista that we have called the Lazy Project Manager. 'Lazy' is normally used as a derogatory term, but here we mean it to be highly complimentary. The Lazy Project Manager does the minimum possible and always has a successful outcome - to the bewilderment of her colleagues.

In detail, the main changes you will find in this edition of the book are the following:

- Since the Ten Steps guarantee success, we have tried to make it as easy as possible for you to begin applying them. Many of the things we provide here are things that our clients have asked us for over the last three years.
- The Probability of Success Indicator, rather than being a bit of a footnote, is now integral to the Ten Steps. Each step's contribution to the PSI is explained more fully. We can do this because we have managed to apply the PSI to nearly 500 projects since the first edition of the book appeared.
- Software estimation has been simplified and made much more usable. Looking back on it I realise that I was confused about software estimation. I still saw it as something which was different somehow from estimating in other disciplines. Now, I realise it is not at all.
- Time management has been integrated with the Ten Steps. This is because we now want you not to be just a successful Project Manager but a *Lazy* Successful Project Manager.

In the evolution of this material over the last three years, I have learned much from many people, and there are some I would particularly like to acknowledge:

Dee Carri and Mary Martin at Elan Corporation; Michael Rice and Colm Quinn of the Kerry Group; Paul O'Dea and Paul Fox of Credo Group; Dermot Gilson of Avid Technology; Tony Mulqueen at ISOCOR; Allan Young from Scottish Equitable in Edinburgh; Sacha Jovanovic of MPA Stuttgart; Guido Haesen and Peter Lowe of the European Commission in Luxembourg; my former bosses at Retix, Tony Fonze and Ron Rudolf; Russell Altendorff of Travelex Corp.; Jan Middleton of SSA Europe, Tim Greening-Jackson of KNX, Paul Renehan of ITP, Dermot Bolger and Redmond Sweeny at Telecom Ireland Software and John O'Leary of BP Exploration in Colombia, all - whether they know it or not - helped me to see connections between things and gain new insights.

The material in Appendix 1 first appeared in an article entitled How to become a world class estimator in issue 4 of the Journal of Structured Project Management. It was then further extended as part of an internal ETP project. However, I would like to acknowledge a number of contributions to its final shape from Telecom Ireland Software, a company which uses this procedure.

Sean McEvoy prepared the Guides to MS-Project and Timeline included in the Appendices, and I am grateful to the Commission of the European Communities who funded this work.

The book is written, and then a small group of skilled, dedicated and talented people bring it to you.

There are the production people - in my case, Ann Greenwood, Louise Wilson (for the last time!) and Val Jones.

There are the editors - three did time on this book:

Viki Williams who did her usual highly professional job, was a pleasure to work with and then, just as I handed in the manuscript, upped and left. Good luck on your travels Viki. I guess I'll never get that £2 now!

Christopher Glennie who held the fort. Jason Dunne, who was the best of project managers - enthusiastic, helpful, creative supportive and - best of all - gave me deadlines I could meet! (If only he'd give me that screen saver, I'd really be happy!!)

There are the cover designers - Maurice Farrell, John O'Regan and Martin Swords. Who knows how many magazines they exhausted trying to get those holes just right!

Myles Dunne, technical author to the gentry, prepared the camera-ready copy with his customary skill and made a book out of a heap of paper, diskettes and garbled notes from me.

Also, the show's not over until the book lands in your lap. For this I have to thank the sales people: Alan, Craig, Delya, Karen, Lesley, Wendy and Sam. I know that books don't just sit there and sell themselves - it's the reps who have to get out and push them. I sell myself, so I know how tough it can be. Thank you for all your hard work on my behalf. It was your commitment and dedication that made the first edition a success.

And finally, there are Hugh and Bernadette. Hugh wasn't old enough to read the first edition, so he had an excuse, Bernadette had none! I'm sure they'll both get endless hours of reading pleasure out of this one!!

And finally, a note on sexist language

This is one area where you can't win. To use 'he' and 'his' throughout, even with a disclaimer that no offence is intended, doesn't wash with some people. To do the opposite and use 'she' and 'her' throughout, one is accused of tokenism or of treating seriously something that should be regarded as trivial. Whatever you chose to do, you can be guaranteed you'll offend or irritate somebody. Sigh!

Here's the policy I have adopted. I have used 'he'/'his' and 'she'/'her' as and when the mood has taken me! I have done this because the juxtaposition of the feminine and masculine sometimes (a) surprises people and (b) conjures up different mental pictures.

Ireland, March 1996

Preface to the first edition

In 1979 I bought Tom De Marco's book *Structured Analysis and System Specification*. At the time, I had been working for about three years as a programmer, but had ambitions to be a Systems Analyst. Those in the know, while applauding my ambition, made it clear that not everyone was cut out to be a Systems Analyst. It was highly likely that I might not have the 'right stuff' - that particular combination of personality, intellect and way of looking at things that characterised the Systems Analyst. In short, the thinking went, systems analysis was very much an art, and in the same way that not everybody was born to be a great pianist, not everybody could be a Systems Analyst.

After reading De Marco's book, it would not be an exaggeration to say that the scales had fallen from my eyes. Or to put it more bluntly, I was gobsmacked! The great mystery of systems analysis was laid bare. It wasn't an art - not much anyway - it was a method, an approach, a technique. While it would be a wild over-simplification to say that anyone could do it, it certainly wasn't sorcery or genius. The book presented a method and if you carried out the method you were doing systems analysis. Systems analysis has long since ceased to have any mystique about it, so now we software practitioners have had to find another black art, another mystery with which to clothe ourselves. That black art is Project Management, and you only have to look at the success statistics for projects to see why the world at large might perceive it to be so. The premise of this book is that Project Management is no more a black art than systems analysis is. Project Management too can be described by a method, and that is what this book is primarily about. De Marco's book had a 7-step method; this one has a 10-step method. The method is derived from studying other projects, why some succeed and others fail.

The argument is simple: If you do enough of the things on your project that have made other projects successful, the chances are yours will be too; and, conversely, if you engage in practices which have been used on failed projects, then God help you.

Parts I and II of the book contain the 10-step method, and are intended to be read sequentially. I'd also suggest you read chapter 20 and score your project(s) on the Project Probability of Success Indicator ('take the PSI test'!). Other than that, you can dip in as you please. While the book uses the software industry to illustrate many of its ideas, the 10-step method isn't unique to software. It can be applied to any venture, in any discipline; and is equally applicable to business or personal projects. Indeed, one person who attended one of my company's courses said that it changed his life. While it may not do that for you, I can pretty much guarantee you will learn new things from it.

Project Management is concerned with bringing about change, about making things happen. In a world where we are in need of much change - and this is true of my own small country as much as anywhere - it is the Project Managers who will make the visions come true. Bad Project Management results in a colossal waste of the world's resources. There is enough of that going on, and we should be trying not to add to it.

But more than anything else, Project Management is FUN. Software people tend to think that all the fun has gone out of their lives when they are promoted from 'doing technical work' to 'managing people'. Nothing could be further from the truth. For infinite variety, constant challenge, unpredictability, adrenalin-burn and ultimate sense of achievement, Project Management is hard to beat; and if this book succeeds in transferring some of that enthusiasm to you it will have been worth the struggle it took to write it.

Many people - customers, students, colleagues, peers, bosses, both current and former - contributed, consciously and sometimes unwittingly, to this book. Rather than changing the names to protect the innocent I have chosen to omit all names. However, two groups of people deserve particular mention. One is those who read and commented on drafts of the book. The other is those who attended courses on the content - while the material was still in its formative years and growing from the 'EOTP Methodology' through 'ETP' to its current simple name of Structured Project Management. There are some people and organisations that I would like to name:

Telecom Ireland Software (TIS) gave me permission to use some of the examples in the text, for which I am very grateful. In addition, Tom Moylan and Eugene Smyth, both of TIS, gave me the opportunity to apply and thereby refine many of the ideas in the book.

Beaumont Hospital were kind enough to allow me to use an example, which one of their staff, Cathy Keany put together.

Whether they know it or not, Ray Welland of the University of Glasgow and Pat O'Reilly of Siemens Nixdorf, both encouraged me at points where I had begun to despair about the material ever seeing the light of day. Often it is small incidents that change lives, and conversations which these people may have forgotten, were crucial in the evolution of the material as well as steadying my will to continue.

As she knows, Viki Williams of Prentice Hall will have a permanent place in my heart for having given me my first break. Viki still owes me £2 from the time we first met, but it's OK, Viki - buy me a pint next time you're in Ireland!

Myles Dunne put the finished product together, ironing the crumpled pages, drying the soggier ones etc. and takes credit for its final appearance.

Bernadette McHugh put up with (relative) poverty and all that that entails, while this was being written. Thanks Bernie for staying with it - and me! *Fortitudinam vincimus.*

Hugh O'Connell and some (furry) friends of his were right there with me when I wrote much of the book, as is evidenced from old drafts that have muddy paw-prints or coloured scribblings on them. Thanks guys - you may not have made it easier, but it was more fun!

Ireland, January 1993

About the Author

Fergus O'Connell graduated with a First in Mathematical Physics from University College Cork. He has twenty years experience in the computer industry, seventeen of those in project management positions. His varied experience covers commercial data processing, microprocessor-based office automation systems, computer networking, data communications and telecommunications. He began his career in the Computer Centre of University College Cork, and since then has worked with companies such as CPT, ICL and Retix, where he was General Manager of the company's European R & D facility. His experience covers projects in Australia, Britain, Denmark, Germany, Ireland, Sweden, Switzerland and the United States.

In 1992 he founded ETP (Eyes on The Prize), a training and consultancy company dedicated to the premise that software projects which succeed can be the rule rather than the exception. He has written on project management for *The Sunday Business Post*, *Computer Weekly*, *DEC Computing* and *The Wall Street Journal*.

He lives with his wife and son, six dogs, two horses, three ponies and a donkey, beside the River Barrow in Ireland where he divides his time between consulting and writing. He is currently working on his fourth book.

Introduction

The Silver Bullet

In 1987, along with most of the rest of the software industry, I read Fred Brooks' famous article *No Silver Bullet*. (For those of you who don't know - it must be my age because there was a time when everyone knew who he was - Fred Brooks is the doyen of software project managers, the author of that most famous of project management tracts, *The Mythical Man-Month*.)

Brooks' point was simple: Despite all the advances in hardware and software technology, there seemed to have been no corresponding '*development in either technology or management technique*' [my italics] that would enable IT people to bring projects in on time, within budget and deliver what was required. Brooks said it and the world agreed, not because it was Brooks, though I'm sure that helped, but more because that seemed to correspond to our experience as well. Brooks saying it merely put the seal of approval on it.

So where am I coming from? In calling this book *The Silver Bullet*, have I discovered the elusive breakthrough? Failing that have I taken leave of my senses? Or more serious still, am I starting to believe my own marketing material?? Most important of all, do I actually have The Silver Bullet?

Well, the answer is yes and no. No, in the sense that I also don't have a development in technology or management technique, some nifty new algorithm, or management technique extracted from the writings of an obscure 12th century philosopher. Sorry to disappoint you on this score.

But you see, I think Brooks and all the rest of us have been barking up the wrong tree. We were looking for a *development*. Because computers and software were new, the thinking went, then we needed some new thing to manage them. For some reason, it never occurred to us that *old* things might work.

Perhaps you might allow me a digression here for a moment, because I think I know how this thinking originated.

People of my generation - people who remember mainframes and punched cards and the term 'data processing' - will remember what it was like in those early days. (I am thinking of the late sixties / early seventies.) I remember the Computer Centre when I was still at college - the air-conditioned room, the machine with flashing lights, and the busy acolytes who tended it - sharp-suited IBM Systems Engineers or the more casually-dressed, but no less boffin-like, Computer Centre personnel. Sometimes the machine went down, or a new operating system release had to be installed, and when we students asked how long it would take, we were told 'We don't know. It'll take as long as it takes.'

We Computer Science students longed to join the ranks of the boffins. To learn the new technology. To tend the machine. To be able to say to those who didn't understand the new technology: 'We don't know. It'll take as long as it takes.'

And so the myth was born. La Grande Illusion, I call it. La Grande Illusion maintains that IT (and especially software) projects are difficult, if not impossible, to estimate. Largely as a result of this, IT projects enjoy the notorious track record that they do.

La Grande Illusion is a fundamental article of faith of the software industry. It's reasoning goes like this: 'Software entities are more complex for their size than perhaps any other human construct'. (The quote is from our old friend Brooks again.) Therefore, all bets are off where estimating software is concerned. Things that would make sense in other areas don't make sense in software.

Thus software people will do things like

- Agree a fixed price contract for something that isn't yet specified; a contract that may well have penalty clauses for late delivery.
- Do plans and schedules based on people working 7-day weeks, 15 hours a day.
- Do 'realistic' plans but then back down on them at the first sign of resistance from their management or a customer.
- Not try to estimate anything at all on the basis that software estimating is only for wimps.

And they will do all of these things without batting an eyelid - all because of the basic article of faith of the software industry which says that software projects are difficult if not impossible to estimate.

(Where else would you find such a career - technically challenging, relatively highly paid, and where, ultimately, we can shrug and say: 'Hey, how could we have known, things take as long as they take'.)

A whole industry has risen up about this article of faith. In Europe, even as we speak, there are research programmes exploring the outer reaches of the problem. I have numerous books - one is nearly 800 pages long, an immense work of scholarship, which propose ways of dealing with it. Around the world, millions, if not billions of research dollars are being spent in the search for the development Brooks spoke of - a way to accurately estimate software projects.

And all of this, I believe, is barking up the wrong tree. Because the answer was there waiting for us all the time.

Attempts - successful to some extent - have been made to compare the building of software to the construction industry. I think, however, a much better comparison is to compare the creation of software to the making of a film. Both take a written vision - a script in the case of a film, a specification in the case of software - and convert it into images on a medium (frames on celluloid or bits on disk or tape).

Now the film industry contains noteworthy examples - *Revolution*, *Heaven's Gate*, *Waterworld*, to name but a few - of films that have gone ballistically over budget and schedule, but these days, routinely, films are shot in a businesslike and highly predictable way to meet specified budget, schedule and quality targets.

And what is the key to this? The key is the pre-production phase. In the book, *My Indecision is Final*, Jake Eberts describes Sir Richard Attenborough's pre-production phase for the film, *Gandhi*:

'He [Attenborough] had to shoot the film during the cool season in India, starting in November and finishing the following April or May. (The summer would simply be too hot: a film crew could not function in 110 degree heat.) But to start in November he had to be making preparations now, six months ahead: hiring the cast and crew, building the sets, sorting out the costumes, getting all the permissions needed to shoot in India, shipping the equipment and so on. These tasks, known as pre-production, are fairly straightforward if you are shooting in your own country, but are horrendously complicated when you are shooting overseas. To take a simple example, if you are going to fly in 125 people to make a movie, you have to book the hotel rooms and pay for them, or at least put down some sort of deposit, well in advance. *That means knowing now exactly where you will want each of those 125 people to be on any given day over the four or six months that the film will be shooting* [my italics].'

If you replaced the 125 people with the size of your particular software team, and replaced the phrase 'film will be shooting' with 'software will be under development', then - essentially - you have the Silver Bullet. And this Silver Bullet didn't come from any 'development' - it came from well-tried techniques that have evolved over the hundred or so years of the film industry, which in turn have come from projects in other disciplines and areas of technology.

This then is the Silver Bullet. The premise of this book is simple.

If you do the things we describe in this book on your projects, then your projects will always be successful. No ifs, ands, buts, maybes, provideds or anything else.

This book is about a method called Structured Project Management. Structured Project Management is the result of over sixteen years of research into why some projects succeed and others fail. While Structured Project Management isn't tied to any particular kind of project, this book focuses a lot on IT and software projects, areas notorious for failures.

Software people will find that Structured Project Management bears the same relationship to conventional project management that:

- Structured Analysis & Design bears to conventional analysis and design
- Structured Programming bears to programming;

that is, it replaces a process which is highly individualistic, with a process that is standard, repeatable, predictable and consistent. We are often asked if Structured Project Management is a 'methodology' - software people love the notion of a methodology - and the answer is yes and no. In their wonderful book, *PeopleWare*, Tom De Marco and Timothy Lister define two versions of the word methodology - 'methodology' and 'Methodology'. Methodology with a big 'M' is defined as 'a general systems theory of how a whole class of thought-intensive work ought to be conducted. It comes in the form of a fat ['a linear foot or more of shelf space'] book that specifies in detail exactly what steps to take at any time, regardless of who's doing the work, regardless of where or when'.

If your question is whether Structured Project Management is such a methodology, the answer is definitely not. For one thing - feel the thickness of the book! Methodology with a small 'm' is a different fish. Methodology with a small 'm' is defined as a 'basic approach one takes to getting a job done. It doesn't reside in a fat book, but rather in the heads of the people carrying out the work'. Structured Project Management is a methodology with a small 'm'.

Though we will deal primarily with software projects in this book, Structured Project Management states that any human endeavour or venture can be treated as a project, and the book could then be used by anybody responsible for leading such endeavours or ventures. Three types of readers are envisaged:

- Project managers managing their first project
- Seasoned project managers who would benefit from the use of a formal project management method
- Seasoned project managers who feel the need for a 'top-up' in their skills; a refresher course; a fine-tuning on how they do things; or some kind of reference point against which to judge their projects.

The book is divided into five parts. Parts I and II present The Ten Steps of Structured Project Management. Parts I and II show you how to run any project successfully.

Most of us don't have the luxury of being able to concentrate all of our efforts on a single project. Most of us are involved in many projects simultaneously, and so Part III shows how to run multiple concurrent projects.

You will see as the book unfolds that most project disasters can be predicted long before they happen. The Ten Steps prove that you pretty much make or break a project during the planning phase. To enable you to assess projects plans quickly and effectively, we have come up with an approach, based on the Ten Steps, which enables you to do this. This is described in Part IV.

Part V, called The Rest of the Wherewithal, presents a series of chapters on subjects of which the Project Manager needs to be aware. Many of the subjects are those covered in other management books or on training programmes. There are chapters on:

- Problem solving / Decision making
- Stress Management
- Picking the Right People
- Negotiation
- Meetings
- Presentations
- Shortening Projects through Accelerated Analysis & Design.

Finally, there are a number of Appendices which are referred to in the text.

With many organisations now moving away from traditional management structures (hierarchical, matrix, etc.) to project-based approaches, it is hoped that this book will become seminal in advancing research in this critical area. The emphasis throughout the book is on

- simplifying and getting to the heart of any issue
- useful and practical ideas
- presenting ideas in an entertaining and stimulating way.

Acknowledgements

The author is grateful to the following for permission to reproduce excerpts from works indicated:

A.P. Watt Ltd, on behalf of Roland Huntford for permission to quote from *Scott and Amundsen* by Roland Huntford.

Verso for permission to quote from *Judgement Over the Dead* by Trevor Griffiths.

Unwin Hyman, of HarperCollins Publishers Ltd, for permission to quote from *The Lord of the Rings* by J.R.R. Tolkien.

Excerpt from *The Fellowship of the Ring* by J.R.R. Tolkien. Copyright © 1954, 1965 by J.R.R. Tolkien. Copyright © renewed 1982 by Christopher R. Tolkien, Michael H.R. Tolkien, John F.R. Tolkien and Priscilla M.A.R. Tolkien. Reprinted by permission of Houghton Mifflin Co. All rights reserved.

Bantam Doubleday Dell Publishing Group Inc. for permission to quote from *Voices of Freedom* by Henry Hampton and Steve Frayer.

After some time they crossed the Water, west of Hobbiton, by a narrow plank-bridge. The stream there was no more than a winding black ribbon, bordered with leaning alder trees. A mile or two further south they hastily crossed the great road from the Brandywine Bridge; they were now in the Tookland and bending south-eastwards they made for the Green Hill Country. As they began to climb its first slopes they looked back and saw the lamps in Hobbiton far off twinkling in the gentle valley of the Water. Soon it disappeared in the folds of the darkened land, and was followed by Bywater beside its grey pool. When the light of the last farm was far behind, peeping among the trees, Frodo turned and waved a hand in farewell. 'I wonder if I shall ever look down in that valley again,' he said quietly.

The Lord of the Rings
J. R. R. Tolkien

Late in the evening on June 6th, Amundsen came out of his house, shut the door behind him, leaving things as if returning in an hour or two, walked briskly through the trees, and boarded Fram. There was a rattle of chains, the anchor was raised, and slowly she swung out into the fjord. 'Sailed at midnight', ran the opening entry of Amundsen's diary ...

Scott and Amundsen
Roland Huntford

One writes in a certain sort of way because one is a certain sort of person; one is a certain sort of person because one has led a certain sort of life.

A. A. Milne

Part One

Analysing and planning projects

The nature of projects

This book deals primarily with software development projects, although much of what we say here will be applicable to projects in any discipline. In particular, the definition of 'project' that we are going to use is that any combination of a noun and verb together constitute a project. Thus, using this definition, any of the following could be a project:

- be the first person at the South Pole
- get a promotion and a raise
- achieve record sales of a new product
- set up a new business division
- cost-reduce a manufacturing process
- build an oil refinery
- put a man on the moon
- develop a new computer system
- build the A-12 airplane

Note that this definition is recursive, i.e. it defines the thing in terms of itself. For example, the project 'develop a new computer system' itself consists of a number of projects:

- develop the hardware
- develop the software
- integrate the hardware and the software
- release the system

Each of these projects can be further broken down. For 'develop the software' we might have:

- identify the requirements
- do the high level design
- do the functional specification
- etc.

The key factor about projects is that they have a birth, a life and a death. They are not ongoing sorts of things. Identifying the birth, life and death - particularly the death - are key to the success of a project. In the course of this book we will use a couple of analogies when talking about projects.

The project as a journey

A project is like a journey; it involves identifying a destination, setting out, travelling and ending up somewhere; hopefully the place you intended to be.

The project as a state change

A project is all about achieving some goal. The universe is in one state before the project, a different state afterwards, and the difference is the goal. In the examples given previously the destinations / goals / state changes are:

- a person has stood at the South Pole
- you have received the promotion and raise
- you have achieved record sales of the new product
- the new business division is up and running
- the cost of the manufacturing process has been lowered
- the oil refinery has been built
- a man has landed on the moon
- the new computer system is available
- the A-12 is operational

This book presents a methodology called Structured Project Management for handling projects. In the terminology used above, Structured Project Management will help you to identify where you want to go. It will then give you the wherewithal to plan your journey, carry out the journey, arrive at your destination. To put it another way, you will achieve your goal.

Structured Project Management - the Ten Steps

The Ten Steps are the cornerstone of Structured Project Management. They are covered in the next ten chapters of the book. I said in the first edition that the first five steps were to do with planning your project, the other five with implementing the plan and achieving the goal. While this is still one hundred per cent true, I realize now that there is a deeper, more intuitive reason as to why the steps are structured in this way.

Steps 1-5 do indeed produce a plan for your project. However, what they also do is to define one possible way in which the project might actually unfold. Let me put this another way. If you build into your project plan the level of intricate detail we are going to ask of you in steps 2 and 4, then your plan will reflect a possible way that the project could actually happen.

The key to all of this is the word 'detail' above. The conventional wisdom is that you can't know much about a project, particularly a software project, at the beginning. This is the I-won't-know-how-long-it-will-take-until-I've-done-it syndrome. I've had people on courses tell me that their plans were criticised for being 'too detailed'. I've heard somebody say that too much detail early in a project is 'inefficient'.

This is complete hogwash

If there is a Silver Bullet in all of this, some new development, then it is the notion of catching every fragment of detail that you can as early as possible. Only in this way can you build a possible scenario of how the project might turn out.

In reality, you do something slightly more fancy than producing a single model. You actually produce *multiple* models.

Let me explain. Steps 1-4 cause you to build a prediction of the way the project might turn out. One part of step 5, step 5a, gets you to build some contingency, or margin for error into your model. This means that - to some extent - things can turn out differently from your prediction, and it still won't be a problem provided the differences are covered by your margin for error. Step 5b then allows for the fact that people - your boss, your customer - may not like what your prediction says. This again, is no problem. What you do then is to use your initial model to produce a whole series of models. So that, for example, if they are not happy with the existing delivery date, you can say 'OK, here's a model showing what we can do by the date you require', or 'Here's what we can do if you give us extra people'.

This process is described in detail in chapters 1 through 5. Each step is described individually. In Appendix 1, we combine all the steps into a software estimating procedure that you could (a) use, and (b) make part of an ISO9000 or other process improvement programme project management procedure.

Having done this much, what we want to do then is to make things actually happen this way, to make reality adhere to the plan, to turn the plan into a self-fulfilling prophecy. That is what steps 6-10 do. And, as you will see, making reality adhere to the plan does not require anything like the god-like levels of ability that such a statement might seem to imply. In fact, you will see that making reality adhere to the plan is one of the most conceptually simple things imaginable.

Thus you get two chances to make your project a success:

- First, by planning your project in intricate detail
- Then, by causing your plan to become a self-fulfilling prophecy

Not all of the Ten Steps are equally important. There is a weighting associated with each step and collectively, these weightings add up to something we call the Probability of Success Indicator or PSI. The PSI, is an instantaneous measure of how likely or not a project is to succeed. You can read the original derivation of the PSI in Appendix 3. However, we can summarise the weightings as follows:

Step	Weighting (Contribution to PSI)
1	20
2	20
3	10
4	10
5	10
6	10
7	10
8	10
9	0
10	0
Total	100

In the chapters describing each of the Ten Steps we will show how that step's individual score is calculated, and how the sum of these scores in turn contribute to the PSI.

In chapter 1 of A.A. Milne's *The House at Pooh Corner* [Ref. 44] we come across the following comments by Eeyore, the down at heel donkey who inhabits that book:

'It just shows what can be done by taking a little trouble,' said Eeyore. 'Do you see, Pooh? Do you see, Piglet? Brains first and then Hard Work. Look at it! That's the way to build a house,' said Eeyore proudly.

Brains first and then hard work. That's not only the way to build a house; it's the basis for a way to carry out any project. Structured Project Management follows this approach in that half of its Ten Steps are to do with planning the project, i.e. they occur before the project really gets moving. This reflects a firm belief of my own: that most projects succeed or fail because of decisions made during this planning phase. Many of the case studies in the pages which follow will serve to illustrate this statement. As for Winnie the Pooh, we will return to him again in Chapter 16, Coping with stress.

Chapter 1

Step 1 - Visualise the goal; set your eyes on the prize

Introduction

The first step in Structured Project Management is to identify your goal, your destination. Visualise what the goal is; set your eyes on the prize. There are a number of reasons why you should do this.

Identifying the goal

Step 1 clearly identifies the goal. In the race to the South Pole between Scott and Amundsen [Ref. 30], Amundsen's goal was identified from the outset. He intended to be the first man to stand at the South Pole. Scott's aims were much more diffuse. His expedition was going to be a scientific one; the Pole was a sideshow. His team would do the scientific work; they would also handle the Pole as and when it came up. Indeed, when Scott discovered that Amundsen was heading south, he disdained any intention of taking part in a race. As project leader of this project, Scott was sending conflicting messages both to himself and to his team. Either the Pole was a goal or it wasn't. If it was, then a project had to be started. If not, then the scientific work was the only project.

Defining the goal

Visualising the goal - stating it, writing it down - immediately starts two related processes. It begins to tighten the definition of the goal, and, it starts the planning process that is the subject of the next chapter.

6

Tighten the definition of the goal

Amundsen's goal - to be the first man to stand at the South Pole - immediately throws up an important point: And bring the team back safely. Ernest Shackleton journeyed to the South Pole in 1909 [Ref. 31] but 97 miles short, with the prize within his reach, he turned back and passed out of the history books. His objective was the same as Amundsen's - to be the first man to stand at the South Pole. Ninety-seven miles short he realised that a shortage of provisions would stop him from bringing his team back safely. He turned back. Thus, for both he and Amundsen, an integral part of the goal was to bring the team back alive.

Visualising the goal tightens the definition of the basic goal identified in previous section. Note that for something like the British offensive on the Somme in 1916 - an example we will use later - the definition of the goal may run to many pages.

The definition of the goal is crucially important. What constitutes completion? For some projects the answer may be as obvious as the nose on your face, but you must consider this issue carefully. If it's so obvious, make a check list of all the deliverables. To put it another way, write down all the state changes that must occur for the project to be considered complete.

Start the planning process

In visualising the goal you start to imagine life as it will be when the project is completed. Mentally you have already made the journey from where you are to this new place. Inevitably, some of the issues that will confront you during this journey start to make themselves apparent.

The reason for the goal

Setting your eyes on the prize gives you your whole reason for undertaking the project. Life is short and we only pass this way once. If you're going to put some period of your life into a project, then you need to feel that it's going to be worthwhile. Visualisation - setting your eyes on the prize - gives you a glimpse of how you will feel when the project completes.

Visualisation involves creating a daydream. In it you start to imagine life as it will be when the project completes. You may dwell on the money you will earn, the recognition of peers and superiors, how your resume will be enhanced, or perhaps the sense of personal achievement. Whatever it is that drives you, you can get a preview of how you will feel when it is all over. If this preview doesn't fire you up, then - for you - the project probably isn't worth doing. But if you do feel the adrenalin starting to flow, then settle into your daydream and allow it to wash around you. Enjoy it. Luxuriate in it. Think of how good you will feel when the project is completed.

Motivating the team

Visualising the goal gives you a vision with which to inspire people who may work on the project with you. It's all very well you being fired up, but what about the people who are going to work on the project with you - and for projects of any size there will always be other people involved?

Visualising the goal gives you a vision, a description, of a place somewhere in the future, for which you are all bound. It draws other people into the daydream. There may be dark days ahead - on most projects there generally are - and the vision of the goal is what will sustain you and your people during those days. The best example I know of setting your eyes on the prize comes from Martin Luther King's Washington speech in 1963 [Ref. 29]:

> ... I say to you today, my friends, so even though we face the difficulties of today and tomorrow, I still have a dream. It is a dream deeply rooted in the American meaning of its creed, 'We hold these truths to be self-evident, that all men are created equal.' I have a dream that one day on the red hills of Georgia, sons of former slaves and the sons of former slave owners will be able to sit down together at the table of brotherhood. I have a dream that one day even the state of Mississippi, a state sweltering with the heat of injustice, sweltering with the heat of oppression, will be transformed into an oasis of freedom and justice. I have a dream that my four little children will one day live in a nation where they will not be judged by the colour of their skin, but by the content of their character ...

Changes to the goal / change control

Nobody, least of all myself, is daft enough to believe that the goal, once set, will never and can never change. In the real world we expect that things will have been forgotten, overlooked, appear differently, change or become redundant as the project proceeds. We have no problem with this provided we have a mechanism for controlling these changes.

Any change control mechanism we institute has to operate within the confines of the First Law of Project Management. You already know the First Law; you just may not have seen it formulated in the following way before. The First Law of Project Management states that on any product or system development project there is a function that relates four variables. These four variables are:

- functionality
- delivery date
- effort (or cost)
- quality

The law says that there is a function of these four variables that is constant, i.e.

function (functionality, delivery date, effort, quality) = constant.

(And if you want to find out more about what this function might be (for software), then you could do a lot worse than reading Laurence Puttnam's and Ware Myer's book *Measures for Excellence* Ref. 47.).

If you change any one of these variables, then all the others will change correspondingly. We have all seen this effect. For example, increase functionality, i.e add a new feature, and delivery date will extend or effort will increase or quality will go down, or some combination of these, for the function to remain true.

Much of what is talked about in this book is opinion (generally mine), or analysis of some event or situation. This, however, is a law - a law like say, gravity. You can certainly pretend that gravity doesn't apply to you. Equally you can pretend this law doesn't apply to you. Both courses of action are about as sensible as one another!

If you believe in the existence of the First Law of Project Management, then it will be your true friend and protector. Pretend it doesn't exist and you will find it the most unforgiving enemy in the world.

One of the immortal phrases from software projects is 'we're absorbing that into the schedule'. The First Law of Project Management is the reason why nothing can be absorbed into the schedule. Later on, in step 5, we will show you a way you can pretend to absorb things, but this is all that it is - a pretence. It is a management convenience as much as anything else, a way of not having to go back to your boss or customer to renegotiate the contract, every time a change occurs. But this is a pretence, an illusion. The law operates and you had better believe that it does.

Change control can be implemented very simply using a change control log. This can be nothing more than a folder containing a page per change, and a table of contents (with one line per change) which summarises all the changes. Each change page basically describes:

- The nature of the change
- An analysis of the impact
- What action was taken

Two sample pages - one for changes and one for the table of contents are presented in Appendix 5.

Ways of visualising the goal

So how do you go about visualising and fixing the goal? Two possible ways are suggested here, one using a checklist which focuses, among other things, on the day the project will end; the other using a method that I like to think of as the and-they-lived-happily-ever-after method.

Visualisation checklist

- What will the goal of the project mean to all the people involved in the project when the project completes?
- What are the things the project will actually produce? Where will these things go? What will happen to them? Who will use them? How will they be affected by them?
- What will the completion of the project mean to the team as a whole and to each of its members?
- Why do they want to do this project?
- Why do you want to do it?
- What will life be like on the day /week the project completes?
- What will you do that day? During that week? What will be your routine? Your schedule? Where will you eat? Whom will you meet? What will be the topics of conversation with these people?
- What will people be saying of the project and its deliverables? You? Your boss? The people who worked on the project? The customer for whom you carried the project out?
- What would you like an audit of the project (see checklist in section 12.2) to be reporting?
- How will you feel?
- What do you think people will be saying about you? Your boss? Peers?

Subordinates? The project's customer? Other parts of the organisation?
- What will be your ambitions / hopes / dreams on that day?
- Will your standard of living have changed?
- Will your position within the organisation have changed?
- Will your view of yourself have changed? If so, how?
- Do you think it is a difficult task you have set yourself?
- Could it fail?
- How would you feel then? What would you do?
- Will you have power you don't have at the moment?
- Will you have changed as a person? If so, how?
- What sort of recognition will you achieve for this project?
- What would you like to do after this project is over?
- What would the best possible outcome of this project be?

The and-they-all-lived-happily-ever-after method

This method involves thinking of the goal of your project in terms of three mutually perpendicular axes as in the diagram.

The first axis is functionality. Low on this axis means minimal functionality, high means all-singing all-dancing. What are you going for here? A lot, a little or something in the middle?

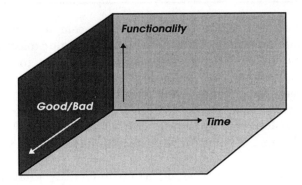

The second axis is time. When in time will your project end? Will it end, for example, when your product is released? Or will it be when your customers have begun to use it and are sending back glowing reports of it? Or will it be when your product has recouped its development costs and is now generating profits for you? Similarly for a system development. Does the project end when the system is released to the users? Or when the users have settled in and become comfortable with the new system? Or when the system has brought the business benefits that were originally set out in the business case? Or what? How you define the end of the project is, to a large extent, arbitrary, i.e. it is up to you. All that is important is that you fix what lies within the scope of the project and what lies outside it; that you know what elements form part of your goal and what elements definitely don't.

Finally, a question that seems to very seldom asked, but is perhaps the most important of all, makes up the third axis. Projects can have lots of different outcomes - bad, average, good, outstanding and the whole gamut in between. What is the best possible outcome from your point of view; the fairy tale ending, the one that would really knock everyone's - the team, your boss, the customer's - socks off? Given that the project can have all these possible outcomes, why opt for an average, scrape-across-the-finishing-line sort of one, when you could have a great one?

Conceptually, the points you select on the three axes fix a point in three-dimensional space which is the goal of your project. Thinking about these three aspects of your project puts a bound around the goal and determines what lies within and outside the compass of your project.

 ## Applying Step 1 of Structured Project Management to software engineering

As I wrote the first edition of this book, my company was managing a project to develop a large software product for a major telecommunications company. The entire project was estimated to be in excess of 600 man-years, and would last several years. The project was in a very preliminary requirements gathering phase.

There was at least one part of the project - about 20 man-years of effort - which had to be delivered by the end of 1993 at the latest. Let's look at the application of Step 1 of Structured Project Management to that part of the project.

As we have seen earlier, it is important to identify what marks the end of the project. To some extent, this can be an almost arbitrary decision we make. For example, we might declare the day the software ships as the end of the project. A slightly better idea might be to declare the ship day plus say 3 months, as the end date. That would give us a chance to see what the customers think of the product. Let's do that then. Let's say that we expected to ship the product at the end of 1993, and 3 months after that, we would declare the project over. By this we mean that we will move the product into a maintenance and enhancement project, and do an audit (see chapter 10) as the last act of our project.

Thus, we expected this to be happening about the end of March 1994, all going well. Let's apply step 1 by following the visualisation checklist at the end of the previous section.

- This project will actually be very significant to all of those involved in it. The organisation my company is working with are a very new organisation, and this will be their first major project and deliverable. All of the people working on it will be new to the organisation, and bringing it in on time, on budget and producing a quality product will be a tremendous fillip to them. It will also enable the organisation with which my company is working, to say to its customer (not to mention its parent) - `we can do it - we have justified the faith you had in us'.

- We have focused very closely on the things the project will produce. We have done this by visualising a software catalogue in which all of the individual items which the project will deliver are listed. There is a core software product, 3 add-on modules, and two sets of documentation. When the project is finished, these things will be delivered to other project teams who will then build the much larger (600 man-year) system around our deliverables. The deliverables will also eventually go to the end customer, but that is a long time in the future.

- We have talked already on what the project will mean to the members of the project team, and what their motivation might be in doing it.

- The reason I want to do it is that this is the biggest project yet to which Structured Project Management has been applied. I am excited to see how it will work.

- What will life be like on the day/week the project completes? This question, and others like it, are ones which enable you to create the daydream we talked about earlier. It is one thing to talk about motivations and other grand notions, but these are things that can change or drift out of focus with time. Thinking, on the other hand, about what you will do one day somewhere in the future, when a certain set of circumstances have come to pass, is a lot more concrete; and creates a vision which you can lock onto and carry with you.

- What then will life be like when this project completes? It will be a day at the end of March. The customer will have had the product three months by then, and we will know from the error reports (or lack of them!) coming in, how successful it has been. What we would like would be that there were no error reports at all. (I once had this experience - for 6 months no errors were reported. And yes, the product was in use!)

- To get back to the daydream: We will probably have planned a meeting for that day in March. There will probably have been a regular meeting ever since the product was shipped, to review how the customer was getting on; but this particular day will be the final meeting.

- I will probably get up early, go for a run and then make my way into the office. I can picture in my head the people who will be at the meeting - people from my company, people from my client's organisation and (perhaps) people from the customer, though it is more likely that they will be indicating their acceptance of the product by fax or phone.

- We expect there to be a lot of happy people around that day. The client organisation, pleased that their customer is saying nice things about the product and its robustness; the members of the project team, some of them perhaps already assigned to other projects but here for the last act but one of the project (the last act will be the audit); people from my company, pleased that we have delivered on what we set out to do.

- The meeting will be brief, reviewing the errors reported over the last 3 months, logging what can be learned from them, spotting where the errors got through our checks, and planning that such things don't happen again. Maybe there will be champagne or cake or some form of little celebration. Maybe there will be bets to be settled (see the chapter on Problem Solving!). Maybe there will be some nice comments about the product that we can savour for a while. Maybe there'll be a celebratory lunch.

- OK, I'm sure you get the idea. This is a picture you can enhance and embellish either on paper or in your head, elaborating it with all sorts of incidents, people and words. What is important is to understand what you will feel when the project ends, because from that will stem your motivation. I know what I will feel - just a great sense of achievement, of happiness for the people who worked so hard to make it happen.

- As regards what an audit will say about it let's write down the answers we would like to be giving to the audit checklist.

- Did we end up where we said we would? Yes. Exactly. The goal wasn't materially different from the predicted goal. It never changed and we were constantly aware that it hadn't.

- Using the Estimating Score Card in chapter 19 (or alternatively, reports generated by our project planning tool) we would have captured estimated vs. actuals for the project, and we would be able to review these to understand where our estimating needed improvement.

- We would like to be able to say that we did lots right and very little wrong, and that here are the lessons we can learn from the things we did do wrong.
- We would like to be able to say that very few surprises of any significance occurred; and again, of those that did, here are the lessons for the future.
- We would like to be able to say that we didn't have to touch our margin for error; and if we did eat into it in any way, that again there are lessons.
- These are all the things we'd like to be saying in a future audit of our project.
- For my company, this project will be a major feather in its cap, and I will be hoping that we can use it as a springboard to other, larger projects. I'll be hoping that people will be saying that only a company like mine could have done a project like this as well as it was done. I'll be hoping that people will be saying it was a pleasure to work on the project and that they would like to work with my company again in the future.
- Will my standard of living have changed? Come on, project management doesn't pay that well!
- I don't think my view of myself will have changed, but it's nice for a relatively new company like mine to add something like this to its track record. I think the task we have set ourselves is difficult enough and has plenty of room for failure. I couldn't bear it if it did fail.

The remaining questions we have probably covered in the course of our ramblings. It's not essential that you answer them all, rather that you get into the thought process behind them. If you end up with a daydream that you can start to carry around in your head, then you can probably press on from step 1.

 Step 1, PSI contribution - 20

Step 1 contributes 20 towards the PSI. You can think of the score out of 20 as being a measure of how completely well-defined or otherwise the goal of the project is. At the beginning, when the project goal is only a vague idea in peoples' heads, the score out of 20 will be close to or at 0. The score only reaches 20 on the day the project ends. Only then will you know *exactly* what the goal of the project turned out to be.

The step 1 score will vary within the range 0-20 over the life of the project. Thus, for example, suppose your project life cycle had a number of phases in it, say:

- Requirements gathering
- Design
- Implementation
- Integration
- Testing
- Release

then the PSI would gradually increase as you completed each of these phases. If you think of the score as a measure of how well-defined the goal of the project has become as a result of each phase, then you might assign values to these six phases as follows:

Requirements gathering	4
Design	9
Implementation	14
Integration	17
Testing	19
Release	20

To use the PSI for your own projects, you should do a similar exercise in which you map the 20 points available onto the phases of your own project life cycle. Remember, the way to do it is to analyse how much more well-defined the goal of the project has become as a result of each phase.

An alternative way would be to break the goal of the project down into blocks and allocate a maximum score per block, the sum of the maximum scores adding up to 20.

Structured Project Management

Planning the Project

1. Visualise what the goal is; set your eyes on the prize

Chapter 2

Step 2 - Make a list of the jobs to be done

Introduction

I had a boss once, a man from the North of England. No project was too daunting for him, whether it was software development or house renovation. I used to pass the house he was then renovating on my way home from work. Often, in all kinds of weather, his children would be out helping him, shovelling, mixing concrete, carrying things.

'Make a list of jobs that need doing', was one of his favourite sayings. He would also refer to his children as 'the sprogs'. In work we put the two sayings together and came up with 'Make list of jobs and give to sprogs', said in a Yorkshire accent. It seemed the only way to explain how he got so much done in his life.

'Make list of jobs and give to sprogs' - make a list of the jobs that need to be done and you've got yourself your project plan. There's only one catch - what if you don't know everything that has to be done?

Not a problem. At the risk of boring you with references to Polar exploration, a project is just like a journey across featureless wasteland. You know where you want to end up and you knew the general direction to take. But you have no idea what lies between here and there; all you can see is the first horizon. What Polar explorers do is steer for a point on that horizon. Only when you get there can you decide how to face into the next bit of the journey.

Projects are exactly the same. The very first thing you do when you start a new project is to make a plan. You may only be able to write down the first one or two tasks, but you're already moving forward. Get yourself to that first horizon and then take stock of what needs to be done next. You will always know in quite a lot of detail what lies between you and that first horizon - even though there will inevitably be surprises. For the rest of the project it is enough that you have mapped out in broad terms the remaining milestones (horizons) along the way.

There will come a time when you have to predict the remainder of the project, but try to postpone that moment for as long as possible, until you have gathered as much information as you can upon which to base your decision.

In the computer industry we call these predictions SWAGs - Scientific Wild-Ass Guesses - but as we shall see, it's not quite as bad as that. Yes, you do have to guess, but by comparing your early guesses against what actually happened, you can start to get a feel for how accurate your guessing is and adjust your plan accordingly.

Your plan becomes the steering compass by which you steer the project. As you reach each horizon, you check the lie of the land and then push on to the new horizon. 'Make list of jobs and give to sprogs'. For us, step 2 of our method is 'Make a list of the jobs that need to be done'.

The list can be in any form. It can be an actual list, like a shopping list; it can be put on to a computerised project planning package - we do this for a lot of our software projects; it can be a chart. Many large companies have a defined standard and layout for a project plan, and you may have to follow this. It doesn't matter a toss what it looks like. It doesn't matter that you don't yet know all the jobs that need to be done. Write down the jobs that you know have to be done to get the project started and leave the crystal ball-gazing until you feel yourself better informed.

You will never feel entirely happy about predictions when you are forced to make them. In some situations, e.g. in business, in the military, you may be forced to make predictions and know that in the first case, maybe your job is on the line, and in the second, lives are on the line. No doubt about it. A lot of projects are about serious things, and a lot of project leaders make decisions which do affect careers and/or lives.

One other thing about jobs. Jobs must be explicit. Think through or write down the sequence of events that must happen for the job to be carried out. If you cannot do this, or if you fudge it, then the chances are you're not being explicit enough. Often this is because what you are treating as one job is in fact a series of jobs. What you should do then is to break it down further, remembering that jobs can be: (a) serial in nature - job A must be done before job B can start; (b) parallel in nature - jobs A and B can be done at the same time; (c) grouped - job A really consists of a number of jobs which all have to complete before job A can be considered complete. (Watch these little guys - they're the ones that will get you if you're not careful.)

Making a checklist

When drawing up your list of jobs, the following may help you to ensure you have covered all possible jobs and areas. Assuming you have drawn up your basic list, then check the following:

- Resources - equipment, products, services, facilities - required.
- Skills required and whether these imply hiring and/or training.
- That you have listed explicit, clearly identifiable milestones.
- Timescales, costs and budgets - that you show how you arrived at your estimates.
- That you have explicitly stated what assumptions you are making.
- That you have explicitly stated what dependencies there are on things which are not directly under your control.
- That you show explicitly who is responsible for what.
- That you have given some thought to what the really high-risk areas are.

Identifying the jobs with form # 1

The form shown in figure 2.1 overleaf can be used to help identify all the jobs in a project. The project is written in the box at the top and then the jobs that go to make up the project are written sequentially underneath. Because of our recursive definition of 'project', any job can then be further broken down by writing its name in the box at the top.

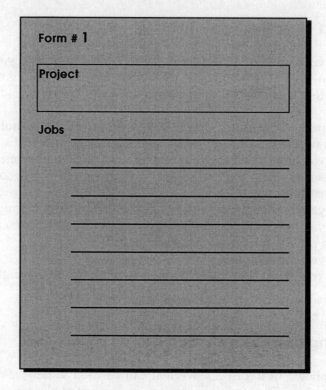

Figure 2.1 Form # 1 - job list

Applying Step 2 of Structured Project Management to software engineering

As soon as a project gives any sign at all of starting, we are in a position to make a list of jobs for it. As we have discussed already, the list should be detailed to the first milestone and give the major milestones thereafter. In addition, what you can do is to add any other available detail to the remaining milestones. This isn't essential, but given that we may have such detail available, and that we will have to put it in some day, we may as well do it now. The advantage of this is that it starts to give us some feel for the magnitude of the remainder of the project. (We will return to this idea in chapter 19 on Software Estimating.)

In the two sections that follow I have given real-life examples of job lists. The first list is a project to achieve the ISO9001 quality standard accreditation [Ref. 49].

The project has four major jobs within it (remember our recursive definition of project):

- Decide to implement ISO9001
- Set up organisation
- Set up and install Quality System
- Apply for certification

The first job has been further broken down into four jobs, and these have been estimated at a total of 5 man-days. The remainder of the job list then gives as much as is known of the rest of the project. Note that we have gone down, wherever possible, to very low levels of detail. This will be the basis of our estimating method in chapter 19.

Example 1: Preliminary plan to get ISO9001 certification

---

1. Decide to implement ISO9001
Develop a Quality Policy statement and have this approved by the board of Telecom Ireland Software and explained to everyone in ACME Software. Total 20 man-days estimated. Includes:

- Develop statement.
- Review internally.
- Take to Board for approval.
- Circulate to everybody.
- Education, i.e. Standards Bodies (videos or other support available?), give an introductory course, ongoing quality training, ongoing awareness of quality program, issues and results.

2. Set up organisation
- Nominate a Quality Manager.
- Set up a quality improvement team.

3. Set up and install Quality System
This involves installing and running a Quality System which is described by a Quality Manual. There are two sides to the work: write the Quality Manual describing the Quality System ('document what you do') and install and run the system described in the Quality Manual ('do what you document').

These two aspects of the work would typically proceed in parallel. A framework for a Quality Manual has already been drawn up. The bulk of the work involved in achieving ISO9001 is to devise the quality system, implement it and document it within the Quality Manual framework.

The bulk of the rest of this document estimates the size of that task, both in terms of setting up / installing the procedure and documenting it in the Quality Manual. Some notes on implementing the Quality System:

- It would be useful to review the contents of the Quality Manual with the Standards Bodies or a quality auditor / consultant.
- Plan should allow for up to 10 man-days of consultant's time.
- Integral elements in implementing the Quality System are:
  - the measurement of the quality of products and the processes which produce them.
  - calculating the cost of quality.
  - taking corrective action based on the measurements above.

Note: In the following example all estimates are in man-days (MD).

	Section in Quality Manual	Set-up/install procedure	Document procedure
1	**Introduction**		
1.1	Company description extract from Marketing brochures	0	0.5
1.2	Place of Quality Manual in overall procedures - written	0	0
1.3	Quality Policy statement (get from 1 above) and education programme	20	1
1.4	Use TIS Organisation chart	0	0
1.5	Define an amendment procedure	0.5	0.5
1.6	Circulation list and procedure	0.5	0
	Totals	**21**	**2**
2	**Documentation**		
2.1	Use Myles' document	0.5	0.5
2.2	Use Myles' document	0.5	0.5
2.3	Document management (2 documents)		
	- Write	5	
	- Review	1	
	- Update	2	
	- Approve	1	
	- Publish	1	1
	Totals	**11**	**2**
3	**Project Management**		
3.1	Project Management Methodology (Adopt? Document wrt book. Project exit criteria, sample Project Plan)	1	4
3.2	Estimating & Scheduling (Document wrt book & MS-Project. Include examples; Historical database)	1	4
3.3	Monitoring & Reporting (Needs an EV system; Project Status report; sample Progress report)	5	6
	Include timesheets and time recording	1	1
	Totals	**8**	**15**

4 Project Life Cycle

4.1	Overview	0	1
4.2	Requirements Spec.	0	
	- Research		1
	- Write (including template)		2
	- Review (possibly by using)		-
	- Rework		1
	- Release	0.5	
4.3	High level design		
	- Research		1
	- Write (inc. deliverables, review/exit criteria, template)		2
	- Review (ideally by using)		-
	- Rework		1
	- Release	0.5	
4.4	Low level design (inc. User Documentation and Test Plans)		
	- Research		2
	- Write (inc. template)		3
	- Review (ideally by using)		-
	- Rework		1
	- Release	0.5	
4.5	Implementation (inc. Code, Unit Test, Integration and Test)		
	- Research (inc. UDFs, walkthroughs, etc.)		2
	- Write (inc. deliverables, review/exit criteria, template)		3
	- Review (ideally by using)		-
	- Rework		1
	- Release	0.5	
4.6	Alpha test		
	- Research		2
	- Write (inc. deliverables, review/exit criteria, template)		3
	- Review (ideally by using)		-
	- Rework		1
	- Release	0.5	
4.7	Beta test		
	- Research		2
	- Write (inc. deliverables, review/exit criteria, template)		3
	- Review (ideally by using)		-

	- Rework		1
	- Release	0.5	
4.8	Operation and Maintenance		
	- Research		2
	- Write (inc. deliverables, review/exit criteria, template)		3
	- Review (ideally by using)	-	
	- Rework		1
	- Release	0.5	
4.9	Configuration Management and Change Control		
	- Research		3
	- Write (inc. deliverables, review/exit criteria, template)		5
	- Review (ideally by using)	-	
	- Rework		1
	- Release	0.5	
	Totals	**4**	**48**
5	**Invoicing and Accounting**		
	Guess	3	5
6	**Training**		
	Will refer to TIS Training Plan (to be estimated separately)	1	1
7	**Subcontractors**		
	Guess	1	10
8	**Orders and Enquiries**		
	Not required by ISO9001 but a good thing to include. Includes Prospects List. Guess	3	5
9	**Personnel**		
9.1	General procedures	5	5
9.2	Organisation chart - done	0	0
9.3	Grading Structure / Job Descriptions	10	20
9.4	Salary Scales	10	10
	Totals	**25**	**35**

10   The Quality System Itself

10.1	Internal audits - review / update of procedures (quality)	5	5
10.2	Cost of quality - maintenance of quality records (guess)	5	5
Totals		**10**	**10**

4. Apply for certification
Sequence of events is:

Run an internal audit (or perhaps a series of them)	20
Submit application form and a copy of the Quality Manual (QM)	2
Standards Bodies vet QM and notifies TIS of any discrepancies which must then be rectified	20
When these are rectified, Standards Bodies audits TIS onsite and again identifies discrepancies	30
Standards Bodies verify remedial action has been taken and recommends award of ISO9001 certificate	10
Total	**82**

Example 2: Plan for a software engineering project

The second example is for a software engineering project. It's actually for a first phase of the project I talked about in chapter 1. This job list was done using Microsoft Project. Figure 2.2 gives day-level detail for an activity called *Restructure 'C' code* and as much detail as is available for the rest of the project.

Don't spend too much time going into these figures in any detail (for one thing, they're not complete - so don't assume that, for example, you'll get ISO9001 accreditation by following the first example!). They are merely snapshots of projects at a particular point in time. They are given here to illustrate the following important points in connection with making job lists:

- Use a project planning tool if at all possible - they give so much more clarity as I think is illustrated by the difference between the plans in

Figures 2.1, page 20 and 2.2, pages 31 to 33. Any of the popular PC ones - Timeline, MS-Project, Microplanner, MACProject, Harvard Project Manager, PMW or others - will do; which one is relatively unimportant. The effort involved in learning and inputting information to them will be repaid a hundredfold in the understanding, flexibility, responsiveness and breadth of vision that this computer model of your project will give you. As I become older and more set in my ways, I venture to suggest that anyone who doesn't use one of these things is nuts!

- Write down the major milestones.
- Fill out the first milestone in complete detail.
- Fill out the remaining milestones with as much detail as is available (you can use the checklist given previously to assist you in doing this).

And what level of detail are we talking about? This is one that always seems to cause people problems. Well, note that the example has about 600 man-days in it. The job list contains about 110 jobs. This means that on average each job covers about five or six man-days. And remember that this is only the beginning of the project. As it proceeds we will accumulate much greater levels of detail, so that it is quite likely that each job will cover five or less days. A pain in the neck? You bet. But this is the only way that success can be assured - by ensuring that no matter how big the project is, that each component is planned and tracked by someone at the day level of detail. It doesn't have to be you, and on a big project it won't be - but someone had better be doing it.

I know the following to be absolutely true: When you break it right down, any project ends up as a large number of occurrences of Joe Soap or Jill Bloggs spending two days here or half a day there or doing job A prior to job B. Now, as the Project Manager, there are two crucial issues that you have to address. These are: 1, Are we consciously going to decide who will work on what when? and 2, If so, when are we going to decide?

The first is not as dumb as it sounds. All Project Managers hand out work assignments which are more or less detailed. There is then an inherent assumption that these assignments will get translated into the 'two days here / half day there' we talked about earlier. If they do, fine. But if they don't then it means that some force other than the Project Manager - let's call it Life - is making these work allocations. The allocations will get done - have no fear about that - because if you don't do them, Life will. But one of the things about Life is that it can be unfair, and if you rely on Life to do your work allocations for you, then you're asking for trouble.

Let's look at the second issue. Assuming you're consciously going to allocate your people to jobs, when should you do this? Well, you have a choice. You can either do it at the beginning, during the planning part of a project when things are relatively quiet, or you can do it in the middle of the project, in the heat of battle, when the bombs are falling and all hell is breaking loose. You will have to do it, so why not make things easy on yourself, and do as much as you can at the beginning when the pressures aren't so bad. And don't worry about it not getting done, because as before Life will intervene and do it for you. But again, you need that kind of assistance like you need a hole in the head.

Let's try to summarise what we're saying here about levels of detail. There is a quote in probably the most famous book on software project management, *The Mythical Man-Month* by Fred Brooks. *'How does a project get to be a year late?'* The answer? '*... one day at a time.*'

Know where your man-days are going, every one of them. Spend them wisely. If you don't, you'll find out just how fickle Life can be.

Once, at a seminar, I was pushing the idea of the plan being at the day level of detail, and somebody asked whether this didn't present an unacceptable overhead. Specifically, the question was whether I had estimated the effort/cost involved in the management of Scott's project versus that of Amundsen. There are two answers to that question. The first is that if we assume that Scott did all the Project Management on his project and Amundsen on his, then both put in almost exactly the same amount of effort - three years. The second answer is this and it is not intended to sound clever. Amundsen had a successful project. Thus whatever the management of it cost, it was worth it. Scott's project cost the lives of five people. At this kind of price there is no such thing as an 'unacceptable overhead'.

 ## Step 2 PSI contribution - 20

Step 2 contributes 20 towards the PSI. You can think of the score out of 20 as being a measure of how completely well-defined or otherwise the plan for the project is. At the beginning, when the project is just beginning, the plan probably contains nothing more than the major milestones with some - probably incomplete - detail thrown in. Then the score out of 20 will be very low. On the day the project ends, the plan will be complete, and will show the myriad little jobs, all strung together, that went into carrying out the project. This is the only time the score can reach 20

Thus, between the beginning and end of the project, the score will vary within the range 0-20. Thus, for example, suppose your project life cycle had a number of phases in it, say:

- Requirements gathering
- Design
- Implementation
- Integration
- Testing
- Release

then the PSI would gradually increase as you completed each of these phases. If you think of the score as a measure of how much closer you are to knowing all of the jobs that have to be done to complete the project, then you might assign values to these six phases as follows:

Requirements gathering	4
Design	9
Implementation	14
Integration	17
Testing	19
Release	20

To use the PSI for your own projects, you should do a similar exercise in which you map the 20 points available onto the phases of your own project life cycle. Remember, the score is a measure of how close you are to knowing all of the jobs that have to be done to complete the project.

As before, an alternative way would be to break the overall project plan down into sub-plans for each of its individual components. Then, allocate a maximum score per sub-plan, the sum of the maximum scores adding up to 20.

Structured Project Management:

Planning the Project

1.   Visualise what the goal is; set your eyes on the prize

2.   **Make a list of the jobs that need to be done**

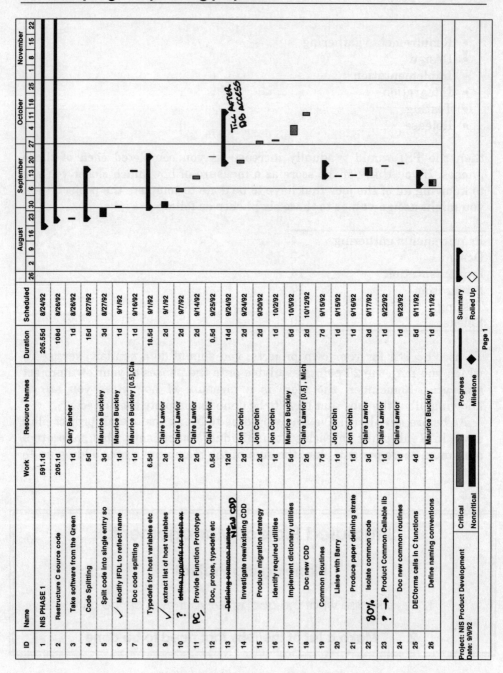

The table content of the project plan figure:

ID	Name	Work	Resource Names	Duration	Scheduled
1	NIS PHASE 1	591.1d		205.55d	8/24/92
2	Restructure C source code	205.1d		108d	8/26/92
3	Take software from the Green	1d	Gary Barber	1d	8/26/92
4	Code Splitting	5d		15d	8/27/92
5	Split code into single entry so	3d	Maurice Buckley	3d	8/27/92
6	Modify IFDL to reflect name	1d	Maurice Buckley	1d	9/1/92
7	Doc code splitting	1d	Maurice Buckley [0.5],Cla	1d	9/16/92
8	Typedefs for host variables etc	6.5d		18.5d	9/1/92
9	extract list of host variables	2d	Claire Lawlor	2d	9/1/92
10	define typedefs for each ex	2d	Claire Lawlor	2d	9/7/92
11	Provide Function Prototype	2d	Claire Lawlor	2d	9/14/92
12	Doc, protos, typedefs etc	0.5d	Claire Lawlor	0.5d	9/25/92
13	Defining common name	12d		14d	9/24/92
14	Investigate new/existing CDD	2d	Jon Corbin	2d	9/24/92
15	Produce migration strategy	2d	Jon Corbin	2d	9/30/92
16	Identify required utilities	1d	Jon Corbin	1d	10/2/92
17	Implement dictionary utilities	5d	Maurice Buckley	5d	10/5/92
18	Doc new CDD	2d	Claire Lawlor [0.5] , Mich	2d	10/12/92
19	Common Routines	7d		7d	9/15/92
20	Liaise with Barry	1d	Jon Corbin	1d	9/15/92
21	Produce paper defining strate	1d	Jon Corbin	1d	9/16/92
22	Isolate common code	3d	Claire Lawlor	3d	9/17/92
23	Product Common Callable lib	1d	Claire Lawlor	1d	9/22/92
24	Doc new common routines	1d	Claire Lawlor	1d	9/23/92
25	DECforms calls in C functions	4d		5d	9/11/92
26	Define naming conventions	1d	Maurice Buckley	1d	9/11/92

Handwritten annotations: "?" (row 10), "PC" (row 11), "New CDD" (row 13), "80%" and "?" (rows 22–23), "TILL AFTER DB ACCESS" (October area)

Project: NIS Product Development
Date: 9/9/92

Critical / Noncritical / Progress / Milestone / Summary / Rolled Up

Page 1

Figure 2.2 Example of project plan

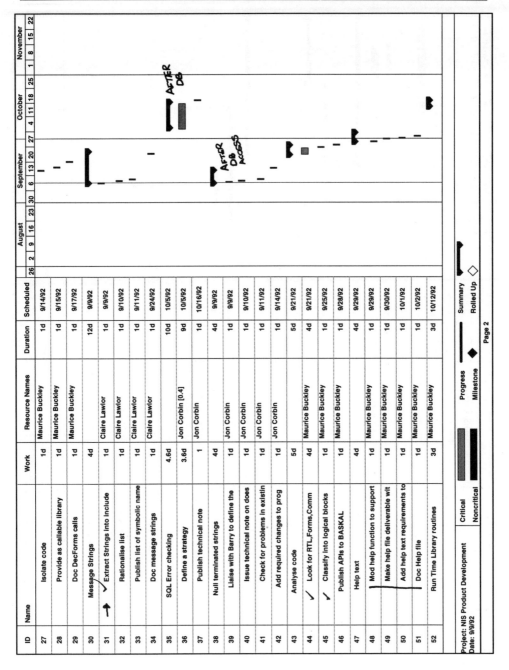

ID	Name	Work	Resource Names	Duration	Scheduled
27	Isolate code	1d	Maurice Buckley	1d	9/14/92
28	Provide as callable library	1d	Maurice Buckley	1d	9/15/92
29	Doc DecForms calls	1d	Maurice Buckley	1d	9/17/92
30	Message Strings	4d		12d	9/9/92
31	Extract Strings into include	1d	Claire Lawlor	1d	9/9/92
32	Rationalise list	1d	Claire Lawlor	1d	9/10/92
33	Publish list of symbolic name	1d	Claire Lawlor	1d	9/11/92
34	Doc message strings	1d	Claire Lawlor	1d	9/24/92
35	SQL Error checking	4.6d		10d	10/5/92
36	Define a strategy	3.6d	Jon Corbin [0.4]	9d	10/5/92
37	Publish technical note	1	Jon Corbin	1d	10/16/92
38	Null terminated strings	4d		4d	9/9/92
39	Liaise with Barry to define the	1d	Jon Corbin	1d	9/9/92
40	Issue technical note on does	1d	Jon Corbin	1d	9/10/92
41	Check for problems in existin	1d	Jon Corbin	1d	9/11/92
42	Add required changes to prog	1d	Jon Corbin	1d	9/14/92
43	Analyse code	5d		5d	9/21/92
44	Look for RTL,Forms,Comm	4d	Maurice Buckley	4d	9/21/92
45	Classify into logical blocks	1d	Maurice Buckley	1d	9/25/92
46	Publish APIs to BASKAL	1d	Maurice Buckley	1d	9/28/92
47	Help text	4d		4d	9/29/92
48	Mod help function to support	1d	Maurice Buckley	1d	9/29/92
49	Make help file deliverable wit	1d	Maurice Buckley	1d	9/30/92
50	Add help text requirements to	1d	Maurice Buckley	1d	10/1/92
51	Doc Help file	1d	Maurice Buckley	1d	10/2/92
52	Run Time Library routines	3d	Maurice Buckley	3d	10/12/92

Project: NIS Product Development
Date: 9/9/92

Critical   Noncritical   Progress   Milestone   Summary   Rolled Up

Page 2

Figure 2.2 cont'd

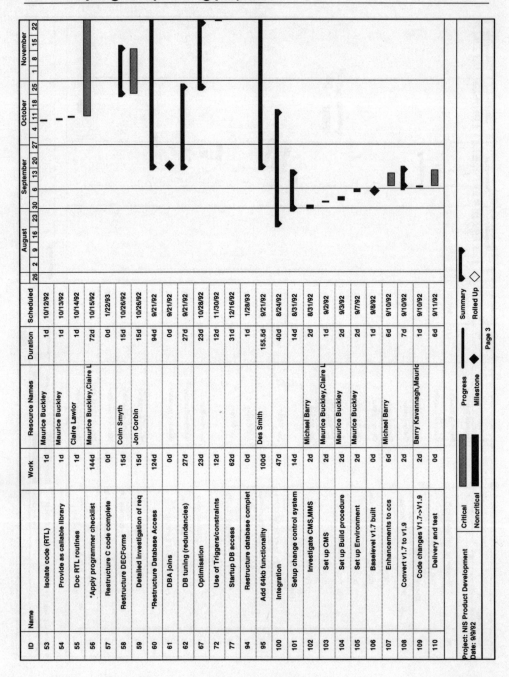

ID	Name	Work	Resource Names	Duration	Scheduled
53	Isolate code (RTL)	1d	Maurice Buckley	1d	10/12/92
54	Provide as callable library	1d	Maurice Buckley	1d	10/13/92
55	Doc RTL routines	1d	Claire Lawlor	1d	10/14/92
56	*Apply programmer checklist	144d	Maurice Buckley,Claire L	72d	10/15/92
57	Restructure C code complete	0d		0d	1/22/93
58	Restructure DECForms	15d	Colm Smyth	15d	10/26/92
59	Detailed investigation of req	15d	Jon Corbin	15d	10/26/92
60	*Restructure Database Access	124d		94d	9/21/92
61	DBA joins	0d		0d	9/21/92
62	DB tuning (redundancies)	27d		27d	9/21/92
67	Optimisation	23d		23d	10/28/92
72	Use of Triggers/constraints	12d		12d	11/30/92
77	Startup DB access	62d		31d	12/16/92
94	Restructure database complet	0d		1d	1/28/93
95	Add 64kb functionality	100d	Des Smith	155.5d	9/21/92
100	Integration	47d		40d	8/24/92
101	Setup change control system	14d		14d	8/31/92
102	Investigate CMS,MMS	2d	Michael Barry	2d	8/31/92
103	Set up CMS	2d	Maurice Buckley,Claire L	1d	9/2/92
104	Set up Build procedure	2d	Maurice Buckley	2d	9/3/92
105	Set up Environment	2d	Maurice Buckley	2d	9/7/92
106	Baselevel v1.7 built	0d		1d	9/8/92
107	Enhancements to ccs	6d	Michael Barry	6d	9/10/92
108	Convert v1.7 to v1.9	2d		7d	9/10/92
109	Code changes V1.7->V1.9	2d	Barry Kavannagh,Mauric	1d	9/10/92
110	Delivery and test	0d		6d	9/11/92

Project: NIS Product Development
Date: 9/9/92

Critical / Noncritical / Progress / Milestone / Summary / Rolled Up

Page 3

Figure 2.2 cont'd

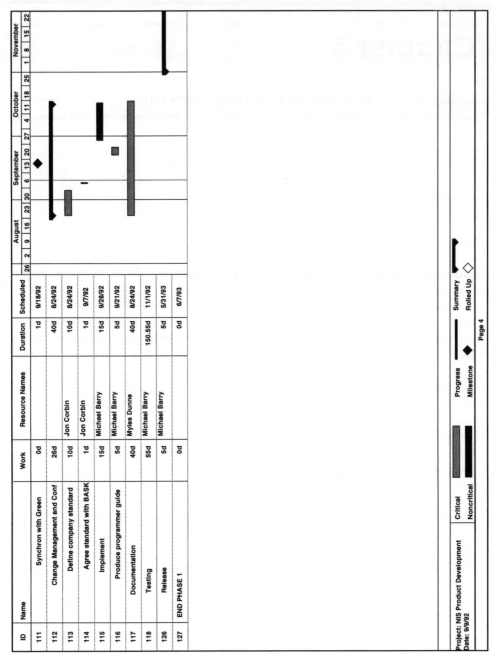

ID	Name	Work	Resource Names	Duration	Scheduled
111	Synchron with Green	0d		1d	9/18/92
112	Change Management and Conf	26d		40d	8/24/92
113	Define company standard	10d	Jon Corbin	10d	8/24/92
114	Agree standard with BASK	1d	Jon Corbin	1d	9/7/92
115	Implement	15d	Michael Barry	15d	9/28/92
116	Produce programmer guide	5d	Michael Barry	5d	9/21/92
117	Documentation	40d	Myles Dunne	40d	8/24/92
118	Testing	55d	Michael Barry	150.55d	11/1/92
126	Release	5d	Michael Barry	5d	5/31/93
127	END PHASE 1	0d		0d	6/7/93

Project: NIS Product Development
Date: 9/9/92

Critical
Noncritical

Progress
Milestone

Summary
Rolled Up

Page 4

Figure 2.2 cont'd

Chapter 3

Step 3 - There must be one leader

Introduction

'But of course there is a leader,' I hear you say, 'it's the first thing we do when we start a new project. We appoint a leader'.

And indeed this may well be true. Whatever else may be said about most projects that we come across, we can pretty much always identify the leader. And isn't it quite a nice sounding title, to give to somebody or to have ourselves? 'Project Leader'. 'Project Manager'. It's a title that settles easily on the shoulders like a fine coat. We walk that bit taller with the responsibility and pressure that we now carry. Yes indeed, we can always point out the Project Leader - if nothing else we can tell him by the way he walks!

Let me re-state the chapter title. The project must have one leader. By that I mean it can't have no leaders and it can't have two leaders or a committee of leaders. THERE MUST BE ONE LEADER.

Let's look at this statement a bit more closely. When I say 'leader', I mean not so much the person with the title, but a person who is going to get the project done. She lives, eats and breathes the project. She is going to get it done or die in the attempt. At any given time she has her finger on the pulse of the project and knows how it's proceeding. Her name is so intimately bound up with the project that when you think of one you think of the other. A fairly negative way of looking at it is that she is the person whose ass is pinned to the project and who will get fired if it doesn't work out. In the terminology of other books she is the project champion.

I have worked on a project where there was no leader, in the sense that I have described it above. I have worked on a project where there was a formal leader, and a person who took over the psychological leadership, thereby resulting in two leaders. Both projects were unmitigated disasters. In the first case, the person with the title Project Leader was fired, and in

34

the second, both the project leaders were fired.

As you can see, sometimes the problem is finding a person, sometimes there are too many contenders.

Case Study 1

One thing that can happen to you as a project leader is that your leadership can be subject to challenge by another member of the team. This means that somebody else tries to take over the psychological leadership of the project from you. If this happens you must neutralise the challenge. If you don't, you will end up with multiple leaders on your project.

Amundsen - the project leader - had a leadership challenge during his expedition to the South Pole in 1911 [Refs 1, 30]. One of his men, Hjalmar Johansen, was a Polar explorer in his own right. He had been on an earlier expedition with Fridtjof Nansen, the father of Norwegian Polar exploration. Together they had made a dash for the North Pole. They hadn't reached it but had gotten 170 miles closer than anybody else had done, reaching 86° 14' North. Amundsen had reluctantly brought Johansen, urged to do so by Nansen.

From the beginning of the voyage, Johansen began to compare Amundsen's voyage unfavourably with Nansen's. Johansen was a better skier and dog-driver than Amundsen and felt he knew more about Polar travel. Often he would correct or contradict Amundsen or volunteer advice. These matters later came to a head when Amundsen set out on his Polar journey: Amundsen was anxious to set out for the Pole, plagued by the thought that Scott might already have started and that Scott had brought motorised transport with him. His colleagues, and particularly Johansen, warned him against too early a start. Amundsen wanted to start on August 24th but having twice put it to a vote - and having been defeated - he yielded. Finally, on September 8th, 1911, which is still the Polar Winter, Amundsen could restrain himself no longer, and the party of men, sledges and dogs set off from their base.

The start turned out to be a disaster. Temperatures plummeted; dogs died from the cold; liquid froze in compasses and the men eventually turned back. At breakfast, after they had all returned, Johansen took Amundsen to task for what had happened. This challenge to his leadership was too much for Amundsen. Johansen was removed from the party going to the Pole. Years later he would commit suicide.

Case Study 2

I have stated that not having one leader will guarantee failure. Unhappily, the converse isn't true - having a leader doesn't guarantee success. Scott [Ref. 30] is a case in point. He was all the things I have indicated above. He did live, eat and breathe the project. He was going to get it done or die in the attempt. Scott reached the South Pole a month after Amundsen and perished with all four of his team on the return journey.

In terms of Structured Project Management, it was his failure to carry out steps (2), (5), (6) and (8) which sealed his fate. To reiterate, there must be one leader. Not zero, not two and not a committee. I believe your project will fail if this is not so.

Case Study 3

I remember my first day on the job in a new company. I was given a copy of the Project Status Book. As the name suggested the book contained the state of every project in the organisation. It was updated weekly, well laid-out and very pretty. Each page had some summary information about the project at the top; name, start and end dates, project leader and so on.

I was amazed to see the same handful of names in all the project leader slots. There were people in there handling ten, fifteen projects. I was young then, and very impressed; I thought these guys must be absolute tigers to be able to stay on top of so many things. It was only later I discovered that they weren't on top of all these things, and that their names up there in the heading meant nothing. Sure they were responsible, maybe their necks were even on the line for those projects, but they sure as hell weren't leading them. There must be one leader.

Case Study 4

One idea I have come across a few times in software projects is that of having a technical leader and a managerial or administrative leader. The managerial leader is more a manager type person who has no interest in things technical, while the technical leader doesn't want to be a manager, but still wants to have a big say in what goes on.

Forget it. Unless there is one manager and he has the final, overall say, then a Laurel and Hardy approach like this won't work. There must be one leader.

A role model

If we are looking for a project manager to act as a role model, we can do no better than to look at some of those old cattle drive Westerns with John Wayne as the trail boss. (You could also read *Lonesome Dove* by Larry McMurtry [Ref. 40].) I'm sure we're all familiar with the scenario. Several thousand head of cattle have to be driven from the Rio Grande to a railhead, usually either Kansas City or Abilene. The entire film then consists of all the incidents that occur on the way.

If we compare the jobs on your job list to the cattle in the cattle drive, the we have a very good analogy for how projects actually proceed. At any given time in the cattle drive, we can probably identify a steady state situation something along the following lines:

Most of the herd are heading generally in the direction of Abilene. (This excludes the mandatory stampede sequence where the entire herd heads off to some place entirely different. Hopefully you will never have a stampede on one of your projects!)

While the majority of the herd are behaving themselves, it is however probably safe to assume that some of the herd are heading backwards to the Rio Grande - they have no plans to go to Abilene or any place the trail boss (John Wayne) has in mind for them

Others have drifted off to a gulch where they've found some sweet grass and are grazing contentedly

Others are at a watering hole and are keeping cool and haven't the slightest interest in getting back on the march under a hot sun

Finally, some cattle have perhaps wandered on ahead and been rustled.

John Wayne, meanwhile, spends the entire film riding around the herd, bringing up the stragglers, scouting on ahead for trouble, and generally making sure that all the cattle are headed for Abilene.

Without wishing to labour the analogy any more, this is exactly what the project leader has to do - to make sure that all the jobs are being pushed forward, and that the entire 'herd' of jobs is moving in the right direction.

Note too that if you decide to be this kind of project leader then this may well generate more jobs for your job list. The logic is simple and unfaultable:

If you want a successful project, then any job that is required for the success of the project is your responsibility. Whether these jobs are formally your responsibility or not; whether the people doing them lie directly under your control or are peers, superiors or members of different organisations entirely; irrespective of any of these considerations, the jobs involved become part of your 'herd' and you have to make sure they happen. We're not saying you *do* them. Not at all. What we are saying, though, is that you have to cause them to happen. And not doing so will be no consolation. If the project ends unsuccessfully, then it'll be small consolation to be able to say 'well, that wasn't my job'.

To repeat the point once more so as to make it crystal clear and unambiguous: If you want a successful project, then any job required for that success is the project leader's responsibility, and she has to take it under her wing and take it forward. *This* is what being the one leader means.

Applying Step 3 of Structured Project Management to software engineering

Here are a couple more examples just to hammer home the point about the need for a single leader. In the software engineering project we've been looking at in chapters 1 and 2; what is the story with its leader?

Well, the setup is that we have a small team of seven people, most full-time but a couple part-time, and one of the full-time people is the leader. Nice. Couldn't be simpler. Now let's look at a more complex example.

Figure 3.1 shows a proposed organisation chart for a large project involving a consortium of three companies - the prime contractor P and two subcontractors S1 and S2.

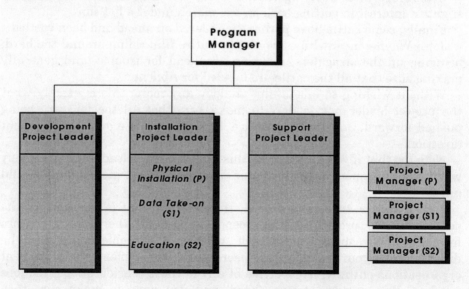

Figure 3.1

There are three logical units in the project:

- Development
- Installation
- Support

Within each of these units, each of the contractors will have certain roles to play. For example, in the Installation unit, let's say for example that contractor P might be responsible for Physical installation of the system, S1 might be responsible for Data take-on and S2 responsible for Education.

Each logical unit will have a 'Project Leader'. In addition, each contractor will have a 'Project Manager' responsible for its components across all three units. What, if anything, is wrong with this arrangement? The test is simple. Each project must have a leader, so let's see how it shapes up.

The project as a whole has a leader - the box marked Program Manager. Each unit also has a leader, the PLs (Project Leaders). Oh, so what are the Project Managers doing?, Nothing - because the Project Leaders are doing it? Duplicating what the Project Leaders are doing? I don't know myself. Clearly, there are two ways to settle this. Either (a) have three people, one responsible for each of the logical units, or (b) have three people, one responsible for each contractor's contribution. All the way down the tree, a single person must be identified whose ass is on the line for each particular part of the project. This is what step 3 is all about.

Thus, in our example, at the next level down, there would be a person responsible for each of the components such as installation, data take-on, education, etc. Be careful of organisation charts. They can give the illusion that there is a single leader at each level in the hierarchy. However, look behind them, look at the one for your own organisation. For example, see if the one leader principle applies, i.e. if there is in reality a person whose ass is on the line for each part of the project that makes up your organisation.

 ## Step 3 PSI contribution - 10

To get most or all of your 10 points here is very simple. The 10 points is a measure of how much you are going to embrace all the jobs on a project and take them forward. Pause for a moment before you award yourself an automatic 10 here.

A 10 means that you are going to move heaven and earth, do whatever has to be done to make a project happen. Irrespective of formal structures, political considerations, resource or personnel constraints, famine, fire flood, pestilence, war, nothing is going to stand in your way.

Now it seems to me that as human beings we may be able to bring such energy to bear on *some* projects. By and large I don't think we can do it on all projects we become involved in. This, of course, merely reflects the rather obvious fact that some projects are more important than others. Thus, there may be some projects under our control that we are going to do everything possible to make them happen. Then, fair play, we draw our 10 points. Similarly, though, there may well be others where we decide that we just aren't prepared to give them that level of energy. There is no inherent problem with this provided we recognise that the lower score we award ourselves here reflects the fact that things may get forgotten or fall between the cracks, and we need to perhaps keep a weather eye out for these.

Structured Project Management:

Planning the Project

1. Visualise what the goal is: Set your eyes on the prize

2. Make a list of the jobs that need to be done

3. There must be one leader

Chapter 4

Step 4 - Assign people to jobs

Introduction

Many of the projects we encounter are too big for one person, and are carried out through using other people. When I first drafted this section of the book, the Gulf War was raging. That was a project which had nearly three quarters of a million people on the Allied side alone.

The overall goal of the project can be thought of as a picture broken down into pieces like a jigsaw puzzle. There are as many pieces as there are people. If each person completes his piece, the picture will complete, and the goal will be achieved. (Note, as an aside, that by our definition, each person becomes engaged in his own individual project; and can apply Structured Project Management to that project.)

There are three things you need to do as part of this step:

- Make sure each job has a name against it
- Take peoples' other commitments into account
- Try to maximise the strengths of the team you've got.

We discuss each of these in turn.

Each job has a name

One of the things we do in our company is to turn around projects that are running out of control. There are basically two phases in doing this. One is to understand why the project is the way it is; the other is to do a new plan (i.e apply steps 1-5) to take the project from where it is now to where it needs to be. One of the first things we do in trying to understand why the project got into a mess in the first place is to take a look at the current project plan.

Sometimes there isn't one! If that's the case then the investigation is pretty much over.

More often through there is a plan of sorts. That being the case, one of the most common things we find is that jobs don't have peoples' names against them. What you find instead are things like the following:

- 'ANO' [also known as 'A.N. Other']
- 'Mr [or Ms] X'
- 'Programmers 1-6'
- 'S/W Eng.'

and other equally mysterious personages. In other words, the jobs were never assigned to anybody. You would have thought that people wouldn't be too surprised then if these jobs weren't done. But, invariably, surprised is exactly what they are.

The first thing then in assigning people to jobs is that every job must have a human being's name against it. Any of the above or organisation names should be avoided as far as is humanly possible. Even if you are subcontracting something so that an organisation is actually working on one of the jobs on your project, the name you should have against that job is the member of that organisation whose ass is on the line for the successful delivery of that particular job.

It may be that at the beginning of a project you don't know who all the people will be, and that's OK, but then one of your priorities as project manager has to be that the unknowns get replaced by warm, living, loving human beings as quickly as possible.

People's other commitments

We once turned around a software development project that was meant to last a year and ended up lasting nearly four years. When we looked back over its history to try to understand what had happened, here's what we discovered.

The original estimates of effort were out by about 50%, which in my experience of software projects, is not too bad at all. Quite creditable actually. But then, we discovered that the project manager had made a kind of unconscious assumption that everyone would be available to the project full time. When we checked back over timesheets and other data, we discovered that people had actually worked on the project on average between 1.5 and 2 days per week. Now, I have a degree in applied maths, but you don't need a degree in anything to figure out that a project like this is probably going to run about three years late, which is exactly what happened. Needless to add, the original assumption about staffing levels - unconscious or otherwise - was lost along the way, and all that everyone saw was a project that was years behind schedule.

The point here is that we have to take people's other commitments into account. PC-based project planning tools have facilities for doing this where you can allocate people to projects a certain percentage of the time, but at its most simple, all you have to do is make a list for each person that looks, for example, like this:

Reggie
- The other project   2 days per week
- Personal development   2 hours (0.25 day) per week
- ISO9001 / Quality   0.5 days per week

- *Therefore, available to my project*   *2.25 days per week.*

Note, in particular, that annual leave, public holidays and sickness are all 'commitment' that have to be allowed for.

This then is the supply side of a supply/demand equation where the demand has been generated by the list of jobs and associated dependencies and effort derived from step 2. Step 2 identifies the pile that has to be moved; step 4 shows how it will be moved.

Note, in particular, that this business also applies to yourself as project leader. Often, especially in software projects, project management is what the project leader does when he has any time left over from doing technical work. A rule of thumb that we offer is that you should reckon on 6-8% of total project effort for project management. 6% would apply to smaller projects - say, about 6 people or less - while 8% would be for larger ones - say, above about 12 people.

This figure is intended to cover work by any member of the project team on:

- Project planning activities including scheduling, estimating and updating of PC-based tool files
- Project meetings to record progress or set targets
- Project reporting
- Day-to-day work assignment
- All project team 'people' issues including staff appraisals and reviews
- Day-to-day problem solving and troubleshooting
- Liaison with any suppliers, both internal and external

- Liaison with management
- Liaison with the customer
- Liaison with related / dependent projects
- Normal ongoing recruitment
- Quality
- Quality Plan / Configuration Management Plan.

Though work by any member of the team is allowed for here, in reality a large proportion of this work (75-80% or even more) will be done by the Project Manager and/or Team Leaders.

Using this rule of thumb it is possible to work out the total amount of project management effort required - in say, man-days or man-months.

By averaging this figure out over the life of a project it is possible to see what daily and weekly levels of project management are required - measured now in hours per day or days per week.

Three examples should illustrate this:

Example 1

A project lasting 6 months and with a total effort of 22 man-months. (Average number of people on the project is 3.7).

Assuming 6% project management overhead, this gives 1.32 man-months = 26.4 man-days (assuming 20 man-days = 1 man-month).

Thus, over the 120 elapsed days (assuming 20 working days in a working month) of the project, the project management overhead = 26.4/120 = 0.22 days (= 1.76 hours for an eight hour day) per day. So, in an 8-hour day, the Project Manager can reckon on this many hours per day being taken up with project management work.

Example 2

A project lasting 12 months and with a total effort of 170 man-months. (Average number of people on the project is 14.2).

Assuming 8% project management overhead, this gives 13.6 man-months.

Thus, over the 12 elapsed months of the project, the project management overhead = 13.6/12 = 1.1 months per month. So, in this scenario, a Project Manager is likely to be busy pretty much full-time doing nothing but project management.

If you don't allow yourself this much time and effort then you are not doing the job properly, and you are actually in breach of step 3: While the project may have a nominal Project Manager, in reality, nobody is doing the job.

The previous examples assume a flat team structure. In that case, a Project Manager carries the majority of the project management responsibility. An alternative to this is to set up some kind of team structure. This will have the effect of spreading the project management load across the Project Manager and the Team Leaders.

The example which follows takes example 2 and does exactly this, breaking the single monolithic project team down into 3 groups, where each group takes responsibility for one-third of the overall project effort.

Example 3

For each team the total project management overhead is 8% of 56.7 man-months = 4.5 man-months, which over the life of the project is 0.38 months per month, i.e. about 3 hours per day.

For the Project Manager who now has a team of three people, the overhead is 3 people for 1 year = 36 man-months by 8%, which gives approximately 3 man-months (2.88) or a quarter of his time over the year.

Note: This calculation assumes that all three Team Leaders are 100% as effective as the Project Manager and that there is no overhead involved in maintaining this hierarchy. In reality the Project Manager would increase his project management overhead in dealing with the Team Leaders.

Examples 2 and 3 both illustrate valid ways in which this project could be managed. In both cases, you should always try to keep team sizes as small as possible. Then, in choosing between flat and hierarchical structures, these are the advantages and disadvantages of each. (There is no better or worse here - ultimately it is the Project Manager's choice.)

Monolithic team / flat structure

Project Manager gets to be totally hands-on. However, this requires a large amount of project management by the Project Manager, *which has to be allowed for in schedules.*

Hierarchy / team structure

Frees up Project Manager significantly to manage other projects and/or do technical work. However, the following points apply:

1. The project management effort required of the Team Leaders *has to be allowed for in schedules.*
2. Handing over responsibility may initially involve the Project Manager in more project management until she is happy that the Team Leaders can be fully relied on.

Maximise strengths

Or to put it slightly more negatively, but more bluntly: Minimise the risk of some turkey screwing up your project!

If you're lucky, you may be in a position where you can identify exactly the person you need to undertake each piece. When I say person, I mean that combination of personality, skills, experience, motivation, personal goals, strengths and weaknesses that go to make up each of us. More often you will be given a group of people and be required to carry out the project with them.

I remember when I was a kid at school, we would have games sessions and teams would be picked. There was a handful of athletic superstars (or so they seemed to me) in the class, and from these would invariably be chosen the captains of the two sides.

Then the captains would pick individuals from a group of solid citizens who made up the bulk of the class. Finally there would be five or six people left and the teacher would split these in two with his hand and allocate half to each side. I was always in this final collection! I mention this because the group you start a project with almost always are a mixed bag of individuals with diverse personalities, abilities, ambitions and motivations and this is the group that you will be trying to mould into your team.

Assigning people to jobs

OK. You have your list of jobs from step (2) of Structured Project Management, you have got a group of people, some of whom are a spectacular match for particular jobs, some less so. You now need to assign the jobs to the people so that the project will get done.

What's the best way to do this? For any job on your list, and for any person in your team, the following possibilities apply. Either the person:

1. can do the job and wants to do it
2. can do the job and is prepared to do it
3. can do the job and isn't prepared to do it
4. can be trained / instructed into doing the job
5. cannot do the job

Category (1)

The first category is the ideal one. If you were to take only one idea away from this book, it is this: if, as part of your project, you can get a person doing what he or she wants to do, you have harnessed the greatest power on earth.

In this category, the person can do the job and likes to do it. Later on, in chapter 14, we will talk about building a team, and I will say that the key question when interviewing somebody is 'what do you want to do?' If you can find people who want to do jobs that exist on your project you're guaranteed a category 1 situation.

Category (2)

The second category is still OK. You're happy that the person can do this job - perhaps they've done it before, or you know it's within their capabilities. There may be more or less persuading to be done to convince them to do it, and in Chapter 11, I present an arsenal of weapons for you to use in resolving issues like this.

However, assuming that you arrive at a category 2 situation, and can maintain that for the duration of the project, you should have no real problems. Let me also say though, as a note of caution, that there is a limit to how often you can persuade people to do things they don't really want to do. If what people are being asked to do doesn't fit in with their own personal plans then in the long term, I believe that you are swimming against the tide.

Category (3)

For the third category, you've got a problem: The person can do the job, but won't. Maybe he's done it too many times before and is bored, maybe he feels he's not being paid enough, who knows what the reason is. Basically what you've got to do here is to cause this situation to revert to either category 2 (he's prepared to do it) or category 5 (for whatever reason he's not going to do it, i.e. cannot do it). Again, you can use the techniques in Chapter 11 to help you to do this.

Category (4)

For the fourth category (can be trained / instructed into doing the job), then provided:

- you're prepared to put in the training time and money
- and you allow for training time in the project schedule
- and you allow for the extra management overhead
- and you're prepared to run with the risk that it might not work out

then this category can often work out very well. In fact, you can often find yourself in a category 1 situation because you may well have pushed the person into a more challenging job that she wanted to move into.

Category (5)

For the fifth category, you have a major problem. It may take you time to arrive at the conclusion that the person cannot do the job, but if you eventually do so, you need to find jobs within your project that the person can do. Failing that, the person belongs outside the project. In this balancing act of matching people to jobs you can obviously get into problems of over- / under-utilising people, and this is where something like a computerised project planning system is useful, though not essential. It may take several iterations before you get everything nicely balanced, i.e.:

- utilisation of everyone less than or equal to 100%;
- all training / instruction needs identified [note that this generates new jobs for the job list];
- a feeling that, by and large, everybody will be happy with the jobs they've been assigned to do.

Case Study 5

It is interesting to read in [Ref. 30] the different ways in which Scott and Amundsen assigned people to their jobs.

First of all there is a large difference in the numbers of people the two leaders took with them on their expeditions. Scott landed 33 people in total in Antarctica; Amundsen landed only 10. To some extent, this difference can be explained by the scientific side of Scott's expedition, but there is still a feeling about Scott's expedition of a general offensive whose aim was to win by strength of numbers. Amundsen's, on the other hand, smacks of a raid.

Scott took some people because they paid to join and his expedition needed the funds. There is a certain amount of logic in his choice of scientists, but he still chose a large number of people with no previous Polar experience.

Amundsen, by comparison, chose his people like a craftsman selects a tool. He needed to get through the pack ice that surrounds the Antarctic continent in the summertime; so, he took an ice-pilot, Andreas Beck. He planned to ski to the Pole so, apart from the fact that every man with him could ski moderately well, he brought with him Olav Bjaaland, who had skied for Norway at international level. Since he was using dogs he needed a skilled dog-driver. He had one in Helmer Hansen.

The lesson for our own projects is clear: put together a small group of highly trained and focused people - as opposed to a large group of generalists with a diffuse objective - and your chances of success are greatly increased.

Assigning people to jobs with form #2

The form shown in figure 4.1 may be of use to analyse the way you have allocated jobs to people. All 1's in the 'Category' column would be ideal but a bit unlikely. A mixture of 1's, 2's and 4's is more likely, with any 3's and 5's being ones for particular attention. This form appears again in chapter 6 where the rightmost two columns are used.

 ## Applying Step 4 of Structured Project Management to software engineering

Figure 4.2 shows an example of the application of step 4 taken from a

real-life project. What the Project Manager has done is to overlay our form on a Gantt chart of the project. This is a neat idea because, for starters, it enables her to check that every job has been assigned to somebody!

Person	Job	Category	Trust	
			Yes	No

Figure 4.1 - Form #2 - Assigning jobs

Looking through the form it looks like we're in reasonable shape. There are some training requirements arising from the 4's and we should check that something has been allowed for these on the job list. If not we should add something. Also the 2's and 4's would want to be watched a bit more closely than the 1's. However, with luck, a lot of the 4's may turn into 1's with the appropriate training and supervision.

You can fill out one of these forms at a number of possible levels:

- for the project team as a whole
- for each person, as we have done above
- or for each person-job, as we talked about at the beginning of this chapter

The deeper you go the more insight you get. Also you can do it at different times in the project, say at the beginning of each phase. A reasonable compromise between not doing it at all and doing it repeatedly for each person-job might be to do it for each team member, either once - when they join the project or, for very long projects, at the beginning of each phase.

Finally, one other thing that's useful is illustrated in Figures 4.3 and 4.4 - charts showing who is allocated to what project over what period. This helps you to keep track of multiple people across multiple projects, and can also assist you with hiring plans. We have given two examples; Figure 4.3 is for a single large project, Figure 4.4 is for a software engineering department. Both were done using Lotus.

 ## Step 4 PSI contribution - 10

You get your points on step 4 as follows:

- Three and a third (3.33) if every job on your list has a human being's name against it. As we said, it may be that early on in a project you don't know who all the people are, but you should be striving to find out as quickly as possible. A score lower than 3.33 here will (hopefully) keep you focused on the fact that there are issues here which haven't been resolved.
- 3.33 if you take people's other commitments, including your own and especially your project management one, into account.
- 3.33 if you do the maximising the strengths analysis that we described earlier.

Structured Project Management:

Planning the Project

1. Visualise what the goal is; set your eyes on the prize

2. Make a list of the jobs that need to be done

3. There must be one leader

4. Assign people to jobs

10 SEP 92

GANTT   CHART
ROSTERING PILOT

PAGE 1

ROSTERING PILOT -JOBS	PERSON	CATEGORY	TRUST YES	NO
PROJECT STARTUP				
CONTRACT FINALIZATION				
SIGN CONTRACT	TONY KENNY	1	✓	
PRE IMPLEMENTATION				
IMPLEMENTATION DAY	CATHY KEANY, TONY KENNY, ATWORK AND A REP FROM EACH PILOT	1	✓	
SOFTWARE AND HARDWARE INSTALL				
DEFINE HARDWARE REQUIRED	CATHY KEANY & ATWORK	1	✓	
INSTALL HARDWARE	OPERATIONS	2	✓	
SETUP SUPPORT MODEM	OPERATIONS	2	✓	
INSTALL SOFTWARE	CATHY KEANY	4	✓	
INTERFACES				
PERSONNEL INTERFACE				
DESIGN PERSONNEL INTERFACE	CATHY KEANY	1	✓	
PROGRAM PERSONNEL INTERFACE				
ANSOS PROGRAMMING USA	ATWORK	2	✓	
BEAUMONT PROGRAMMING	CATHY KEANY	1	✓	
TESTING				
ANSOS TESTING UK	ATWORK	2	✓	
BEAUMONT TESTING	CATHY KEANY	1	✓	
PROGRAMMING PART 2				
ANSOS PROGRAMMING UK	ATWORK	2	✓	
BEAUMONT PROGRAMMING	CATHY KEANY	1	✓	

Figure 4.2

10 SEP 92 GANTT CHART ROSTERING PILOT PAGE 1

ROSTERING PILOT – JOBS	PERSON	CATEGORY	TRUST YES	TRUST NO
PAYROLL INTERFACE				
DESIGN PAYROLL INTERFACE	CATHY KEANY	1	✓✓	
CONFIRM DESIGN	CATHY KEANY AND (FIN)	(2)	✓✓	
PROGRAM PAYROLL				
ANSOS PROGRAMMING USA	ATWORK	2	✓✓	
BEAUMONT PROGRAMMING	CATHY KEANY	2	✓✓	
TEST PAYROLL				
ANSOS TESTING UK	ATWORK	2	✓✓	
BEAUMONT TESTING	CATHY KEANY AND (FIN)	1		
PROGRAMMING PART 2				
ANSOS PROGRAMMING UK	ATWORK	2		
BEAUMONT PROGRAMMING	CATHY KEANY	2		
SET UP PERSONNEL INTERFACE				
TEST ANSOS	CATHY KEANY AND (PER)	1 (2)	✓✓✓	
TEST ANSOS AND BEAUMONT	CATHY KEANY AND (PER)	1 (2)	✓✓✓	
REPORT PROBLEMS	CATHY KEANY	1	✓✓	
PROGRAM ANSOS UK	ATWORK	2		
PROGRAM BEAUMONT	CATHY KEANY	1		
TEST AND ACCEPT INTERFACE	CATHY KEANY AND (PER)	1		
IMPLEMENT PERSONNEL INTERFA	CATHY KEANY	1 (2)	✓✓	✓
SETUP SYSTEM IN WARD				
DATA COLLECTION	WARD AND CATHY KEANY	4		✓✓✓✓
TECHNICAL TRAINING UK	CATHY KEANY	1		
CONTROLLER VISIT	CATHY KEANY, WARD AND ATWORK	1		✓✓
DATA ENTRY	WARD	4		
POLICIES AND PROCEDURE DEVEL	CATHY KEANY AND (WARD)	1 (4)	✓✓	
REPORTS DEFINITION	CATHY KEANY AND (WARD)	1 (4)		
REPORTS GENERATION	CATHY KEANY AND (WARD)	4 (4)		
SCHEDULAR VISIT	CATHY KEANY, ATWORK AND WARD	1 1		
TEST ROSTERS	CATHY KEANY AND (WARD)	1 (2)	✓	✓
STAFFER VISIT	CATHY KEANY, ATWORK AND WARD	1 1	✓	

Figure 4.2 cont'd

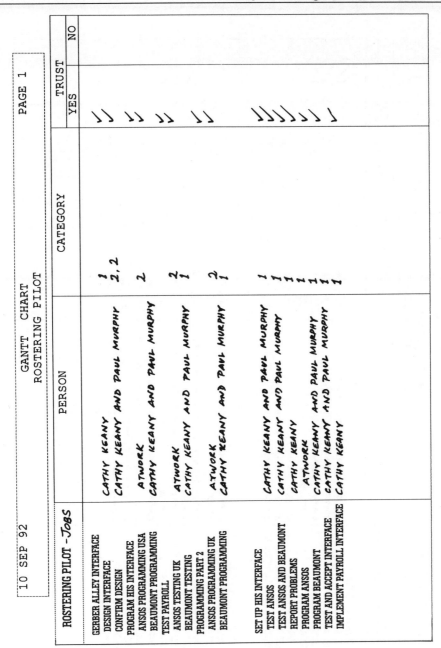

Figure 4.2 cont'd

10 SEP 92

GANTT CHART
ROSTERING PILOT

PAGE 1

ROSTERING PILOT – JOBS	PERSON	CATEGORY	TRUST YES	NO
SET UP PAYROLL INTERFACE				
TEST ANSOS	CATHY KEANY AND (FIN)	1, (4)	✓✓✓✓✓✓	(✓✓)
TEST ANSOS AND BEAUMONT	CATHY KEANY AND (FIN)	1, (4)		
REPORT PROBLEMS	CATHY KEANY	1		
PROGRAM ANSOS	ATWORK	2		
PROGRAM BEAUMONT	CATHY KEANY	2		
TEST AND ACCEPT INTERFACE	CATHY KEANY AND (FIN)	1, (2)		
IMPLEMENT PAYROLL INTERFACE	CATHY KEANY	1		
SET UP CATERING ROSTERS				
IMPLEMENTATION REVIEW	CATHY KEANY, CATE AND TONY KEANY	1 1 1	✓	
DATA COLLECTION	CATE	4		✓✓✓
CONTROLLER VISIT	CATHY KEANY, CATE AND ATWORK	1 1 1	✓	
DATA ENTRY	CATE			
POLICIES AND PROCEDURES DEV	CATHY KEANY AND CATE	1, 4	✓	
REPORTS DEFINITION	CATE	4		
REPORTS GENERATION	CATHY KEANY AND CATE	1, 4		
SCHEDULAR VISIT	CATHY KEANY AND CATE AND ATWORK	1, 1, 1	✓✓✓✓	
TEST ROSTERS	CATHY KEANY AND CATE	1, 4		
STAFFER VISIT	CATHY KEANY, ATWORK AND CATE	1, 1, 1		✓
CATERING PILOT LIVE				

Figure 4.2 cont'd

10 SEP 92	GANTT CHART			PAGE 1

ROSTERING PILOT

ROSTERING PILOT *Jobs*	PERSON	CATEGORY	TRUST YES	TRUST NO
PILOT WARD LIVE				
SET UP NCHD ROSTERS	CATHY KEANY, TONY K, AND NCHD	1, 1, 1	✓✓	✓
IMPLEMENTATION REVIEW	CATHY KEANY & NCHD	1, 4		✓✓✓
DATA COLLECTION	CATHY KEANY, ATWORK NCHD	1, 1, 1		
CONTROLLER VISIT	NCHD	4		
DATA ENTRY	CATHY KEANY AND (NCHD)	1, (4)	✓✓	
POLICIES AND PROCEDURES DEV	" "	1, (4)		
REPORTS DEFINITION	" " AND ATWORK	1, (4)	✓	✓
REPORTS GENERATION	" "	1, 1, 1		
SCHEDULAR VISIT	" " AND ATWORK	1, 1, 1		
TEST ROSTERS	NCHD	1		
STAFFER VISIT				
NCHD PILOT LIVE				

Figure 4.2 cont'd

ACME SOFTWARE - BIGPROJECT STAFFING PROJECTION
16-May-93

PROJECT	1992							1993												1994												1995			
	6	7	8	9	10	11	12	1	2	3	4	5	6	7	8	9	10	11	12	1	2	3	4	5	6	7	8	9	10	11	12	1	2	3	4
Feasibility Study	2	2	2	2	2																														
Functional Spec.						8	8	8	8	8	8																								
Design										3	3	11	11	11	11	11	11	11	11																
Implementation												1	4	8	8	22	22	22	22	33	33	33	33	33	33	33	33								
Integration																												12	12	12	12	12	12	12	12
TOTALS	2	2	2	2	2	8	8	8	8	11	11	12	15	19	19	33	33	33	33	33	33	33	33	33	33	33	33	12	12	12	12	12	12	12	12

Figure 4.3 Example of large project staff allocation

ACME SOFTWARE - STAFF ALLOCATIONS

GROUP/PROJECT	16-May	May	Jun	Q3	Q4	
BASE TECHNOLOGY (Fred)						
Management		1	1	1	1	Fred
Project A		3	3	2	2	Roy, Steve
Project B		11	11	12	12	Jill, Greg #1, Greg #2 etc.
Working in H.Q		1	1	1	1	Eleanor
		16	16	16	16	
PRODUCTS (Steve)						
Product A		2	2	2	2	Alan, Kathy
Product B maintenance		1	1	1	1	Noel
		3	3	3	3	
CUSTOMER SERVICES (Milton)						
Management		1	1	1	1	Milt
High end products		5	5	5	5	Tracy, Lisa, Sid, Mike, Bert
Low end products		1	1	1	1	Jim
Mid-range						New hire
		7	7	7	7	
ADMIN. & MGMT. (Alex/Jim)						
General Manager		1	1	1	1	Bert
Personnel / Admin		5	5	5	5	George, Tammy, Niki, Viki, Lee
		6	6	6	6	
CUSTOM SERVICES						
Technical Director		1	1	1	1	Mark
Software Dev. Mgr.		1	1	1	1	Alan
Pre-sales		1	1	1	1	New hire
EEC Projects		6	8	8	8	Lou, Joe, Al, Robin, Tony, Dick
U.S Projects		5				Gary, Harry, Anne, Tim, Davin
Major customer projects		2	3	3		Steve, Linda
Available			4	5	8	
		16	18	19	19	
TOTALS		48	50	51	51	

Figure 4.4 Example of software department staff allocation

Chapter 5

Step 5 - Manage expectations, allow a margin for error, have a fallback position

Introduction

By the time you have completed steps 1-4 you have actually finished the planning for your project. If you have carried out the steps as we have described, then what you have done is you have built a working model of how your project might unfold over time. In a sense you know the 'answer'. You know what's going to be delivered, you know when it will complete, you know how many people you need and a whole load of other useful information. In theory now, you could come scampering out of your office, go in to your boss or customer, and announce 'we know the answer. It'll be November 27th' - or whatever.

You could. However, stay your hand for a moment while you consider one other thing. What will you do if it doesn't turn out like your model predicts?

You see it's all too easy, especially if you've gone into things in excruciating detail like we talked about, and even more so if your plan is now being output by a PC-based project planning tool, to forget that everything that's in the plan is a *prediction,* a guess, a shot in the dark, a gamble. You know nothing in your plan for a fact. In fact the only thing you do know for a fact is that *your plan is definitely not right*. It couldn't be - it's a prediction of the future. Given that this is the case, the most you can hope for is that you get a lot of it right, and that where it's wrong it's not too far wrong. You need to ask yourself the question 'what will I do if it doesn't work out like this?' And the answer you have to give yourself is to build in some contingency. That's what the first part of step 5 - call it step 5a - is about. It's about allowing yourself a margin for error, a fallback position.

Having done this, having built in some contingency for yourself, then you need to sell your plan to the powers that be and create the expectation to which you will then deliver. This is the other part of step 5, step 5b. We describe each of these in turn.

Contingency - allow a margin for error, have a fallback position

Explicit or hidden contingency

If you were a Project Manager and you worked in construction, then on your plans people would expect to see a line item called 'Contingency'. It might be set, for example, at 15% of the project budget and/or elapsed time. If people didn't see this, they would assume one of two things. The more charitable of the two would be that it was an omission on your part. The other would be that you had taken leave of your senses. They would believe this because in omitting contingency, it would imply that you felt confident you could predict the future.

There are some software companies - regrettably few, I have to say - where a similar ethos applies. The management and the customers of those companies expect to see contingency built into plans. Not doing so is regarded as project management practice somewhere in the range improper to criminally negligent.

So what happens in the rest of software companies? Well, in these, contingency is actually what the management or the customer take the red pencil to first. 'OK, now where can we shorten this baby [or make it cheaper]?' ponders the Big Cheese, the Great Gorgonzola. 'Ah, contingency, you won't need that for starters'.

If your organisation is one of the enlightened ones, then put in the contingency explicitly, and put plenty of it - as much as you can get away with.

If, on the other hand, your organisation is of the red-pencil variety, then you need to hide the contingency in there. PC-based tools are very powerful in helping you to do this quickly. Another useful way of doing it - and they'll never spot it - is to put in fake activities. You can couch these in technobabble - there are numerous software packages that will generate buzzwords and acronyms for you - and so you have activities like:

- Update table lookup
- Memory maintenance
- Changes to existing
- Decision on tool
- Re-work

you know the kind of thing I mean - just find some applicable to your particular application area and you can re-use them time after time. Of course it's better if you can put your cards on the table and set out the contingency explicitly, but failing that you have to get it in there somehow.

Not so long ago, I did some consultancy for a company. It essentially ended up with me spending an afternoon working with a Project Manager helping him to hide contingency in an MS-Project plan. It was his management who were paying my fee and here I was preparing material to, in a sense, hoodwink them. I have to tell you that I felt entirely morally justified in doing what I was doing, on the basis that one day they would thank me for it.

They did too. About a month ago; when their project came in on time and within budget - the time and budget that *included* the contingency.

Finding contingency

You can use the four parameters we first identified in chapter 1 to help you build in your contingency. Remember that these were:

- Functionality
- Delivery date
- Effort (Cost)
- Quality

Functionality

Some projects get structured such that on some happy day in the future, somebody will pull the great lever and the whole system will power up and work perfectly. (The nuclear deterrent system operated by the superpowers during the Cold War was such a system! I had a friend who ran a small software house. He was a veteran of more payroll system installations than you could shake a stick at. Based on his experience on these, he was confident that there could never be a nuclear war. He'd never seen a payroll system work right first time; why should thermonuclear Armageddon be any different?) Either it all works perfectly on the promised delivery date, or ... it doesn't work at all. That's how some projects are conceived.

You can certainly organise your project this way, but then you're really asking for trouble. You've given yourself no room for manoeuvre, no fallback position.

As an alternative to this you can do what is called phased delivery. Is there some minimal set of functionality your project can deliver which will get your customer off the ground; start them doing useful work, while at the same time, familiarising themselves with, and debugging the system? Then can you add some more and some more and some more. At any point if you find you've reached for a milestone too far, you can always fall back on the last version you delivered.

Delivery date and effort (cost)

You can add contingency using either of these merely by adding on an additional percentage to allow for contingency. Typical numbers tend to be in the range 10-15%, but I suspect the only significance of these numbers is that they tend to be what people can get away with. As a general rule, I would say the more you can get the better. Certainly the more chance you have of your model being seen to be right and hence, of having a successful project.

You can add the contingency:

- On a blanket basis, across the entire project
- On a per phase basis, i.e. to each phase
- To those jobs on the critical path

Also it's probably better to aim for adding a percentage onto the delivery date, because in doing so, it often means you can get to hold onto people for that extra period of time, and so achieve an even bigger contingency on the effort.

Quality

If you can measure the quality of your project deliverables, then you can use these as bargaining counters in the contingency game.

For example, in the development of a software system you might use mean time to defect (MTTD) as a measure of quality. (For an excellent discussion on this, see *Measures for Excellence* [Ref. 47].) Then you might aim for an MTTD of say, 2 days, but in a pinch you'd be prepared to settle for 1 day or 1.5 days. Thus you again gain some room for manoeuvre, some margin for error.

Manage expectations

OK, you've built the model of your project using steps 1-4. You've built in contingency using step 5(a). Now you're ready to go to the powers that be, be it your boss or your customer, and tell him the answer. Typically, this is the point at which you announce the answer and your boss or customer does the equivalent of slapping their thigh and saying 'you've got to be joking. It's going to be *when*?' Or 'You want *how many* people?' And so on. I'm sure you've been there before; and, if not, if you've just joined this business, then it'll only be a short space of time before you will be.

So now what do you do? Well, for starters, let's be quite clear that the one thing you don't do is to agree to whatever *they* propose. That is unless your model shows it is possible.

The way forward is conceptually simple. It may well, however, require plenty of guts on your part. Here's what you do.

The model shows one possible way that your project could work out. If you either (a) anticipate that the powers that be won't like that way, or (b) find out they don't like it when you tell them, then you can use the model to generate other possible scenarios. How do you this? Easy, by varying our four trusty parameters:

- Functionality
- Delivery Date
- Effort (Cost)
- Quality

So, you might for example, ask what the effect is of adding more people. Or see what (reduced Functionality) can be achieved by the delivery date that Sales have already promised. Or see if you can get people to buy into an extension on the Delivery Date. Or you can try combinations of these. At all times you use the model you have developed to generate these new possible scenarios - think of them as flavours to the basic vanilla model. Using the model keeps you honest. It stops you from signing up for something that is patently impossible.

If you don't use the model - if you merely succumb to pressure - then you are doing precisely that. You are signing up for a mission impossible. You are opting for a quiet life now and trying to put out of your mind the certainty that a hydrogen bomb is going to fall on you when the chickens come home to roost - as they inevitably will, because your model says that they will.

The one thing you cannot do in this game is to sign up for a mission impossible - no matter how much and how severe is the pressure that is applied to you. And, your model will act as your protection. Often, in the traditional way that this game is played, the negotiation becomes an emotive confrontation between two sides. Using the method we propse, it becomes a logical discussion of facts. The Roman writer Sallust said, *ubi res adsunt, quid opus est verbis*, 'when the facts are at hand, what is the need of words'. People can be as emotive as they like in our version of the game and it doesn't matter. The models you develop will coldly and logically show what can and cannot be done. Hold your ground and ultimately the good guys should win.

Another stratagem that the powers that be may adopt will be to question your model, to try to chip away at the estimates contained in them. 'It couldn't possibly take two weeks to that,' they will say, 'you're overestimating everything here'. Your answer to this is reasonableness itself. 'They're only estimates,' you will say, 'so they're definitely not 100% right. They may indeed be too high.' Pause for dramatic effect. 'But they might also be too *low*. We don't actually know. We think there's a fair chance, because of the detail we've built in [via step 2] that they're accurate, but they are only predictions. Why don't we run it for a couple of weeks and see how things turn out? Then, when we make our final decision, we've a better chance that it's the right one.'

The key to all of this is discussion, negotiation, trying to keep the whole thing on a civilised level. In *Applying step 5 of Structured Project Management to software engineering*, later in this chapter, we offer some additional tactics you can adopt to try to keep things on this civilised plane.

Ultimately, however, there may just be someone out there crazy enough to say 'I don't care about models, figures or anything else - just do it - or else'. If that happens, you should take your courage in your hands and walk away from the whole thing. A glib statement, you may say, with mortgages to pay and families to support, but what's the alternative? The alternative is that somewhere down the line you're sitting in a blackened smoking ruin and you're being spotlighted as the person responsible for it all.

Come on, life is too short for that kind of unhappiness. And anyway, there are still enough unsuccessful projects out there that good project managers are still in demand. So let's just summarise the process:

- Steps 1-4 build the basic vanilla model
- Step 5(a) adds contingency to the vanilla model
- Step 5(b) creates a number of possible 'flavours' of the model. It is one of these - and only one of these - that your boss or customer can buy

- Once they have chosen the one that they want, this becomes the one that you try to make happen. This is the expectation you create.
- Finally, the chosen option is documented so that it is clear to everybody involved who signed up for what.

A word on committing

Sooner or later in projects we have to 'commit'. In doing this, we basically make a promise and then try to make that promise happen. If everything turns out as we predicted, then we are heroes; otherwise our name is mud.

The first thing that should be said about committing is that you should try and leave it to as late as possible in the project. The longer you can get away with not having to make this promise, the better for all concerned. Each day that passes you find out more about the nature of the project, and all of these details, when fed into a model of your project, increase the likelihood that the promise you make will come true.

Sooner or later, though, the fateful day will come and you will have to make the promise.

It is both my belief and my experience that if you use the planning techniques we've described here in steps 1-5, then there is a fair chance that the project will just run through to a successful completion. If so, then fair play to you and God bless us all.

If this doesn't happen, however; if you find that you have eaten up all your contingency and that there is no way that your promise can now be met, then you've got to come clean. Our instinctive reaction is perhaps to do the opposite - to cover the whole thing up, pretend that nothing is wrong and hope it'll all be alright on the night. Not to put too fine a point on it, this is madness.

Coming clean won't be pleasant. On my courses I liken it to exploding a 500 lb. bomb around everybody. But again, what's the alternative? The alternative is that blackened smoking ruin we spoke of earlier. Think of it as exchanging a 500 lb. bomb now for one of about 20 megatons later!

So you come clean. You carry out steps 1-5 again. You make a new commitment, set a new expectation and off you go. Ultimately your conduct will be seen for what it was - professional project management.

Some final thoughts on this subject:

- Know what your customer is expecting. What he is expecting will be based entirely on what you have led him to believe. Can you trim back from this without affecting him unduly? Sure you can. Check and see what he could actually put up with at a pinch. Be sure that your development schedule enables you to deliver this first.

- Build a number of demonstrations and/or prototypes into your schedule so that your customer can get her hands on the system early and you can verify that you have read her expectations correctly.
- See what is required to go beyond her expectations and plan to go there if at all possible - that'll really wow her. But it will only wow her if you have given her all of what her basic expectations were.
- Don't spring surprises on your customer. Customers are very forgiving people once they are treated as intelligent human beings. It is only when they get the impression you are not being straight with them that they react badly.
- Some things have no margin for error. Know which things on your project are like this, watch them like a hawk, and make sure they happen.
- A retreat to a fallback position need not be an ignominious thing; it can be presented as a master stroke of planning and forethought - another example of managing expectations.

Case Study 6: manage expectations

Scott left England in a blaze of publicity. The British Empire was at its height - to any rational outside observer it was clear that the British would be first to the South Pole. Amundsen slipped quietly away, and it wasn't until he was long beyond anyone's reach that his objective was made known to the world. If he failed then he would disappear quietly into oblivion. If Scott failed, then it would be a very public failure.

Case Study 7: allow a margin for error

Scott moved 1 ton of supplies out onto the path he would follow to the Pole. These depots were indicated by cairns of snow and single marker flags. Scott allowed just about the amount of food and fuel that he needed. When at the last minute he switched the number of people in the Polar party from 4 to 5, this put all his calculations awry. A hastily drawn up plan was put in place to offset this problem, but Scott and his companions were to die of starvation, scurvy (caused by vitamin deficiency) and exposure.

Amundsen put 4 tons of supplies on his path. His depots were marked by sets of marker flags radiating out from the depot. Each marker flag had a note attached to it indicating the distance to, and direction of, the depot. On his return, Amundsen's men put on weight and left 2 tons of food behind them in depots.

Case Study 8: have a fallback position

We referred previously to the opening of the Battle of the Somme during the First World War, when the British launched an offensive which they hoped would end the war [Ref. 39]. The British commander's plan was admirable. Quite simply, he hoped to give his men a walkover.

He would do this by submitting the Germans to the biggest artillery barrage of the war, or indeed of any war. It would last continuously for a week. At the end of that time, his men would quite literally walk across to what would remain of the German lines. Well, of course, there was no walkover. The German lines were very much intact and nearly 60,000 British soldiers were killed or wounded on that one day alone. Over 19,000 of them were killed, most of them in the first couple of hours of the battle.

The British project plan was based on the premise that there would be a walkover. When that failed to materialise, there was no contingency plan. You are doing one of the most risky things imaginable if you take a project forward on the basis of no contingency plan, no fallback position.

It's human nature, you tell somebody you're going to do something, you do it and they're pleased. You do more than what you said - give them an added bonus - and they're delighted. But fail to do what you said and your name is mud. Once you've done your plan you need to look at it and ask:

- What are people - you, the project team, your customer, your boss, your peers, the rest of your organisation, people outside the organisation - expecting to happen when the project completes? Can you deliver on what they are expecting?
- What if something goes wrong? Spend a while analysing what can go wrong - use Brainstorming or some of the other techniques in chapter 11 - and see how well you are set up to deal with these eventualities. There are some things upon which you will have no margin for error, and these become crucial jobs for you. Many things, however, are less critical and you can perhaps live without them for a while. Identify the critical and less critical things. Do these then cause people's expectations to be modified?
- Is there a fallback position? If something disastrous happens can you still save your skin and the project? If you can't then at least you go forward consciously knowing the risks you run; but often there are things you can do.

You should do this for the project as a whole and for each job in your job list. Try to categorise the risk associated with each job as high, medium or low. Then focus on the high-risk ones and make sure, if nothing else, that these have a margin for error and a fallback position. We have said that managing expectations, allowing a margin for error and having a fallback position are all facets of the same issue. There's an argument that says:

- define your goal
- identify a fallback position
- set expectations equal to the fallback position
- then your margin for error is everything between the fallback position and the real goal

There is some merit in this approach. The big danger is that the fallback position now becomes the goal; so that you are still left with a situation where you have a goal and no fallback position. Here's a final example from history showing all three things - manage expectations / allow a margin for error / have a fallback position - as facets of the same issue.

Case Study 9

The 'unsinkable' [expectation] *Titanic* was launched in 1912. She could carry 2,000 - 2,500 passengers and crew and had lifeboat capacity for 1,100 [no margin for error]. When she struck an iceberg on the night of April 14, 1912, over a thousand people lost their lives [no fallback position].

 ## Applying Step 5 of Structured Project Management to software engineering

We promised you some additional tactics to help protect yourself from predatory bosses and customers while at the same time keeping things civilised. Here they are:

Bosses or customers often want to know at the beginning of the project when it is going to end and what it will cost. Often too you are required to bid fixed-price for a job when you are very early in the product development life cycle. What do you do in these cases?

I would maintain that the only time you can accurately estimate a project, i.e. commit to a fixed schedule and effort, is when all the design is finished. At that point I would be quite happy to give a fixed-price estimate to a customer, i.e. to pin my ass on a particular delivery date and staffing level. *Before that you can't.* I repeat, before that you can't. If you are being pressurised to commit earlier, then there are a few stratagems you can employ:

Two fixed-price quotes - I'll give you a fixed price bid for the design phase and at the end of that I'll give you a fixed-price bid for the rest. You'll have your design so that if you don't like my bid for the implementation you can take the design elsewhere. Another way of looking at this is 'I can only give you a date/effort by which the design will be done. At that point I can give you a date/effort for the rest'.

Parkinsonian estimating - Often pressure is applied by telling you the end date by which the system must be ready and the size of the team you're being given to deliver. A Parkinsonian Estimate, worked back from the end date, can show the impossibility of what you are being asked to do. It can be done very quickly. You fit your six (or whatever number you use) phases back from the end date. Typically the effects you get are things like:

To make the deadline the development should have started two months ago. The deadline can only be achieved if coding takes two days. Or, the deadline can be achieved if we don't do any testing.

Load the estimate - If you are put in a position where you have to give a fixed price quote, then you must load the estimate to give yourself sufficient room for manoeuvre. And it's OK to tell the customer you're doing this and why. 'We don't know how big the job is Mr Customer, so given our estimates - see - and our level of knowledge at the moment, we have to assume worst case and so this is the reason for our pricing. If, at the end of the design phase, we find that we overestimated we'll be more than happy to pass the reduction on to you. Oh, and by the way if anyone is telling you differently ... they're wrong'.

You have to stick to your guns. If you have done your estimates properly and believe in them, then you hold the moral high ground. If you commit to something you cannot achieve then you will preside over a catastrophe and you will be left looking fairly silly.

I don't know of anyone who has been fired for refusing to budge from their estimates. I know of numerous instances where people were fired for screwing something up!

Play the change control game - If you are forced to make a fixed-price bid, be sure you deliver it with all the relevant fine print. State explicitly, and in excruciating detail, what was and wasn't included and the assumptions you made. Then as other items come to light in the course of the analysis and design phases, you can play the change control game where every new item becomes a change to the contract.

Tell 'em it's impossible - Here you take on the project but none of the associated guilt or responsibility. Nice prospect, huh ? In this scenario, somebody asks you to take on what looks like an impossible mission and you say yes! Not yes unconditionally, however, but a yes with certain provisos.

Imagine the scene. You've looked at what they're asking you to do, and your model and all associated reason tells you that it's impossible. They're adamant, however, it's been promised - it has to be done. So you make the following offer. You say: 'I've looked at what your asking me to do and I believe that it's impossible for reasons that I've outlined to you. However, given the squeeze you're in I'm prepared to do whatever I can to help. Here's my offer. I'll take on this project and run it for you. I can't guarantee you I'll make those commitments, but I will guarantee you that as soon as I know *for a fact* that the commitments are impossible, I'll let you know. Then you can decide how you want to present that to your customer.'

There now. They can't accuse you of not being a team player. Note too, the repeated use of the word 'you' during this little speech, ensuring that the guilt stays well and truly where it belongs.

Step 5 PSI contribution - 10

Contingency, or margin for error, can be thought of as the gap between your fallback position and your actual goal.

You get a score out of 5 points on step 5 if you've built in some contingency into your plan. The more the contingency the higher the score out of 5.

You get the other 5 points if you can show that the expectation you've created lies somewhere between the fallback position and the goal. The closer the expectation lies to your fallback position, the higher your score out of 5.

If your project has no margin for error, then you lose 15 off your cumulative score here.

Structured Project Management:

Planning the Project

1. Visualise what the goal is; set your eyes on the prize

2. Make a list of the jobs that need to be done

3. There must be one leader

4. Assign people to jobs

5. Manage expectations/allow a margin for error/have a fallback position

Part Two

Reviewing and implementing the plan; achieving the goal

Introduction

At this point in the proceedings you have spent all your time planning your project; you have still not set out on the journey. It is not an exaggeration to say that the fate of your project has been, to a very great extent, sealed by the work you may or may not have done so far. If you have applied the steps of Structured Project Management to your project, then you will:

- Know in intimate detail the goal of the project
- Have a plan - very detailed for the immediate future, less so thereafter, but at least showing the remaining important milestones
- Have identified who is going to be the leader
- Have assigned the members of your team to the jobs on the list of jobs
- Have ensured that everyone understands the big picture and how their particular piece fits into the jigsaw
- Know what everyone is expecting and have some room for manoeuvre between that and what you plan to deliver

You can now begin the journey secure in the knowledge that you are starting from a secure base, and that you have done as much as you could do at this stage to expect the unexpected. If you have not done some or all of these things, then there is a startling amount of very bleak news for you, which I had better begin to recite. If you have tears to shed, prepare to shed them now. Your project may not fail. After all life is full of surprises - that's part of what makes it so enjoyable.

If your project does not fail, then you will have pulled off a major success. You will have succeeded against the odds. I'll bet it won't have been very pleasant and there were times when it was just awful, and I'd say nobody enjoyed themselves all that much. But if you did it, hats off to you is what I say. I do wonder why you would choose to put yourself and your team through an experience like that. And I also wonder why you choose to do projects in this way, since it can't get any easier from one to the next, never knowing whether it's going to work out or not. Anyway, it's your call and good luck with the next one.

That was the good news. The bad news is that I believe your project is bound for disaster, speeding towards it as surely as the *Titanic* towards its encounter with the iceberg. Your project will be a disaster and you as project leader will have a monumental mess on your hands that will make you wish you had never become involved with the project. Whatever you had hoped to gain from it - money, promotion, prestige, an enhanced résumé, fame, recognition, whatever it was - will be lost in the appalling shambles that lies ahead of you. There are only two possible pieces of advice I can offer you. Either do a proper plan or get out while you are still untarnished.

Assuming you have done a proper plan, with all of the detail that we've stressed so much, then what you have done is you have identified one possible way that the project could unfold. What we are now going to do, in steps 6-10, is to make this plan into a self-fulfilling prophecy. We are going to try to *force reality to adhere to the plan*. And if that sounds as though you would have to have god-like qualities to make it happen, forget it, you need nothing of the sort.

The plan says that certain sets of jobs are going to have to get 'bitten off' every month, every week and ultimately every day. If the jobs are bitten off exactly as specified in our plan; in other words, if we reach the monthly, weekly and daily targets that our plan specifies, then the project will remain on schedule. Amongst other things we can use the interaction of our four parameters:

- Functionality
- Delivery Date
- Effort (Cost)
- Quality

to try to ensure that this happens. Thus, for instance, if a particular milestone has to be met on a certain day, then we can say, add people (increase effort) or reduce functionality to try to ensure that this happens. If we do this for every milestone, large and small, throughout the life of the project, then the project will remain on schedule, and our plan will indeed turn into a self-fulfilling prophecy. Reality will indeed have adhered to the plan. These comments apply completely too, to cost or budget.

This is what steps 6-10 as well as the material in part III about running multiple projects is all about.

There is another thing on offer here as well. At one point I wanted to call this book 'The Lazy Project Manager', but Viki, my editor, wasn't at all keen on the idea. The word 'lazy' is normally used in a pejorative sense, but in this context I intend it to be highly complimentary. The Lazy Project Manager doesn't just have successful projects. She has them *by doing the least amount of work possible*.

You see, the Ten Steps don't just guarantee a successful project. They also are *the least you have to do for a successful project*. Mathematicians would describe them as a 'necessary and sufficient condition' for a successful project. 'Necessary' - you have to do these things; 'sufficient' - these things are enough - once you have done these you need do no more.

The Ten Steps stop you from fretting about whether you have done enough project management. They stop you from waking in the middle of the night in a cold sweat wondering whether you have missed something. They tell you when you have done enough, when you have done your job as well as it can be done.

In chapters 6-10 and in part III, we will show you how you become a Lazy Project Manager.

Finally, there is one last use for the Ten Steps worth mentioning. When I first began managing projects, and when I took over or started a new project, the first thing I did was to 'read myself in'. This involved laying my hands on every document that I could find related to the project, everything related to the technology the project used, and any other background information that seemed remotely relevant. The I would read and highlight away to my heart's content. Often the stuff was non-existent or out of date, and then you ended up with an incomplete or skewed picture of what the project was all about.

With the Ten Steps, 'reading-in' is at an end. The first five steps tell you exactly the things you need to know:

Where can I find a description of the goal of the project and evidence that the detail in this goal is being developed (specs, designs, etc.)?

Is there a plan? [If there is you can use the material in part IV to analyse it.] Who's leading the project - if it's not meant to be you?

Are all jobs assigned to people? Have people's other commitments been taken into account? Where are the potential weaknesses in the work assignments?

Is there contingency and a fallback position? What expectations have been created? How do the goal, the fallback position and the expectations all relate to one another?

Applying Structured Project Management to software engineering

At this stage you should have the following:

- a detailed description of the goal of the project (from step 1)
- a job list, complete to the first milestone, and as detailed as you can be thereafter, but with the major milestones included (from step 2)
- a project leader (from step 3)
- an allocation of your team to the jobs on the job list, so that all jobs are covered (from step 4)
- some contingency plans (from step 5) if things go wrong

In other words, you have all the things that a good project plan should have, and you are ready to set forth into the great unknown. Just as a final cross-reference, here's a proposed table of contents for a Project Plan, into which you could structure all the information you have gleaned by applying steps 1 through 5.

SECTION IN PROJECT PLAN	INFO. FROM STEP
0 Related Documents	
1 Introduction	1
2 Project Description	
2.1 Statement of Work	1/2
2.1.1 Requirements Specification	
2.1.2 High Level Design	
2.1.3 Low Level Design	
2.1.4 Implementation	
2.1.5 Alpha Test	
2.1.6 Beta Test	
2.2 Deliverables	1
2.2.1 Software	
2.2.2 Documentation	
2.2.3 Services	
2.2.4 Acceptance Criteria	
2.3 Completion Criteria (i.e. how do we know when it's over)	1
3 Development Plan	
3.1 Work Breakdown Structure (WBS)	2
3.1.1 Requirements Specification	
3.1.2 High Level Design	
3.1.3 Low Level Design	
3.1.4 Implementation	
3.1.5 Alpha Test	
3.1.6 Beta Test	
3.2 Work Plan	2
3.3 Effort	2
3.4 Schedule	2
3.5 Milestones	2
3.6 Resource Loading / Project Ramp-Up	2,3,4
3.7 Budget	2,3,4
3.8 Critical Items	5
3.9 Project Organisation	3,4
4 Resources Required	
4.1 People	3,4
4.2 Equipment	2,5

Finally, software projects fail for a variety of reasons, but often they fail just because:

- things took longer than expected
- requirements kept changing in an uncontrolled way
- something came up that nobody had anticipated
- nobody estimated - in any kind of a common-sense way - how long the thing was likely to take or what it would cost
- technical problems, that nobody had foreseen, caused delays

Admittedly, some of these things can be valid. But often they are presented to cover up an absence of basic planning and forethought. Carry out steps (1) - (5) of SPM on your project and you give yourself some kind of a fighting chance. If you inherit a project, insist that you be allowed to carry out these steps, and don't be surprised if your management are alarmed at the result.

However, don't you be alarmed. SPM provides you with the proof that what you say is true, and anyway, at this point in a project, you have the moral high ground. Hold your nerve and if the project is important enough, they'll let you do it the correct way. This is also true if you are dealing with a subcontractor. Ensure that at the very minimum, his proposal contains the elements already outlined, and kick him out if it doesn't.

You have done all your planning and your project has hit the road. The next five chapters talk about what things you need to do during the journey to your destination.

 ## Steps 1-5 Significance of PSI at this point

Two points need to be made here. First, you should notice that 70% of the

PSI is accounted for by steps 1-5, the planning steps. If this is true, and all the evidence we have gathered to date suggests that it is, then this confirms what we said earlier about the fate of your project being sealed in the planning phase.

Secondly, the projects we have analysed to date reveal that 40 is the threshold from the planning steps. What we mean by this is the following. When the project starts, during it's very first moments of life, things like the goal [step 1], the list of jobs [step 2] and so on will register little if anything in terms of scores. For example, you might have little more than a one or two line sentence describing the goal of the project, and this would earn you a score out of 20 of perhaps 1 or 2, if you were lucky. Similarly for the other four steps.

The 40 threshold says that the first things you have to do in the project - *the absolutely first things you have to do to the exclusion of all others* - are to go through the processes of

Defining the goal in successive levels of detail. (If you think about it, the first few phases of any project life cycle - Requirements gathering, Design and so on - are concerned with doing precisely this.) [Step 1]

Refining the plan as the goal becomes more definite and detailed. [Step 2]

Ensuring that one person is driving the project, setting up the project organisation structure and installing the processes and procedures that are going to operate throughout the remainder of the project. [Step 3]

Getting your hands on people (real warm bodies) and allocating them to jobs. [Step 4]

Structuring your plans such that you have a fallback position and a margin for error. [Step 5]

Creating the right expectations. [Step 5]

In doing these you will gradually raise your PSI scores until they reach the critical 40 level. Until you get to 40, you should be trying to expend as little effort as possible on the project, since you won't be sure of anything like a successful outcome until you get past 40. Also, doing anything else, other than the things mentioned above is wasting time, effort, resources, money and energy.

Chapter 6

Step 6 - Use an appropriate leadership style

Introduction

Your team is moving forward; a mixed bag of individuals as we discussed previously. Some seem to be megastars, some are good solid players, some look decidedly dodgy. There may only be a small number of them, so you are like a close family; or there may be thousands of them. Each person is an individual with his or her own wishes, fears, desires, prejudices, skills, experience, relationships, problems, ambitions. How can you even begin to set about leading such a complex organism? How can you allocate work? Find out what's going on? Keep a check on morale? How can you even measure morale?

Beats me, is probably the most accurate answer to this question. *It is an incredibly difficult thing to do.* It is probably safe to assume that at any given time some of the people in your team will be unhappy. It is probably equally safe to assume that at any given time some of the people will be behaving in such a way as to contribute nothing or even to retard your project.

The best any of us can do here is to apply those management talents we have as best we can. There are no rules here, only guidelines; and I present mine under the general heading of 'Use an appropriate leadership style'.

Each job on your list will be carried out by a person. This makes the combination of job and person unique, i.e. the same job would be done differently by different people. This means there will be hundreds or perhaps thousands of unique job-person events happening on your project, all of which you have to manage. The sum of how you handle all these events is what makes up your leadership style.

Each of us will have a basic style - autocratic, democratic, 'soft', 'hard', etc. - but we will have to vary our style depending on the job-person event that we are dealing with. Does this mean we have to have hundreds of different styles? And if not, how do we know what styles there are and when to use them. Here's how. We discussed earlier the five situations that could arise with regard to a person and a job. These were:

- can do the job and wants to do it
- can do the job and is prepared to do it
- can do the job and isn't prepared to do it
- can be trained / instructed to do the job
- cannot do the job

There is another concept we need to introduce at this point. This is the idea of trusting somebody to do a job. Let us use the following definition. If, when you ask somebody to do a job, you can regard the job as being done, then we will say that you trust that person. Obviously if this applied to all the people and all the jobs on your project, there would hardly be a need for you at all - the whole thing would go swimmingly and complete according to plan. It is precisely because you generally do not trust some or all of the people on your project that you are needed, and that projects go awry.

What would cause you to trust somebody as we have defined it above? You might trust them because you had worked with them before and knew they could be relied upon to carry out any job. Or perhaps other people whom you trust might have spoken highly of them. Or maybe you would try them out on your project: tell them what you expect from team members - that when you give a person a job you want to be able to assume it will be done - and try them out with two or three tasks. If they perform then you can start to build up trust in them. A good test is to ask yourself whether you feel confident entrusting your reputation to their judgement and performance. Another is that you can identify some solid evidence as to why you believe you can trust them.

If they cannot pass these tests, then you don't trust them. Simple as that. As the project progresses, you may come to trust them. That's a different issue. Also you may trust them on some jobs but not on others. I repeat the test - if you don't feel you can entrust your neck completely to them or have no solid evidence, then for the purposes of this discussion, you don't trust them.

Table 6.1 overleaf then shows the ten possible scenarios and the leadership style I suggest you adopt in each case. Where it says 'Resolve into a (2) or a (5)', we will discuss methods in chapter 11 whereby you might do this.

Table 6.1

Case	Trust	Don't trust
(1) Can do it/likes to do it	(A)	(B)
(2) Can do it/prepared to do it	(A)	(B)
(3) Can do it/won't do it	Situation same as (E)	Resolve into a (2) or a (5)
(4) Can do it with training	(C)	(D)
(5) Cannot do it	(E)	Resolve into a (2) or a (5)

(A) You trust the person to do the job. Perhaps they've done it before or if not something similar to it. They like doing it or at worst they're putting up with doing it. In short, they're the experts and can make all the decisions internal to the job. Leave them to it. Don't concern yourself with it, other than to tick it off your list on the day when it completes on schedule. Even if something does go wrong we will catch it because of *No Surprises* as discussed in the next chapter.

(B) They're doing it, their hearts are probably in the right place, but you're not super-confident that they'll do it right or on schedule. You have to watch them: your neck depends on it. There's no need to bug them to distraction - a bit of gentle hand-holding will do the trick. If there are decisions to be made then you need to work with them to arrive at the correct conclusion.

(C) They've done other things well in the past and now you're trying them on something new. They've come through on everything so far, but this is a new ball-game. Another case of watching them gently, as in (B). Remember that your neck depends on it. You may have a decent relationship with them anyway - from which the trust has arisen - and know what level of monitoring to apply. Decisions can be made democratically as in (B).

(D) They've never done it before and you have no reason to believe they can / will do it. It's back to school, guys. Hand-holding. Inching forward with mini-goals spelled out in detail. Constant monitoring for trouble signs.

(E) Here we have a problem. In fact we have two problems. First, there is the problem of what will happen to the job that this person was meant to be doing. This job isn't happening - we need to make alternative arrangements about it. Then there is the problem of the person. On at least one of the jobs on our project this person isn't performing. This potentially means there are others where this is also, or will become the case. We need to determine what we are going to do about this person. But as Project Managers, especially a Lazy Project Manager, our first priority is the job. First we have to get that squared away. Then, as a secondary priority, we can worry about the person.

You can use form #2 from chapter 4 which is reproduced in Figure 6.1 to understand which management style to use in which job-person situation.

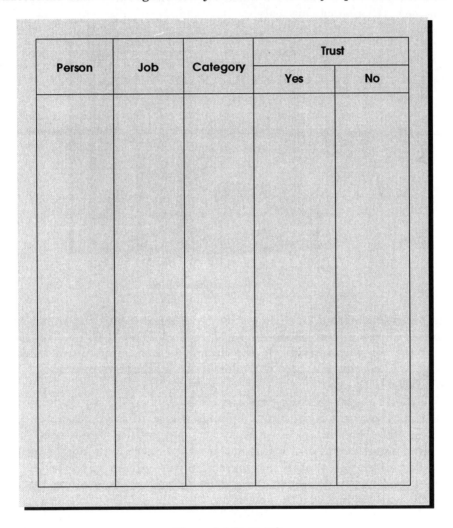

Person	Job	Category	Trust	
			Yes	No

Figure 6.1 Form # 2

The Lazy Project Manager

Let's for a moment rate these five different styles on the following scale. The vertical axis is a measure of how much management time and effort you put in to a particular task. It is a measure of how much micro-management you do, how much you are in your peoples' faces, how much you stick your nose into their business. We have rated each of our five styles (A) - (E) against this scale.

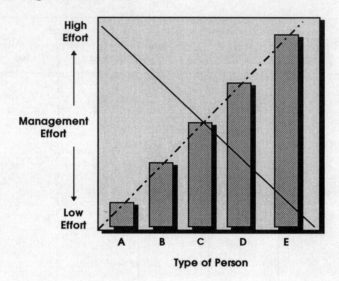

The *ascending dotted* line shows the gradual increase in management effort as we move from leadership style (A) through style (E). Now it seems to me that as warm, living, loving human beings, our natural tendency would be to allocate our time and effort in a way that is represented by the *solid descending* line.

We would enjoy spending time and effort over on the (A)-(B) end of the spectrum. Over here is the happy uplands where all good men agree. Over on this side are competent, motivated people. It's milestones being achieved and commitments being met. It's good news, high morale, forward progress; all that great stuff that we dream will happen on our project. We could spend happy days over here and go home in the evening thinking that the world is indeed a fine place.

Over on the (D) and especially (E) end of the spectrum, on the other hand, is the twilight zone of project management. Here is the land of permanent bad news, cock-ups, screw-ups, SNAFUs; having to tell bad news to bosses and customers; having to eat humble pie; having to give people bad performance appraisals or no salary rises; having to fire people; having to coax people painstakingly through things; having to confront, annoy, argue, and generally dissipate vast amounts of emotional energy trying to keep things on the rails. Over here is feeling that you have been let down by people. We want to be here - in short - like we want a hole in the head!

And so - I don't know if you've been guilty of this, but I certainly have - we spend our time on the (A)-(B) end and procrastinate, delay and generally avoid doing things on the (D)-(E) end. We spend time having really interesting conversations with the good guys - and in the process wasting our time and theirs; and we avoid dealing with issues which are rotting away inside our project.

The Lazy Project Manager has no time for such foolishness or dithering. She knows that spending time in the shaded zone, while it may be enjoyable, *is of no value whatsoever in progressing the project.*

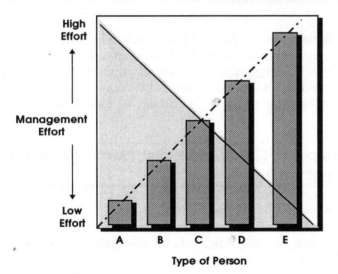

Indeed, if you spend lots of time trying to *manage* people who should really be treated with an (A)-(B) style, not only is it a waste of time and effort, it can actually be counter-productive. Such people end up feeling that you don't trust them, their expertise and their judgement, and can become very demotivated with lots of what they perceive as interference.

Instead, the Lazy Project Manager puts in the effort where it counts: in the shaded zone. Here every ounce of management time and effort contributes directly to the forward progress of the project.

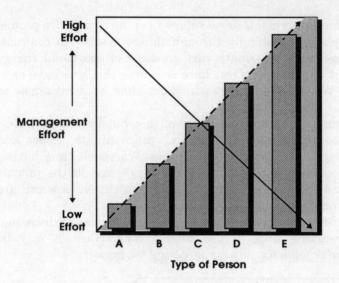

Type of Person

The Lazy Project Manager becomes an object of complete bafflement and irritation to her colleagues because she seems to have an uncanny knack of knowing how to leave well enough alone, and to get in where the problems are. In short, the Lazy Project Manager not only always has successful projects but, in the process, she makes it all look like a piece of cake.

Applying Step 6 of Structured Project Management to software engineering

Here we fill in form # 2 which was introduced in chapter 4. We have filled out the form categorising a team of people in accordance with the scheme introduced in chapter 4. From the form it looks like we're in reasonable shape. There are some training requirements arising from the 4's, however, it is the rightmost two columns which interest us. This form shows exactly where the project manager ought to expend management effort and suggests the management style that will be right in any particular situation.

In Figure 6.2 we see that everyone appears in the 'don't trust' column of the form - the reason might be that this is a brand new team with which the Project Manager has not worked before - and everyone has been classified as either a category B or a category D. This team will require intensive monitoring on the Project Manager's part. There is no part of the project he will not have to stick his nose into. If, after a period of time, he finds that he has come to rely on some people, and finds that they consistently deliver, he may have reason to revise his rating of them and place them in the 'do trust' column. However, until then he will have to keep a careful eye on things to make sure nobody drops the ball.

Person	Job	Category	Trust	
			Yes	No
Snow White	Project Manager	1		B
Grumpy	User Interface	4		D
Sneezy	New Functions	4		D
Dopey	Programmer	1 - ish		B
Sleepy	Programmer	1 - ish		B
Happy	Designer	1		B
Bashful	Database Specialist	4		D
Doc	Testing	4		D

Figure 6.2 Using form # 2

 ## Step 6 PSI contribution - 10

If your style tends to be static - either constantly hands-on or always hands-off - give yourself a low score here. If you vary your style with the circumstances, well done, and give yourself a high mark.

Structured Project Management

Planning the Project

1. Visualise what the goal is; set your eyes on the prize

2. Make a list of the jobs that need to be done

3. There must be one leader

4. Assign people to jobs

5. Manage expectations / allow a margin for error / have a fallback position

Implementing the plan / Achieving the goal

6. Use an appropriate leadership style

Chapter 7

Step 7 - Know what's going on

Introduction

In this chapter we talk about three things:

- Using your plan as instrumentation to guide the project. In doing this, in particular, we will describe how the Lazy Project Manager spends her day
- Positive and negative signs on a project
- The doctrine of 'no surprises'

Using your plan as instrumentation / The Lazy Project Manager's day

We're all familiar with instrumentation. In a car, for example, we have a series of gauges, clocks and other display devices that give us quantitative information about what is happening out in the world. We then take actions based on this information.

We can use our plan in exactly the same way to give us information about what is happening on our project. We can then make sensible decisions and take appropriate actions to control the progress of our project towards its goal. Fancier project management books than this one call this process project monitoring and control.

It is in this process that all of the hard work that went into steps 1-5, and notably step 2, begins to pay off. Note too the way the plan we developed during the planning steps has multiple uses:

- The plan we developed with steps 1 through 5(a) enabled us to estimate the project

- Applying steps 5b to this plan enabled us to generate versions of it from which our management and/or customers could pick
- Now we are going to use the chosen version again as the instrumentation with which we will guide the project.

The myriad uses we make of our plan are yet another reason why it is well worth putting time and effort into producing a good one. And we see yet again the central position of planning in having a successful outcome to our project.

You can use your plan as instrumentation whether it is on paper or stored on a PC-based planning tool. Everything I am going to say here will apply in either case. The advantage of using a PC-based tool is that you will get results quicker and your work will not contain the errors that will almost certainly creep in if you do things manually on paper. I am going to illustrate things here by reference to a PC tool, but I reiterate that everything that I say here can also be done manually.

Let us assume then that you have your plan and you have entered it into a PC tool such as Microsoft Project or Timeline. Every morning when the Lazy Project Manager comes into work, she fires up her PC and brings up the plan on the screen. Now, the plan may well have many activities in it. Four to five hundred wouldn't be uncommon for the levels of detail we have said you should produce.

But remember the format of our plan. It contains all the major milestones and then is very detailed to the next milestone. So when we look on our screen, and we look at those jobs clustered around today, we probably won't see more than a few dozen that fit within say, a week either side of today. Then, when we look to the right on our screen, we will see those other jobs which are part of the big milestones off in the future.

The Lazy Project Manager then has two things she has to do. Once she has done these she has quite literally finished her project management for the day. These two things are (a) check on the current stuff, and (b) look off into the future and try and unearth more detail about those future milestones. We discuss each of these in turn.

Check on current stuff

The few dozen jobs clustered around today give the Lazy PM her to-do list for the day.

First there are the finishers. These are the jobs that the plan says should have finished. Have they? Go and see. Is there a deliverable you can hold in your hand? If so, then they're done. If they're not done, then you update your plan to reflect this fact. This change causes a ripple through the rest of the project. We will discuss this ripple in more detail in a moment.

Next there are the starters. These tasks should have started. Again, have they? Is somebody beavering away on it, doing exactly what the plan says? If so, fine. If not, what *are* they doing? Does the plan need to be changed? Or do they need to be refocused.

Finally there are the jobs that are in progress. Depending on the leadership style you are adopting in particular situations (see previous chapter), you may want to go check on some of these. On the other hand, you may be happy to leave the people to it. Note that this is the Lazy Project Manager at work again.

All of these items may generate additional off-line activities - meetings, memos, faxes, phone calls, and so on - that you have to do. These are your project management tasks for the day.

Open up the surprise packages

Each day that passes you find out more information about the project. Almost like a detective gathering clues, you get more and more information about things which lie in the future, and which up to now had been hazy or guesses or assumptions or just plain unknown.

Having checked on the current stuff, you now look through the stuff that lies in the future and try to fill out any additional details that you can. Remember that what you are trying to do is to achieve the *man-day* level of detail in all of your plan, i.e. that you can say what each person on your project is doing for each day over a particular period of time. Once you have added all the detail you can, then you're finished.

Doing the two things just described may have a number of possible effects on the schedule. These are:

- No change
- A slip which can be recovered
- A slip which can't be recovered

Let's look at these in turn. The first is trivial. It means that you have managed to keep your project on schedule for another day. You can ask no more. Go home - you've done your project management for today.

In the second case, the changes in the schedule generate a slip. However, by using our plan as instrumentation, we can do things like move people around, work some overtime, drop some feature which was a bit of a 'frill' or similar actions to bring the project back on course. Note that those four parameters of the Apocalypse:

- Functionality
- Delivery Date
- Effort (Cost)
- Quality

show us what our options are. Note too how our model, which we have put such a lot of work into, is serving us well again. Our model tells us what is and what isn't possible. It stops us making foolish assumptions such as the one that says we can always recover from any slip just by working harder - a well-worn recourse of software practitioners. As Caesar said, 'Men usually willingly believe what they wish'.

The third possibility is that we have a slip and we can't recover from it, no matter how much we tweak our four parameters. Now, we have a problem. This means that we have run out of contingency. The only thing that can help us now is a lucky break, and we might indeed let things go for a few days, a week, a couple of weeks to see if such a thing happens. Remember that our model is still only a prediction and so, occasionally, the gods smile on us and things take less time and effort than we anticipated. Occasionally! It may be we get such a break which puts things to rights.

However, if at this stage things are not improving - this technique I'm describing is the way some people, including myself, manage their overdraft! - you have to come clean with the powers that be.

Will this be pleasant? Almost certainly not. Humble pie rarely is. *But you have to*. The alternative is unthinkable. You can be caught in a small explosion now or a thermonuclear one down the line.

Go on. Go break the news to your boss and/or customer. Whichever of these situations occurs, once you have worked your way through the business we have just outlined, your project management, your project monitoring and control, your know-what's-going-on, is finished for the day. You can do no more. You have done everything that needs to be done. You can go home and rest secure in the knowledge that it is all under control. Even if things went wildly awry, you caught it at the earliest possible moment. Now, that's a professional Project Manager for you.

Positive signs

The following are all indicators that should be regarded as positive signs on a project.

People are having fun

Roland Huntford's account of Amundsen's return journey Ref. 26 makes exhilarating reading. Amundsen knows he has won, all he needs to do now is return his team to safety and announce his achievement to the world. He has food and fuel aplenty and for the last 200 miles marker flags, that he deployed during his outward journey, now make the return trip more like an extended ski race. Doing 20-30 miles per day - three to four times what Scott is doing - his men career into Framheim, their base, on January 26th 1912. It is a good sign if your project gets to a point where:

- people are strutting around a bit
- their confidence is up
- morale is high, pretty much independent of working conditions on the project
- they feel the worst is behind them
- their belief in their own abilities and those of the team, has increased
- there is less tension and ill-temper
- there are more practical jokes
- people enjoy being in the team environment; in short, people are having fun
- milestones are being met

Amundsen laid out his plan in terms of daily milestones that all his team could understand: Each day they would travel 20 miles, a quarter of a degree of latitude, and stop. Thus every 4 days they were a degree closer to the Pole. Also as soon as they had done their 20 miles, they could stop. Milestones completing and being ticked off is a good sign of progress as well as being a significant morale booster, since it implies that the estimates that were made before the project got under way, appear to have been good ones.

Independent feedback

You may receive an early indication from a source independent of the project team that the project is working. 'Independent' is the key word here. This is sometimes called 'putting your fingers in the wounds'. In the case of a project to develop a product, this could mean a demonstration version, a prototype, an early release or a partially working system. There was a period in Operation Desert Storm where we in the West were receiving no such independent feedback from the Allies, with the result that we were very unclear as to how that particular project was progressing. [Note: (before you write to complain!): I first drafted this particular chapter of the book in mid-February, 1991. At that time the land war in the Gulf had not yet started and it was unclear exactly what was going on.]

People leave the team alone

This one is more from the project team's point of view. If the project is going well, there will appear to be fewer outside interruptions, people sticking their noses in, meetings, and so on.

Life after the project

Again, more from the team's point of view; people start to talk of a life after the project ends. They have been bound up with it for so long but now they can begin to see a light at the end of the tunnel.

Common vision

The goal has stabilised; there is complete accord and no confusion as to what the ultimate objective is.

Few crises

Nothing appears to have been forgotten; there is very little firefighting; everything is calm and efficient.

Negative signs

The following are indicators, any one of which should make a Project Leader extremely nervous about a project.

Milestones are not being met

Things aren't working out according to plan. Estimates appear to have been whacky. Milestones which were reported as done somehow become undone. The same milestone gets rescheduled several times.

'Everything's under control'

It's a negative sign if somebody, particularly the Project Leader, uses this phrase!

Low morale

High staff turnover or sickness. People looking dour or moaning a lot. An apparent absence of anything that could be termed 'team spirit'. Nobody appears to be enjoying things very much. A loss of confidence in the team.

Personality clashes

These would be worrying particularly if they occur in the upper echelons of the project's management.

Nobody's having fun

A really extreme instance of this is Scott's return from the Pole which makes appalling reading: It takes colossal effort from his weakened and demoralised men to move what have now become light loads, a few miles. Nerves are wracked as meagre supplies run low and depots are difficult to find. One of the team, P.O. Evans, dies. Oates, the horse handler, is suffering from an old leg wound he received during the Boer War. He too dies; he walks out of the tent, never to be seen again. Finally, 14 miles short of a supply depot, Scott and his two remaining companions, held up by a blizzard, pitch camp. They are never to set forth again.

Procrastination

You ask about particular jobs several times, and each time you find an excuse why the job hasn't been done. An interesting historical example of this is General George B. McClellan's command of the Army of the Potomac during the early part of the American Civil War, where Lincoln kept asking him to advance on the Confederate Army and McClellan kept finding reasons not to (this earned McClellan the sobriquet 'The Virginia Creeper'! [Refs. 9-11]).

Goalposts keep shifting

The goal has never stabilised. Each time you thought you had identified it, it got changed or expanded in some way. Note that this can happen through the process of 'creeping elegance': Lots of small changes to the goal are made. Each one in itself is small and can probably be accommodated without too much difficulty. However, the sum of all the changes represents a dramatic change to the goal.

Mistakes are being made

Lots of things seem to have been forgotten; mistakes become more frequent; there's a lot of carelessness about.

Lots of crises

There appears to be a crisis every other day. Panic meetings are commonplace. Firefighting is the order of the day.

No independent feedback

All you have is the Project Leader's assurances that things are under control. There is nothing you can see and feel for yourself.

The Slough of Despond

A feeling, either amongst the team or the customer that there is no end in sight. A good historical example of this is the World War One Battle of Passchaendale fought between June and November 1917 in Flanders [Refs 38 and 54]. In popular memory it has become the classic World War I battle. The summer of 1917 was one of the worst on record, and the rain turned the low-lying Flanders land into a sea of mud in which men literally drowned.

The Battle of Passchaendale actually consisted of a number of smaller battles and the result, from the infantryman's point of view, was that time after time he was asked to cross a churned-up morass in the face of withering machine gun and artillery fire to attack German lines protected by vast belts of barbed wire. Those men who survived one battle were soon thrown into the next one, with the result that men lost hope. The war would go on for ever. They would all die - it was just a question of when, and better to do it sooner rather than later and avoid the awful suffering of living and fighting in a quagmire. If your project gets to the point where people are repeatedly being asked to work overtime, put in 'one more effort', come in at weekends, and if they feel that no real progress is being made, then your project is in trouble.

The rumour machine

If the normal grapevine that exists in any organisation suddenly gets replaced by a rumour machine, and that machine seems to be spewing out wilder and wilder rumours as the days go by.

Things are not as expected

As you have planned your project you will have gone through the process of visualising every step of the journey. As a result of doing this you will be expecting certain things to be a certain way, i.e. there will be signs you will be looking out for and expecting to see. If you do not see them or if the signs are not what you expected, this could be a cause for concern. An example of this from history is the Battle of the Somme. Part of the aim of the artillery bombardment that we discussed previously (chapter 5) was to cut the enemy's barbed wire entanglements. It was confidently predicted that these would be cut by firing shrapnel. However, on the eve of the infantry assault, scouting parties were reporting large tracts of barbed wire intact. These reports were ignored by headquarters staff - being put down to nerves - with the resulting disaster that we have already described.

'No surprises'

Run your projects on the basis of 'No surprises'. This means that there should only be one real 'crime'. That is to be aware of some impending problem on a project and not to alert anybody to the fact. This applies to anyone connected with the project - leader, team or customer. Mistakes can and will be made and this is all allowed for, but to keep some time-bomb hidden, for whatever reason, is to cause a major threat to the project and to let down the other people involved in it.

Applying Step 7 of Structured Project Management to software engineering

How do you know what's going on? On a large software project there may be scores or even hundreds of people beavering away on components of the system. These components may run into many thousands, all of which have to fit together in an intricate and perfect way. How do you know how well the system is coming together; how complete it is and how much remains to be spent to complete?

As well as all the qualitative things outlined above, there are a couple of very quantitative ways you can track progress on your project. The most obvious one is, assuming that you have your plan on a computer-based project planning tool, that you can now track progress by marking off jobs done, adding in new jobs and changing existing ones. The advantage of the tool is that it is unforgiving. If there is a slip it shows you - in a depressingly clinical way. Correspondingly though, it illuminates the critical path - the way of recovering from slips - if recovery is possible.

The whole plan can be laid out for you in as much or as little detail as is relevant to your particular interest and the analysis you want to do. As I've said earlier, anyone who runs any kind of a project, no matter how small, without the use of one of these tools is nuts. An even more sophisticated way of tracking progress, particularly on large projects, is through the use of the earned value concept. You will find a good discussion of this in *Software Engineering Economics* by Barry Boehm [Ref. 3]. In addition, the particular project planning tool you are using will explain how it has implemented the concept, and what earned-value-based reports and analyses are available.

Basically, earned value allows you to determine whether the costs incurred on a project up to the present time are in proportion to its current level of completion. In other words, it tells you if you are spending more than you planned to spend given the work that has been completed up to this time. It also enables you to predict what the project (or any job within it) will cost at completion if the current trend continues. Remember, however, that earned value is not a panacea. Get many of the other things right and earned value is useful, effective and gives you a very fine finger on the pulse of your project. But if the basic, simple stuff that we have been describing in the rest of this book isn't carried out, all the earned values or fancy financial reporting systems in the world won't save you.

Step 7 PSI contribution - 10

If you do what we have said and keep your finger on the pulse of your project then you get a high score here. Otherwise, if from day to day, you're out of touch with what's happening, score low.

Structured Project Management

Planning the Project

1. Visualise what the goal is; set your eyes on the prize

2. Make a list of the jobs that need to be done

3. There must be one leader

4. Assign people to jobs

5. Manage expectations / allow a margin for error / have a fallback position

Implementing the plan / Achieving the goal

6. Use an appropriate leadership style

7. Know what's going on

Chapter 8

Step 8 - Tell people what's going on

Introduction

In this chapter we talk about Status Reports, and we tell you how the Lazy Project Manager spends her week.

We are told that knowledge dispels fear. Amundsen and Scott provide conflicting examples of how to handle information dissemination within a project. Amundsen explained the objective and his plan to achieve it. The plan was explained, discussed, posted up in the mess for everyone to see. As we have seen the plan enabled people to visualise progress and set a finite limit on what they would have to do each day.

Scott by comparison would remain unclear as to his plan until well into his journey to the Pole. Whatever plan he eventually evolved was not shared with anybody until the moment when people had to know. At the last moment he changed one of the cornerstones of the plan - the number of people who were to come on to the Pole with him. Even his backup plan, such as it was, was hastily put together, and the result was that when he got into serious difficulty, whatever hope he had of rescue was ruined by the poorly laid and confused plans he had given to his subordinates.

What we are saying here is that people are thinking creatures. Everyone has inputs to give, everyone has elements of creativity and everyone feels more self-worth if they know what's going on. People will operate at their best if they know what the big picture is and how their component, no matter how trivial, fits into it. One assumes this is particularly true in a military situation if you are asking people to make extraordinary and sometimes final sacrifices for you.

So step 8 is 'Tell people what's going on'. Having said this I will now proceed to contradict it. There is the concept of the leader acting as a filter. Think of it as a fort with the project team inside and the leader acting as a sentry on the gate. The world outside is in a constant state of change.

During the life of the project, some of these changes will have implications for the project and the team. The leader needs to determine how much of this change to let through to the team.

Some change has to be let through. Some is healthy and as I have said in the paragraphs above, the team will feel more self-esteem for knowing that they are being treated as intelligent people. However, there will be changes that might, or definitely would, cause a major problem in the progress of the project, if the team got wind of them. These changes you must either:

- block
- or failing that, censor so that their threat is reduced
- or finally failing that, to relay to the team in such a way as to minimise the effect on them

and you have to do all of this without hiding true realities from them. A tall order? You bet! The foregoing is equally true of outgoing information. There will be ups and downs on a project, and the outside world needs to be apprised of progress. But there may be things which occur on the project that you must either:

- stop from going outside
- or failing that, to water down so that when they get outside, their true effect is reduced
- or failing that, to transmit so as to minimise the effect on the outside world

and all of this without hiding true realities. All of this is A VERY TALL ORDER. What this book does is to try to give you an armful of methods and ideas that you can apply in just such circumstances. In Chapter 11, we present a whole bunch of ideas that you can apply. In any particular situation you will be able to apply more than one of them with differing results. It will be up to you to pick the one that suits you and the situation best.

The analogy is with a carpenter's tool box. Pretty much anything in it - a hammer, the handle of a screwdriver, the flat side of a plane - will drive a nail into a piece of wood, but some of the tools are better suited than others. So too with the tools in this book. Several will achieve the effect. It will be up to you to judge which effect is best for you.

Status Reports

It's funny the things that seem to be constant across lots of different cultures, and one of them, I've discovered, is that during their school days, many people have written an essay entitled 'A Day at the Seaside'.

Perhaps you did too, and if so, maybe you remember how it went. All human life was there - the weather, the personalities, the events, the emotional highs and lows, the interplay of characters - and, at the end of it all, we tumbled into bed, sand between our toes, badly sunburned, covered in calamine lotion, tired but happy after a tremendous day.

I mention this because most status reports seem to bear striking similarities to 'A Day at the Seaside' essays. They might as well be called 'Here were all the dead interesting things that happened on the project last week'. As we read on excitedly we find out all the minutiae that occurred on the project and invariably - just like in our essay - there is the happy ending; the upbeat conclusion that says everything's OK, all's right with the world.

But is the project on target? Hey, I don't know. And you certainly won't find out from reading a 'Day at the Seaside' status report. If you want to come away with a permanent warm feeling, then a 'Day at the Seaside' is just for you. But if you want some useful information, you will have to look elsewhere.

The Status Report we propose is a top-down creation, going from the most high level to the most detailed. It says in no uncertain terms what the status of the project is; and you can perhaps see why people might not want to write these - they are completely unforgiving and clinical in terms of what they reveal.

Here, then, is a structure you might follow in writing a Status Report.

Level I

Is the project on schedule? Yes or No. Your Status Report template could have two boxes where you tick one. If the project is on schedule, people may not want to know any more.

Level II

At this level you present some high level information on the state of our four parameters:

Functionality
A couple of sentences stating at a high level:

- what the functionality started off at
- any major changes that have occurred

and pointing at the change control log (see chapter 1) where the detailed changes and history of changes can be seen.

Delivery Date

Here's what is was originally   dd/mm/yy
Here's what it is now   dd/mm/yy
Here's how it changed

Change no.	Date	Reason for change	New del. date
1	dd/mm/yy	xxxxxxxxxxxxxxxx	dd/mm/yy
2	dd/mm/yy	xxxxxxxxxxxxxxxx	dd/mm/yy
...	...	...	...
n	dd/mm/yy	xxxxxxxxxxxxxxxx	dd/mm/yy

Effort

Here's what is was originally   nnnn man-days
Here's what it is now   nnnn man-days
Here's how it changed

Change no.	Date	Reason for change	New effort (in man-days)
1	dd/mm/yy	xxxxxxxxxxxxxxxx	nnnn
2	dd/mm/yy	xxxxxxxxxxxxxxxx	nnnn
...	...	...	...
n	dd/mm/yy	xxxxxxxxxxxxxxxx	nnnn

Quality
If you are measuring quality say, with something like Mean Time To Defect (MTTD), then a similar originally - now - change history thing could be applied here. (If you're interested you'll find a good discussion of MTTD in Ref. 47).

Finally, at this second level, you should make some general statement about the state of health of the project. Even though it may be on schedule there may be some calamity looming. Here you can say in a few sentences what the big issues / known risks / problems outside your control are, and what you are doing / would like done about them.

Level III

At level III, if you're feeling a bit like a frustrated novelist because you haven't been able to get into a day at the seaside, then this is your chance for a bit of narrative. If you like, you can write down the things that are currently happening. This would correspond very much to the 'current stuff' we talked about in the previous chapter. Do it by person maybe, and that way everyone gets something said about him and feels loved and wanted.

Level IV

Finally, at this level, you can throw in everything and the kitchen sink. Here you can throw in a copy of the current plan - the Gantt chart - showing all the detail in the world.

Finally, the last question is who do we give this great opus to? Well, in the spirit of what we said in the Introduction to this chapter, it seems to me that we should give it to as many people as possible. Clearly there may be things that we don't want the team or the boss or the customer to see, but there's nothing to stop us doing a sort of 'vanilla' report for general consumption with a little note attached if there are things we want to report to a specific audience.

By giving it to the team, we enable every person to see the big picture and how their part fits in. Other people may spot things that we haven't seen. The more problems are identified now, the fewer problems we'll have down the line.

Equally, by giving the status report to bosses and customers we avoid the project becoming a black hole where money is poured in, and someday something may come out. We not only do a good job but are seen to do a good job.

As an example of what I mean here - and this is very much by way of illustration rather than a rule - on the last project I ran for a client, I produced two versions of the status report. One - the same one - went to the team and my boss, i.e. *my* client. The other went to my client's client, i.e. my customer. There were two differences between the reports:

(1) All references to who was working on what were removed from the customer's version on the basis that this was my client's business and not the customer's.

(2) Any downbeat or ominous messages were removed from levels II and III of the customer's version. This however, was because the project was generally going well. If it had been otherwise then we would have been passing those messages on to the customer. Had we had to do this, then, amongst other things, we would have been preparing the customer for bad news. And in doing this, we would have been following the principle of 'no surprises' that we talked about in step 7. If we had had to break bad news to the customer, what he would have seen all the way would have been professional project management of the situation.

The Lazy Project Manager's Week

The Lazy Project Manager's week goes like this:

Monday

Monday, or the first day back after a bank holiday weekend, is a long day for the Lazy Project Manager. On Monday she has three things to do.

Set targets
The first is to set targets for the week. Do this as early as possible on the first day of the new week. This not only gives the team as much time as possible to achieve their targets, but also gets people back to work mentally, i.e. it brings their heads back from the weekend. (We're assuming that their bodies have already arrived!)

Use your plan, your instrumentation to do this. Do it on a one-on-one basis or in a team meeting or a combination of the two, whichever makes the most sense. Each has advantages and disadvantages. One-on-one means everybody spends the least amount of time with you; meetings are synergistic - you catch things where dependencies exist between people. Use your common sense. Then let everyone get on with it.

Daily stuff
As we described in the previous chapter, Monday is no different from any other day and so you have to do the Lazy Project Manager's daily tasks.

Any other business
Many organisations have their own regular things that happen on Mondays - timesheets have to be filled out, regular meetings for various

things take place, there are routine administrative things that have to be done. These make up the third element of the Lazy Project Manager's Monday.

Tuesday - Thursday

These three days are fairly quiet for the Lazy Project Manager. All she has to do is the daily stuff (from chapter 7, *The Lazy Project Manager's Day*) and then she's finished.

Friday

Friday is busier than the preceding three days but not as busy as Monday. First there is the daily stuff to be done as before.

Then, as late as possible in the day, i.e. as close as possible to close of business, run round to the team, find out what happened and write a status report. These results should also be recorded in the *Actual Schedule and Effort* columns of the project Gantt chart or on an estimating Score Card (see Appendix 4). Here we are recording whether or not the targets set on Monday were met. Those who haven't met their targets have the option of the two weekend days to make them up.

Notice a couple of things here. The first is the surgical use of overtime. Many software organisations make unlimited overtime a feature of the job. If, at your job interview, they say things like 'we work hard, we play hard' or 'we run aggressive schedules here', you can safely assume that they expect you not to have a life outside work. The Lazy Project Manager has no time for such foolishness, but equally she recognises that overtime is occasionally needed in the real world. The use of overtime by 'work hard play hard', 'aggressive schedule' companies is done with all the finesse of a chainsaw operator. The Lazy Project Manager uses overtime like a surgeon with a scalpel, making fine cuts to superb effect.

The other thing to notice is that in doing this overtime, we are actually adding some contingency back into our project. Thus, contingency is not just something you get one crack at, but a little reservoir that you can top up repeatedly. Think of it like those old arithmetic problems where a tank of water has a hole in it, so that water is flowing out, but also a running tap is filling up the tank. If you can keep some water in the tank at all times, then you will never run out of contingency, and you will never have to go back to the powers that be to renegotiate a commitment.

A variation on the Lazy Project Manager's Week

Dee Carri, a friend of mine, invented the following variation of the Lazy Project Manager's week.

Monday

As well as doing everything else on Monday, why not write the Status Report on Monday as well? A friend of mine told me about this. She writes it and pins it to the wall. She says 'This is what I want to be reporting on Friday, and once I've written the report I don't like to change it. You can be sure I'll move heaven and earth rather than go back and have to edit that report'.

Tuesday - Friday

If you write the report on Monday, then there is nothing to do on the other four days but follow the Lazy Project Manager's day.

Some people like to do the goal setting and the status reporting in the one meeting, but I don't think this is a good idea. It tends to blur the distinction between a target and an achievement. People say things like 'I didn't quite get that done by then, but don't worry it'll be ready in the next few hours'. Note that in this situation you already have a slip on your hands. By separating the two things there is no ambiguity, fuzziness or confusion about what was and was not achieved.

Applying step 8 of Structured Project Management to software engineering

Nothing more to be added here - just go to it !

Step 8 PSI contribution - 10

High marks here if you let all the players know what's happening on the project. Encase your project in a glasshouse and score high. Keep it all close to your chest and score low. Also you should remember what happened to Captain Scott!

Structured Project Management

Planning the Project

1. Visualise what the goal is; set your eyes on the prize

2. Make a list of the jobs that need to be done

3. There must be one leader

4. Assign people to jobs

5. Manage expectations / allow a margin for error / have a fallback position

Implementing the plan / Achieving the goal

6. Use an appropriate leadership style

7. Know what's going on

8. Tell people what's going on

Chapter 9

Step 9 - Repeat Steps 1 to 8 until Step 10

Introduction

Your job as a Project Leader involves repeating these first eight steps of Structured Project Management until the project is complete. How often do you do this? Every month? Every day? Every hour? In chapter 12 we will talk about how to spread your time across projects, but basically the answer is yes! Every month, every day, every hour - as often as it takes to get the job done. This means that

- Everyone is permanently focused on the goal. The team members have heard the 'dream', the vision, so often that any one of them could give your speech!
- You are using your list of jobs, your plan, like a steering compass, pushing on to each new horizon. This means that you are constantly scanning the plan, adding new jobs as unexpected things arise, changing the nature of jobs as more information about them become available, marking jobs off as they complete, deleting jobs if you find they are now no longer relevant and moving people to where they are most effective. At all times you are using the style most appropriate to the situation.
- You are checking to ensure that there is one and only one leader on the project.
- You are constantly thinking of the expectations you have set and considering fallback positions. Each job has associated with it an expectation and a fallback position, and it may be possible to fall-back on a number of these without affecting the overall project.
- You are out in front scouting, scanning the horizon for danger, asking 'what can go wrong?' Behind you, you know what progress the team is making and you report back to them of new perils, obstacles, challenges ahead.

When should we update the plan?

This is a question that gets asked on almost every project management workshop that I run, and I think it's the result of a number of different issues being mixed in together and confused.

There are three different answers to the question, depending on what the questioner meant.

Constantly

As we have seen already, the plan is constantly being updated, throughout the Lazy Project Manager's Day.

Weekly

These days, I would never run a project without using a PC planning tool. You may know that if you use one of these tools, then the plan, i.e. the Gantt chart, is stored in a file; and for example, in Microsoft Project, this file is a .MPP file. It is this file that I make the constant changes to as described above.

It is useful though, to keep copies of previous versions of the plan, so you can look back and see how things unfolded. I do this on a weekly basis. The convention I use is that last thing on Friday I copy the current plan (i.e the current .MPP file) to a new file. This, then, becomes the one I operate on in the coming week.

I name the files using the Monday of the week in question. Thus, XX170495.MPP would be the file for the week of Monday 17 April ('XX' is a project code) and on the Friday of that week, I would create a new file XX240495.MPP which I would then operate on in the week of Monday 24 April.

Only if there's a slip

At the outset of the project we write a plan, we agree it with all and sundry, everyone gets a copy and the plan then becomes our contract with the powers that be. This document need never be changed again unless a slip occurs which can't be recovered (see chapter 7).

If there is never such a slip, then this particular document never changes. Status reports keep everybody posted about what's happening; tell everybody how we're progressing against this original document.

If there is an unrecoverable slip, then this means we are in a position where we must renegotiate our contract. Then a new version of the plan document will get produced, a version 2.0 say, and this becomes the project's new contractual basis.

Applying Step 9 of Structured Project Management to software engineering

Software projects have a notorious reputation for going out of control. We mentioned earlier the US Navy's A-12 attack plane. (By the way, while this book was being written, the A-12 project was cancelled!) One of the elements cited in the A-12 cost overrun was software; and increasingly, as software intrudes into more and more areas of our lives, and as we use software to do increasingly complex (not to mention life-threatening!) things, we find that software projects go haywire.

That this should be so is hardly surprising. Software development as a discipline is less than 50 years old. When you compare it with something like the construction of buildings which has been going on for several thousand years, it seems only to be expected that software development should still have the status of a cottage, almost a craft industry. It is one of the few labour intensive industries remaining, and to all intents and purposes, every element of a software product is still hand-made. (Even pre-processors or code generators require hand-crafted input!) This is not to say that there have been no efforts to move the discipline forward. A rash of methods appeared during the 1970s and 1980s, and as a result of this it was judged that software development had now achieved the status of an engineering discipline. Hence the phrase 'software engineering'. Note that in the process, a lot of phraseology from other disciplines - for example, 'sub-assemblies' (from manufacturing), 'architecture', 'build' (from the construction industry) - drifted into the software engineering vocabulary.

We talked in chapter 2 about making a list of jobs to get you to the next horizon. Software development has already defined the main horizons for you. There is the concept of a Product Development Life Cycle (PDLC) and the horizons correspond to phases in the PDLC. Anyone who has ever worked on a software project will be familiar with PDLCs. In large organisations PDLCs are an end unto themselves and departments exist to maintain them. For the purposes of this chapter, we are going to assume a software development life cycle consisting of six phases. These six phases are:

- A Plans and Requirements phase.
- A two step design phase. The first step we will call high level design. This will include the commencement of user documentation and test plans.
- The second step, low level design.
- An Implementation phase. This will include coding, unit testing, integration, integration testing and the completion of test plans and user documentation.
- Alpha test - a test of the system, preferably by an independent team, using the test plan.
- Beta test. A real-life test by a controlled group of final users of the system.

Note: don't worry if your software development life cycle doesn't correspond exactly to the one we are using here. Once you have seen what we do, you will see that it will fit easily on to whatever life cycle standard is used by your organisation. The rest of this chapter shows Structured Project Management operating on the project as a whole and within each of the phases.

Plans and requirements

Visualise what the goal is; set your eyes on the prize
The first step on all software projects is (or should be) a statement of requirements; called in our PDLC a Requirements Specification (RS). The RS gives the requirements that the software system to be developed will satisfy. Thus it describes:

- what the system will do
- how it interacts with the world outside it
- the performance levels expected of it

Properly written, the RS is a statement of the prize. There are various ways you can approach writing a RS:

- At its most basic, the above three items constitute a checklist for a RS.
- There are also numerous checklists in the literature; as well as an increasing number of methodologies for identifying, documenting and tracking requirements. All of these fancy tools have their place and can help, particularly in controlling the vast amount of information which results from a system development effort.
- My company, ETP, offers a consultancy service called AAD

(Accelerated Analysis and Design) which is basically a 5-10 day brainstorming session in which all of the requirements and some of the design of a system can be carried out, provided that all the decision-makers on a project are involved.

Also, irrespective of what checklists or tools you may be using, you should still go through the visualisation described in chapter 1.

Make a list of the jobs that need to be done
Treating the RS as the first horizon very quickly enables us to identify the jobs we have to do to get there. This list is very straightforward, and is probably something like:

- Get the RS written
- One or more levels of review (internal / external)
- One or more levels of rework
- Signoff

Visualising the prize enables us, to some extent, to see beyond that first horizon and build our job list. We know what the next big horizons are because our PDLC gives them to us. Also the last few jobs to be done (put the software on to a disk, ship it, install it at the user site, etc.) are very apparent. The bit in the middle will be a trackless waste of pretty much Polar proportions, and all you can do at this stage is to estimate it. Estimation is discussed in detail in the next chapter.

There must be one leader
There is nothing more to say here over and above what was already said in chapter 3.

High level design

We have reached the first horizon: The RS is written and, more importantly, we can picture the goal in shining detail. However, our immediate interest now focuses on getting a high level design (HLD) done. If the RS describes what the system will do, what it looks like on the outside, the HLD describes what the major bits of the system's internals look like - the heart, lungs, liver and so on.

Visualise what the goal is: set your eyes on the prize
The HLD can be pictured as a block diagram showing your system's major components. Eventually this block diagram will 'decompose' into many smaller blocks, right down to the program or module level, but for the moment it just has the big blocks.

Make a list of the jobs that need to be done
A cycle similar to that for the RS, i.e. write / review / rework / signoff is probably all that is required here.

Low level design

Second horizon reached. We must now decompose the HLD down to a sufficient level of detail that the system can be coded.

Visualise what the goal is; set your eyes on the prize
In our PDLC we have done our design in two jumps, high level design (HLD) and low level design (LLD). Irrespective of how many jumps you take to get there, and what you call these jumps, you must end up with a picture of your system. The picture is a block diagram showing all the components of the system to be built, right down to the smallest one. For large systems this may occupy many pages and have its own internal hierarchy. This now becomes the prize.

Make a list of the jobs that need to be done
The familiar cycle of write / review / rework / signoff is what you need. I try to make it a rule never to commit to delivering anything until the LLD is complete. Most customers are happy with this, or if they insist on a fixed-price, cast-in-concrete estimate sooner than that, you make it clear to them that they are going to pay a heavily loaded price, so that you can allow for your own risk and exposure (we discuss this problem again in chapter 19 in a section entitled The Politics of Estimating).

Your job list will be a living thing, constantly changing to adapt to circumstances. New jobs will appear, jobs will complete, jobs will be found to be unnecessary and jobs will end up differently from what you originally envisaged. (This is why a computerised project planning system is very useful.) All these changes are good, routine stuff. Your list will be highly detailed for the short horizon and less so for the longer one.

Tell people what's going on
The only new point to be made here is this: if, during the design process, something emerges which significantly modifies expectations, then it needs to be made public. Good surprises you can keep secret until the moment you feel is best for you and your purposes. Bad ones - unfortunately - have to be made public, so that the outside world can adapt to the new situation.

Implementation

Design is complete and so we move on to writing and testing the code.

Visualise what the goal is: set your eyes on the prize
The goal is now a working system. If you are building your system as a series of increments, each having gradually more functionality than the previous one - always a good way to proceed because of the fallbacks it allows you - then this phase will contain a number of mini-phases each of which will represent an horizon along the way.

Alpha test

Your system is complete and works to the developer's satisfaction. The Test Plan is now run against the system, preferably by somebody other than the developers.

Visualise what the goal is; set your eyes on the prize
The goal is a working, bug-free (insofar as is humanly possible) system or product.

Beta test

Your system or product is released to a limited number of users/customers. It operates under field conditions and corrections/enhancements are made to it by the developers.

Visualise what the goal is; set your eyes on the prize
The goal is what you laboured for all this time - a system or product that the users love and/or that sells in thousands.

Step 9 PSI contribution - 0

It's 0 because the score is contained in steps 1-8.

Structured Project Management

Planning the Project

1. Visualise what the goal is; set your eyes on the prize

2. Make a list of the jobs that need to be done

3. There must be one leader

4. Assign people to jobs

5. Manage expectations / allow a margin for error / have a fallback position

Implementing the plan / Achieving the goal

6. Use an appropriate leadership style

7. Know what's going on

8. Tell people what's going on

9. Repeat steps 1 to 8 until step 10

Chapter 10

Step 10 - The Prize

"What is now achieved was once only imagined."
William Blake

The Prize

Finally there comes the day you dreamt of, the day that was at the heart of your vision, the day when the project is completed. Amundsen and his companions arrived at the South Pole at 3:00 in the afternoon of Friday, December 15th 1911. They recorded different feelings in their diaries. Bjaaland, the ski-champion, was delighted to be there before Scott, and celebrated with a big meal. Hanssen, the dog-driver, was just glad that the wind wouldn't be blowing into his face any more, but would now be at his back.

Trevor Griffiths, in his screenplay for the television series *The Last Place on Earth* {Refs. 28 and 32], about Scott and Amundsen, puts the following words into Amundsen's mouth when he is asked by his companions to make a little speech.

> I thank you. From my heart. For your work. Your commitment.
> Your craft and your comradeship. I have ... no grand emotions, no
> profound thoughts to share with you, I have to confess it. I experience
> the excitement, of course ... But above all what I feel is ... not large
> or deep at all, it's just: how good it is. To be alive.

The Reckoning

We humans have short memories; and there is nothing more easily forgotten than the experiences learned on a project. If it was a bad project we want to blot out those awful memories, while if it was a good one, we are euphoric and just want to take on something bigger and better. Pause just for a short while. Look back over the project and ask yourself questions like the following:

- Did you end up exactly where you said you would, or was the goal achieved different from the goal predicted? Where did it change? Were you aware that it had?

Document how your estimates turned out against what actually happened:

- What did you do right and wrong, particularly with regard to people? What mistakes did you make? Were there things that just couldn't have been done better? If you could do it over again, what would you do differently?
- What surprises occurred? What things did you not anticipate?
- Did you have to eat into your margin for error? Did you have problems with people's expectations? Did you have to actually go to your fallback position? What lessons do these hold for the future?

Write down the answers to these and questions like them, and have them there beside you when you set out to plan the next project.

PSI - Thresholds / The Second Law of Project Management

Since the first edition of this book appeared, we have found out essentially three things about the PSI.

Threshold for Steps 1-5

A score of 40 gained from steps 1-5 appears to be a threshold. Initially, when a project starts, it will score little, if anything, on the PSI scale. We expect this to happen.

Your priorities on the project then are to firm up the goal [step 1] - what is to be delivered - and the plan for delivering it [steps 2-5]. You do this by going through those early project phases - requirements definition, analysis, various levels of design. If these are done properly, they will have the effect of raising the step 1 score and this will in turn enable you to increase the scores from the other four steps. The score should eventually go above 40 as these various phases are completed.

If you cannot register a score above 40 it means that the goal is not sufficiently well worked out and agreed. *Unless you take steps to firm up the goal in as much detail as possible, you should not go any further in the project.* You should certainly not begin implementation type activities. *Your project will not succeed.*

Threshold for Steps 1-10

A score of 60 gained from steps 1-10 appears to be a threshold. Initially, when a project starts, it will score little, if anything, on the PSI scale. We expect this to happen.

From then on, the low scores will always point you at your most important tasks. If you are a person who has difficulty prioritising, then the low scores on each step will show you what your absolutely most important jobs are. If, at any given time, you are focusing on these, you are doing exactly the right things.

The Second Law of Project Management

In [Ref. 6], the author cites Brook's Law: 'Adding people to a late project makes it later'. Note that this law involves two of our four parameters - Delivery Date and Effort.

The relative balance of the two PSI thresholds described above implies that a much more general version of this law exists. I have called this law The Second Law of Project Management. It works like this:

- If you got a very high score out of steps 6-10, say you got 9 out of 10 for each step, a total score of 27, this would imply an extraordinary level of sensitivity in handling staff (step 6), monitoring and control (step 7) and reporting (step 8).
- Now, if you get a low score out of steps 1-5, a score that is under the 40 threshold, then the extraordinary score from steps 6-10, added to the low score from steps 1-5, won't be enough to bring you over the 60 threshold.

Or to put it more bluntly:

- 'Doing anything you like on a poorly planned project won't make the blindest bit of difference.'

The Second Law of Project Management involves all four of our parameters and is, I believe, a more general law, of which Brook's Law is a particular instance or occurrence.

 ## Applying Step 10 of Structured Project Management to software engineering

The last act of the drama is the achievement of the final horizon - The Prize. When it comes it all seems so familiar, and it should be, because it is a daydream in which you have lived ever since you first set out on the road. It's time for you to celebrate in whatever way you had planned to. With luck, they'll give you time to do an audit. (Insist on it, even if they don't!) After that they'll probably put you on a new project - even more challenging, even more exciting, with even more outrageous deadlines and delivery dates - but that is tomorrow.   Today, you can bask in your achievement, and marvel at how easy you made it look.

 ## Step 10 PSI contribution - 0

It's academic now - you're finished.

Structured Project Management

Planning the Project

1. Visualise what the goal is; set your eyes on the prize

2. Make a list of the jobs that need to be done

3. There must be one leader

4. Assign people to jobs

5. Manage expectations / allow a margin for error / have a fallback position

Implementing the plan / Achieving the goal

6. Use an appropriate leadership style

7. Know what's going on

8. Tell people what's going on

9. Repeat steps 1 through 8 until step 10

10. The Prize

Part Three

Running multiple projects simultaneously

Chapter 11

The Lazy Project Manager's monthly routine

Introduction

In the Introduction to Part Two, we put forward the (rather glaringly obvious) argument that if we could 'bite off' the amount of a project that our plan required of us every day, every week and every month, then our project would remain on target. The same applied to the project budget. Clearly the same argument applies to multiple projects. If the Project Manager can succeed in meeting each of his or her project's successive monthly, weekly and, ultimately, daily cost and schedule milestones, then the projects will remain on schedule.

The procedures described in this and the following two chapters enable the Project Manager to do exactly that.

These three procedures *must* be used in conjunction with each other in the way described here. An individual procedure can not be used in isolation.

Project Manager's monthly routine

If a Project Manager has planned all of his/her projects using the approach described earlier, then each project will consist of a plan which is very detailed to the next milestone - probably no more than 4-6 weeks away - and as detailed as it can be thereafter.

The Project Manager's monthly routine involves the Project Manager taking a month long 'bite' out of each project and then trying to organise his/her time such that all the tasks in this month long bite are carried out.

To do this, go through the following steps either at the beginning of a new month or the end of the preceding one:

1. For each project identify where the project has to be by the end of the month.

2. Identify how much effort is involved *by you personally* - not your team - in each of these projects. Include in your tally time that will be spent in things like:

   - Trips
   - Pre-arranged meetings
   - Training
   - Annual leave
   - Public holidays
   - Personal tasks
   - Quality issues
   - Support
   - Miscellaneous tasks, e.g. dealing with the in-tray, interruptions, general administrative things that can't be tied to any particular project

   Everything you do in your job needs to be accounted for in this tally.

3. Add up this effort required by all the projects and tasks and convert the resulting figure to man-days.

4. Compare this against the number of working days available.

5. If (3) is less than or equal to (4) then proceed to step (6). Otherwise, you need to determine how the shortfall will be made up. Basically, there are four choices open to you:

   - Do less - delegate it
   - Do less - drop it
   - Work more hours
   - Delay things and extend deadlines.

   Note that the latter may have the effect of delaying projects. The demand (from step (3)) needs to be less than or equal to the supply (from step (4)) before you can proceed here. Once this is true you can proceed to step (6).

6. Now schedule everything on a personal Gantt chart as shown in Figure 11. 1. (This can be done on paper, but a spreadsheet is very useful for doing this, and makes changes from month to month much easier.)

August	1st - 5th	8th-12th	15th-19th	22nd-26th	29th-31st	Total days	Actual days
	1st - 5th	8th-12th	15th-19th	22nd-26th	29th-31st	21	21
New System							
Installation process		3				3	4
Integration							
Meeting	0.5					0.5	2
Plan	2					2	4
Pick supplier				3		3	0.5
DBA							
Install client upgrade					2	2	0
Routine work	0.5	0.5	0.5	0.5	0.5	2.5	0.75
Admin							
Management	0.5	2	1.5			4	1.5
General Admin	0.5		0.5	0.5	0.5	2	3
Assistance	0.5	0.5	0.5	0.5	0.5	2.5	8
Interruptions	0.5	0.5	0.5	0.5	0.5	2.5	2
Total	5	6.5	3.5	5	4	24	25.75

Figure 11. 1   A personal Gantt chart

7. Now, when changes occur in the course of a month or new requests / demands are made on the Project Manager's time, (s)he can schedule these into the overall monthly view using the options described in (5) above, rather than making unreasonable or unachievable commitments.

Chapter 12

Project manager's weekly routine

Introduction

The monthly view shows what jobs have to be done each week for the Project Manager's projects to stay on schedule. The weekly routine involves extracting from the monthly view a week's worth of work. This should be done at the end of a particular week or at the very beginning of the next week.

To build a weekly schedule, the Project Manager reads from the monthly view the contents of the coming week, and schedules this over the five (or six or seven, but ideally five) days of the week. To take a week from the previous example:

Week of 1-5 August

The Project Manager will spend about half the week involved in routine work, but there is one big job, the Integration Plan, that is going to require 2 days' solid work. If this is the case, then the Project Manager might set 2 specific days aside for this, e.g. Tuesday and Thursday. On these days (s)he would be saying that no routine work will be done, and anyone requiring these things will have to wait. Thus his/her week would look like:

Monday	Routine stuff
Tuesday	Start Integration Plan
Wednesday	Routine stuff
Thursday	Finish Integration Plan
Friday	Routine stuff

128

Again, if changes occur in the course of the week, or new priorities arise, the Project Manager can reschedule across the week, and if necessary, into subsequent weeks, using the monthly view as an overall context within which to make decisions.

Specific weekly jobs

There are two specific jobs which should form part of every Project Manager's week. These are Monday morning project planning meetings and producing a Project Status Report last thing on Friday. These were described in detail in chapters 7 and 8 respectively. We summarise them again here.

Monday morning planning meetings

Planning meetings should be held as close to the beginning of the week as possible. Their aim is to agree what proportion of the project schedule each person is going to bite off that week. Delays, people absences and unforeseen things occurring on projects can all be dealt with at this meeting. The Project Manager can use the PC-based model of his/her project to make sensible decisions about how to deal with unexpected events.

Friday project status report

The status report should be done last thing on Friday and the report itself, or versions of it, delivered to customer, management and the project team. Where the Monday project meeting sets targets, the Friday status report records results.

These results should also be recorded in the *Actual Schedule and Effort* columns of the project Gantt chart or on an Estimating Score Card.

Chapter 13

Project manager's daily routine

Introduction

Ultimately, whether projects stay on schedule or not will be determined by what the Project Manager does or doesn't do on a daily basis. The daily routine tries to ensure that those jobs which are key to the success of each project get done. The daily routine involves choosing those jobs which are going to get done every day. This should be done first thing in the morning or last thing on the preceding day.

1. Draw up a list of all the jobs that are contenders to be done on the particular day. To do this consider the following sources:

    (a) Projects will have generated jobs, through the monthly and weekly routines already described.
    (b) Projects will have generated jobs through the Project Manager looking daily at the plan for each project under his/her control, and determining which jobs require some action to be taken.
    (c) Projects will have generated jobs through the Project Manager trying to generate more detailed task lists about parts of the project which still lie in the future and which have not yet been reduced to a man-day level of detail.
    (d) There will be other jobs - in-tray, meetings, faxes, e-mails, mail, yellow stickers, reminders, phone calls to be made.
    (e) There may also be personal jobs.

2. Having developed the list of jobs, categorise them according to the following scheme:

    'A'   HAVE to get this done today

      'B'   Nice to get this done today
      'C'   Not going to get this done today
      'D'   Delegate this job

3. Now, do all the 'D's, and all the 'A's. Everything else can be moved to later in the week or month.

Note: Note that this approach only works where you have first done the monthly and weekly analyses. If you don't do these, then the only result will be that a great backlog of tasks will build up for later in the week or month.

As described earlier, if changes occur in the course of the day, or new priorities arise, the Project Manager can reschedule simply by categorising the jobs again, and doing the 'A's and 'D's as before. If 'A' jobs end up not getting done, then, by definition, they couldn't have been 'A' (HAVE to get done) jobs to begin with.

Part Four

How to assess Project Plans

Chapter 14

Assessing Project Plans

Introduction

You will have gathered by now what our angle in all of this is: If you plan it right, then the doing will be very straightforward. The key measure of how well a project has been planned is the quality of the Project Plan that has been produced. In this chapter we will show you how to assess such plans - your own or other people's. By learning how to do this you will stop potential disasters from becoming real ones.

As you also know by now, we are anxious to make you into not just a successful Project Manager, but a Lazy one. The method we will show you in this chapter will be a key weapon in your Lazy Project Manager's arsenal. If the plan is a poor one you will find out within a few minutes. Then, only if the plan is good, will you spend time analysing it more closely. The tests contained in the method we will describe will smoke out the turkeys with the least amount of effort on your part.

As you would expect the tests in our method are directly derived from the Ten Steps.

At the highest level there are four things you need to need to look for in assessing a Project Plan. These are:

- That the project has a clearly defined goal
- That there is a plan for achieving the goal
- That the project has a leader
- That there is some sort of backup plan or room for manoeuvre

All of the checks we will describe will be to determine the existence of otherwise of these.

It may be convenient for you not to do all of the checks we describe on every plan you encounter. In particular, it might be useful for you to have a first battery of checks that a plan must pass, and only if it passes these would you analyse it further. Ideally, too, the amount of work involved in carrying out this first battery of checks wouldn't be all that great.

This is exactly the way we have organised the checks in this method. In all, there are ten checks, and these are listed in the following table. Opposite each check is an assessment - small, medium, large - of the amount of work required to carry out the check.

Five of the checks require relatively minor amounts of work. We suggest you use these as your first level of analysis. The five of these could probably be done in under 30 minutes.

Another three of the checks can be done with modest amounts of work. To do them all might take up a couple of hours of your time. However, as we have said already, you would only do them provided the plan being tested had already passed the 30 minute test.

The remaining check could, depending on the scale of the plan, turn out to be very time-consuming indeed. Whether or not you would do such a check is, of course, entirely up to you. If you personally decided not to, it would still be important that somebody - and this is most likely to be the Project Manager - should do it. The checks we will consider are these:

Check	Effort involved
First level checks	
Contents	Small
WBS	Small
Gantt - Overview	Small
Resourcing #1 and #2	Small
PSI	Small
Second level checks	
Schedule and Effort	Medium
Gantt - Critical Path	Medium
Resourcing #3 and #4	Medium
Third level check	
Gantt - All jobs	Large

First level checks

Project Plan - contents analysis

The first quick and very simple check you can do on a Project Plan is to check its table of contents. (If it doesn't have one send it back!) This is likely to take no more than 5-10 minutes and can tell you whether it is worthwhile your spending any more time than this assessing the Plan.

They may have different names but the table of contents should contain the following elements:

1. Management summary - some sort of overview or summary
2. Statement of what is to be done (The goal of the project)
3. Deliverables (Also part of the goal). These may come under a number of headings:
   - Software
   - Hardware
   - Documentation
   - Services
4. Completion criteria - how do we know when the project is over? (A key part of the goal)
5. Acceptance criteria - how does our customer decide the project is over? (Also a key part of the goal)

The next six are all part of the plan and the backup plan.

6. Work Breakdown Structure - a list of all the jobs that have to be done to complete the project together with estimates of their associated effort and any assumptions made.
7. A Gantt chart - showing the Work Breakdown Structure phased over time, and stating any assumptions made.
8. Milestones - a list of key dates extracted from the Gantt chart.
9. Resources required - human and otherwise.
10. Resource loading - how the resources are phased over time.
11. Project budget [OPTIONAL] - derived from the effort in the Work Breakdown Structure and section (8) on Resources.
12. Project organisation chart [OPTIONAL] - amongst other things, this serves to identify the project leader.
13. Backup plan / margin for error. Sometimes called Risk Analysis.

The Project Plan represents a prediction of how things will go in the future with regard to this project. The intention of this section is to show that the author of the plan has given some thought to what he will do when what happens in reality differs from the Project Plan.

Match these 13 elements against the table of contents of the Plan you are assessing. Without delving too deeply, this will give you your first indication of how well put together the Plan is.

Project Plan - work breakdown structure analysis

The next thing you need to see is whether or not the plan is complete - in the sense that it contains all of the various work elements that make up the project. The checklist displayed in *Example 1* below allows you to do this. Use it as a guide to highlight missing Project Plan elements. The checklist is presented in the form of a Work Breakdown Structure (WBS), a structure that breaks down all of the project elements from a high to a detailed level.

The WBS tries to make the most general possible assumption about the lifecycle that the project follows. The lifecycle can be described as follows:

1. The requirements for the system are developed.
2. Following on from this, an overall architecture for the system is developed. This architecture gives the major blocks of the system.
3. The system is programmed (3a) and a working (integrated) version (3b) of it is produced.
4. Testing is planned (4a) and carried out (4b). 4b is often referred to as Alpha Test.
5,6. Both while the system is under development and after it is released, accepted, and has gone into maintenance, elements 5 and 6 (project management and configuration management) operate on the system.
7. Manuals are developed.
8. The system is released and implemented and accepted.
9. Training, initially of project team personnel and eventually of system users takes place.
10. The system, having been accepted, goes into maintenance.

The WBS is presented in such a way that you can add in your own WBS checklist elements, gathered from your own experiences over time.

Example 1 - work breakdown structure

1 Requirements Analysis

1.0 Reviews

1.1 Requirements document(s)

1.2 Request for Proposal

2 Product Design

2.0 Reviews

2.1 High level design (Basic architecture)

2.2 Low level design (Detailed design / Program specs.)

2.3 Possible development of prototypes

3 Programming

3.0 Code walkthroughs

3.1 Code and unit test
  3.1.1 Write code element
  3.1.2 Clean compile code element
  3.1.3 Unit test code element (including element Test Plan)
  3.1.4 Code element documentation

3.2 Integration

3.3 Test environment development

3.4 Development support
  3.4.1 Database administration
  3.4.2 Development environment
  3.4.3 System build

4 Testing

4.0 Reviews

4.1 Write Test Plans

4.2 Alpha Test (System Test)

4.3 Beta Test (Acceptance Test)

5 Project Management

5.0 Reviews

5.1 Production of initial Project Plan and ongoing project monitoring and control

5.2 Management of subcontractors

6 Configuration Management

6.0 Reviews

6.1 Ongoing Configuration Management

6.2 Release

7 Documentation

7.0 Reviews

7.1 User (different types)

7.2 Administrator

7.3 Release Notes

7.4 Technical manuals, i.e. manuals describing how the software works

7.5 Help texts

8 Implementation

8.0 Reviews

8.1 Installation
8.1.1 Plans
8.1.2 Activities
8.1.3 Test

8.2 Conversion
8.2.1 Plans
8.2.2 Activities
8.2.3 Test

9 Training

9.0 Reviews

9.1 Familiarisation by project personnel

9.1 Training of project personnel

9.1 User training

10 Maintenance

11 Staffing

11.1 Recruitment

11.2 Staff training

12 Quality

12.1 Quality Management

12.2 Quality Plans

13 Administration

13.1 Public holidays

13.2 Annual holidays

13.3 Sick

13.4 Meetings

Match these WBS elements against those in the plan you are assessing. This will show you what, if anything, has been forgotten in your plan.

Project Plan - Gantt Chart Analysis - High Level Overview

The Gantt chart is the heart of your Project Plan. (If there isn't one in the Plan you are assessing, then send it back now, because there's not much point in going any further).

The Gantt chart can be assessed at a number of different levels, each one becoming progressively more detailed than the previous one. The more detailed the assessment the more likely you are to catch potential flaws in the plan. However, more work is required on your part to do this detailed analysis.

The three levels we will look at, working from the highest to the lowest are:

- High level overview
- Critical path
- All jobs

At this stage, however, we will only concern ourselves with a high level overview.

The Plan should present an overall high level overview of the project. In other words, the Plan should show:

- What the main phases of the project are
- How long these phases last
- How they relate to each other
- The amount of work in each phase

It doesn't take long to check this, and there are a number of advantages to doing do.

First this overview gives you milestones - points in time at which the project has to be in a particular state. If, when a particular milestone comes, a project isn't the expected state, then this is early warning that something is wrong.

The presence of a high level overview also implies clarity of vision on the part of the Project Manager. It indicates that the Project Manager has clearly thought through - at least at a high level - what he is being asked to do.

An example of a plan which has exactly the kind of overview we are looking for is shown in figure 14-1. Figure 14-2 shows one which is almost the direct opposite of what we mean. Both plans are taken from real life.

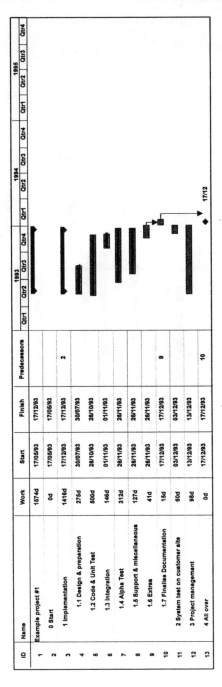

ID	Name	Work	Start	Finish	Predecessors
1	Example project #1	1574d	17/05/93	17/12/93	
2	0 Start	0d	17/05/93	17/05/93	
3	1 Implementation	1416d	17/12/93	17/12/93	2
4	1.1 Design & preparation	275d	30/07/93	30/07/93	
5	1.2 Code & Unit Test	500d	26/10/93	26/10/93	
6	1.3 Integration	146d	01/11/93	01/11/93	
7	1.4 Alpha Test	312d	26/11/93	26/11/93	
8	1.5 Support & miscellaneous	127d	26/11/93	26/11/93	
9	1.6 Extras	41d	26/11/93	26/11/93	
10	1.7 Finalise Documentation	15d	17/12/93	17/12/93	9
11	2 System test on customer site	60d	03/12/93	03/12/93	
12	3 Project management	98d	13/12/93	13/12/93	
13	4 All over	0d	17/12/93	17/12/93	10

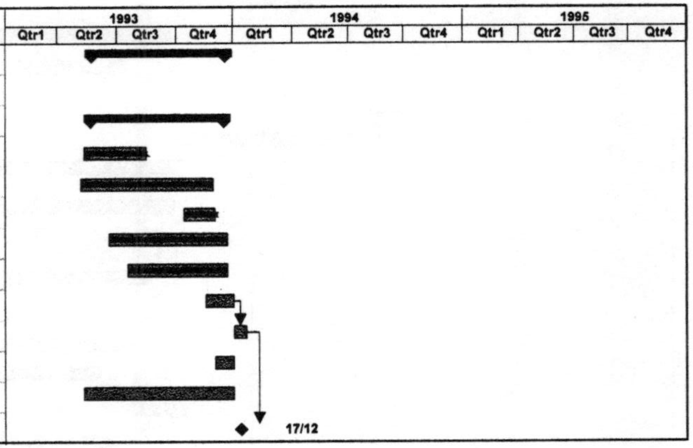

Figure 14-1

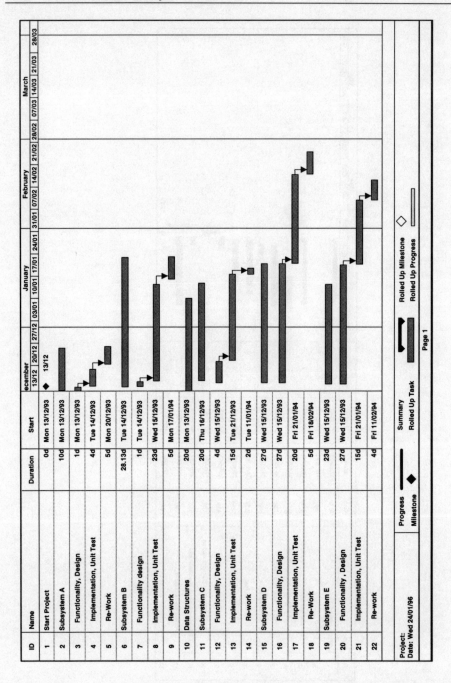

ID	Name	Duration	Start
1	**Start Project**	0d	Mon 13/12/93
2	**Subsystem A**	10d	Mon 13/12/93
3	Functionality, Design	1d	Mon 13/12/93
4	Implementation, Unit Test	4d	Tue 14/12/93
5	Re-Work	5d	Mon 20/12/93
6	**Subsystem B**	28.13d	Tue 14/12/93
7	Functionality design	1d	Tue 14/12/93
8	Implementation, Unit Test	23d	Wed 15/12/93
9	Re-work	5d	Mon 17/01/94
10	**Data Structures**	20d	Mon 13/12/93
11	**Subsystem C**	20d	Thu 16/12/93
12	Functionality, Design	4d	Wed 15/12/93
13	Implementation, Unit Test	15d	Tue 21/12/93
14	Re-work	2d	Tue 11/01/94
15	**Subsystem D**	27d	Wed 15/12/93
16	Functionality, Design	27d	Wed 15/12/93
17	Implementation, Unit Test	20d	Fri 21/01/94
18	Re-Work	5d	Fri 18/02/94
19	**Subsystem E**	23d	Wed 15/12/93
20	Functionality , Design	27d	Wed 15/12/93
21	Implementation, Unit Test	15d	Fri 21/01/94
22	Re-work	4d	Fri 11/02/94

Project:
Date: Wed 24/01/96

Progress
Milestone ◆

Summary
Rolled Up Task ◆

Rolled Up Milestone ◇
Rolled Up Progress

Page 1

Figure 14-2(a)

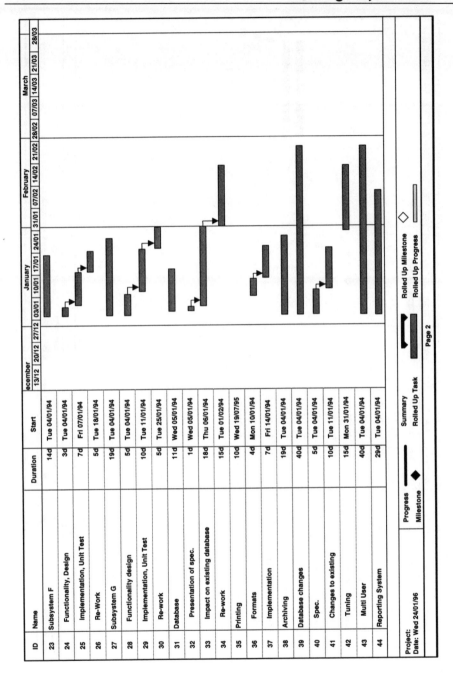

Figure 14-2(b)

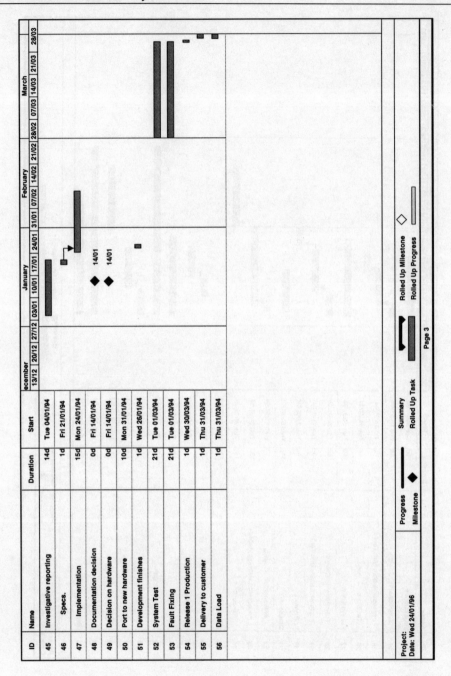

The following appears within the Gantt chart figure:

ID	Name	Duration	Start
45	Investigative reporting	14d	Tue 04/01/94
46	Specs.	1d	Fri 21/01/94
47	Implementation	15d	Mon 24/01/94
48	Documentation decision	0d	Fri 14/01/94
49	Decision on hardware	0d	Fri 14/01/94
50	Port to new hardware	10d	Mon 31/01/94
51	Development finishes	1d	Wed 26/01/94
52	System Test	21d	Tue 01/03/94
53	Fault Fixing	21d	Tue 01/03/94
54	Release 1 Production	1d	Wed 30/03/94
55	Delivery to customer	1d	Thu 31/03/94
56	Data Load	1d	Thu 31/03/94

Project:
Date: Wed 24/01/96

Progress	▬▬	Summary	⬱
Milestone	◆	Rolled Up Task	▭
		Rolled Up Milestone	◇
		Rolled Up Progress	▭

Page 3

Figure 14-2(c)

One other thing to watch for at this level is the amount of activities being paralleled. Sometimes if a project has a very tight deadline or a deadline which has been set in advance of the plan being drawn up, the way people try to allow for this is to run several activities in parallel. There is nothing intrinsically wrong with this unless the activities that are being run in parallel are actually ones which in fact cannot be. For example, a number of potential system suppliers can't really be assessed until a Request For Proposal (RFP) has been drawn up. It may be possible for some of the assessment jobs, e.g. gathering information about particular products or systems or suppliers to be done while the RFP is still being drawn up, but it is certainly not possible for the RFP and the supplier assessment to complete at the same time!

Project Plan - Resourcing Analyses #1 and #2

Two quick checks that should be done on a project are to examine its resourcing. At its simplest what this means is that the scheduling of people on the project takes account of some basic realities.

The first of these realities (check #1) is that the allocation of people to jobs takes into account the fact that people can only work 5 days a week, and that there are certain holiday periods when they don't work. Thus you should check that the effects of:

- Annual leave (especially for projects running over the summer)
- Public holidays
- Long weekends
- Seasonal holidays (Christmas, Easter)

have been accounted for.

Also, projects or phases of projects which end on Saturdays and Sundays should be looked at with some suspicion. They can imply that some basic thinking things through has not been done.

Check #2 is to check that every job in the project plan has a human being's name against it (see chapter 4). If this is not the case, then that is not necessarily a problem provided there are jobs elsewhere in the plan, e.g. hiring, recruitment, internal transfers, agreeing of subcontracts, and so on, to supply these human being's names.

Project Plan - PSI Analysis

If you've read the earlier chapters, 1-10, you'll know what the PSI is. (If not, you could take a quick scan through Appendix 3 which will give you an overview.)

The PSI is quickly calculated - you can use figure 14-3 to help you - and will not only show you what kind of shape a project is in, but the low scores will enable you to say in your review of the Project Plan, where the Project Manager should focus his energies.

The Ten Steps

Planning the Project   Weight

1. Visualise what the goal is; set your eyes on   20 [   ]
   the prize
2. Make a list of the jobs to be done   20 [   ]
3. There must be one leader   10 [   ]
4. Assign people to jobs   10 [   ]
5. Manage Expectations/allow a margin for   10 [   ]
   error/have a fallback position

Implementing the plan / Achieving the goal

6. Use an appropriate leadership style   10 [   ]
7. Know what's going on   10 [   ]
8. Tell people what's going on   10 [   ]
9. Repeat steps 1 through 8 until step 10
10. The Prize

Total   100 [   ]

Current Projects   1-5   5-10

_____   [ ]   [ ]
_____   [ ]   [ ]
_____   [ ]   [ ]
_____   [ ]   [ ]
_____   [ ]   [ ]
_____   [ ]   [ ]
_____   [ ]   [ ]
_____   [ ]   [ ]

Figure 14-3

Second level checks

Project Plan - Schedule and Effort Analysis

A very effective way of finding out if a project has been planned out and thought through properly is to examine the distribution of effort and schedule over the life of the project. By comparing this distribution against that of previous completed projects, you can get a feeling for the accuracy or otherwise of the estimates in the plan being reviewed.

Obviously projects vary widely, from organisation to organisation and within organisations. Thus, the distribution of effort and schedule over the life of the project will also vary. However, finding that the distribution of the project being assessed is roughly comparable to that of a previously completed successful project will add to your confidence in the Project Plan being assessed. Conversely, finding a wide discrepancy between the two distributions will cause you to ask questions about the various estimates and how they were arrived at.

Obviously you can only carry out this analysis if you already have some distribution figures that you can use as a basis for comparison. Unfortunately, it is still something of a rarity in the IT industry to find this done with any degree of consistency. Thus, to make the most effective use of this test will require you to start recording distribution data on your completed projects. A form which makes it easy for you to do this, called an Estimating Score Card or ESC, is described in Appendix 4.

In the absence of data of your own, you can still apply the analysis by using data supplied by us. The comparison will not be as accurate, because our data are, by necessity, 'vanilla' data culled from many different projects. However, they will enable you to get started with this analysis, and can be used until data of your own become available. Our data are presented on an ESC in figure 14.4. The points to note are:

- The ESC covers all but two phases of the life cycle described in section 5.3 These are 8 *Release Implementation and Acceptance* and 10 *Maintenance*.
- The first column of figures shows what proportion of the elapsed time of the project should go in to each of the phases. Thus, for example, 26% of the elapsed time of the project would go into the Requirements and Design phases of a project.
- The second column of figures shows what proportion of the project's effort should go in to each the project's phases.

Estimating Score Card

Project | Schedule & Effort Analysis - Example

Author

Revision No.

Date

Phase	Schedule (months)	%	Efffort (MM)	%	Schedule (months)	%	Effort (MM)	%	Schedule (months)	%	Effort (MM)	%
Reqs & Design (1, 2)						27		18				
Code & test (3a)						37		36				
Int (3b)						18		9				
System test (4)						18		20				
Proj Mgmt (5)						-		6				
Doc & Support & CM (6, 7, 9)						-		11				
8, 10-						-		-				

Figure 14-4

Note: Just to repeat again that these are general-purpose figures and so, should be treated with caution. Figures on the project being assessed may vary considerably from these, and could still be right because of the peculiar nature of that project.

Now, let's see a sample analysis. Let's say that the Project Plan that you are assessing contains the distribution of effort and schedule shown in figure 14.5.

Estimating Score Card

Project   *Schedule & Effort Analysis - Example*

Author

Revision No.

Date

Phase	Schedule (months)	%	Efffort (MM)	%	Schedule (months)	%	Effort (MM)	%	Schedule (months)	%	Effort (MM)	%
Reqs & Design		17		7								
Code & test		55		52								
Integration		0		0								
System test		28		35								
Proj Mgmt		-		6								
Doc & Support & CM		-										

Figure 14-5

If the author of the Plan hasn't presented such a distribution, there are two choices open to you. Either (a) send it back and ask for it or (b) work it out yourself from the estimates of effort and schedule on the Project Plan's WBS and Gantt chart.

Estimating Score Card

Project   *Schedule & Effort Analysis - Example*

Author

Revision No.

Date

Phase	Schedule (months)	%	Effort (MM)	%	Schedule (months)	%	Effort (MM)	%	Schedule (months)	%	Effort (MM)	%
Reqs & Design		17		7	A	26		18				
Code & test		55		52	B	36		36				
Integration		0		0	C	18		9				
System test		28		35	D	18		20				
Proj Mgmt	-			6	E	-		17				
Doc & Support & CM	-											

Figure 14-6

Figure 14.6 shows the distribution from the Project Plan compared against our general-purpose figures. *Significant* differences between the two sets of figures are marked and discussed below.

1. There doesn't appear to be enough time or effort allowed in the project being assessed for Requirements gathering and design.
2. Too much of the project elapsed time and effort is being taken up by the actual writing of the software.
3. Integration hasn't been allowed for at all.
4. System Test also looks too high. Is this because not enough Design will have been done and so lots of problems are expected?

These are questions to which you will have to get answers before you can give this project the go-ahead.

Project Plan - Gantt Chart Analysis - Critical Path

As we mentioned earlier, the Gantt chart can be assessed at a number of different levels, each one becoming progressively more detailed than the previous one. The more detailed the assessment the more likely you are to catch potential flaws in the plan. However, more work is required on your part to do this detailed analysis. The level we will look at in this check is the Critical Path level.

The Critical Path is the shortest path through your project; in other words, it is the shortest time in which the project can complete. If any of the jobs on the Critical Path are delayed then the project will be delayed.

If you want to delve deeper into the project, without actually going through it job by job, then the Critical Path is both a convenient and a crucial way of doing exactly that.

To do this, the plan you are assessing should show clearly what the Critical Path is. PC-based project planning tools do this automatically. If the Gantt chart hasn't been done using such a tool, then the author of the plan needs to have worked out the Critical Path manually. If the plan doesn't show the Critical Path then you would be quite justified in sending it back, as the implication would be that the Project Manager hasn't thought it through.

Assuming that the Gantt chart does show the Critical Path, then for each job on the Critical Path you should check all of the following:

- Does the amount of effort associated with the particular job seem reasonable?

- Do the calendar days on which the job is due to be carried out make sense? For instance, have tasks been scheduled on bank holidays or are unrealistic assumptions being made about what will get done over a holiday season like Christmas?
- Does each job on the Critical Path have somebody's name against it - not the name of an organisation, but the person who will cause the work to be done?

The same comments made earlier about paralleling of tasks also apply here. Are tasks which actually have a dependency between them, being run in parallel?

All of these tests applied to each task on the Critical Path will generate review comments of the Plan.

Finally, if you wanted to, you could do a simple risk analysis using the four parameters from the First Law of Project Management:

- Elapsed Time (when the job must be done)
- Effort (how much work is involved)
- Functionality (i.e. what is to be done)
- Quality (how well it is done)

You would do this by asking yourself questions like:

- What happens if the job runs over? [Elapsed Time]
- Can the job be shortened? [Elapsed Time]
- What happens if the job is bigger than we estimated? [Effort]
- What would be the effect of adding more people? [Effort]
- Is this job doing something which is crucial to the project? If not, could it be put into a later delivery? [Functionality]
- What happens if this job isn't done perfectly? [Quality]

Project Plan - Resourcing Analyses #3 and #4

These are two further checks to see whether the resource loading has been done correctly, and that the project takes account of some basic realities.

Check #3 is to see that people have not been scheduled more than 100%, i.e. that they are not scheduled to be in two places at once or working more than 5 days per week.

Check #4 examines whether the amount of people's effort that has been scheduled onto a particular project takes into account their other commitments. Thus if a person has been scheduled 5 days per week, then it means that *they will be doing absolutely nothing else* during their time on the project. Often people have several commitments and these have to be taken into account.

It should be said again that the use of a PC-based tool by the Project Manager makes checking all of these things very straightforward. In particular, a PC-based tool can supply resource loading charts showing how much work each person is scheduled to do, and when.

Third level checks

Project Plan - Gantt Chart Analysis - all jobs

As we mentioned earlier, the Gantt chart can be assessed at a number of different levels, each one becoming progressively more detailed than the previous one. The more detailed the assessment, the more likely you are to catch potential flaws in the plan. However, more work is required on your part to do this detailed analysis.

The level we will look at in this check is that of all the jobs in the plan.

The Gantt chart analysis can be applied to all jobs in the project. This is something that could be quite time consuming. While you might expect the Project Manager to do it, you probably wouldn't do it in a plan you were assessing. What you might do, however, would be to do it in the form of spot checks on particular jobs. For instance, you might spot check:

- Particularly large jobs
- Jobs to be done by an outside contractor
- Jobs to be done by somebody new to an organisation
- Jobs that are known to be technically complex
- Jobs that are ground breaking, i.e. that haven't been done by an organisation before,
- And so on.

Whatever you choose to do, the steps are laid out here again. Check:

- Does the amount of effort associated with the particular job seem reasonable?
- Do the calendar days on which the job is due to be carried out make sense? For instance, have tasks been scheduled on bank holidays or are unrealistic assumptions being made about what will get done over a holiday season like Christmas?

- Does each job have somebody's name against it - not the name of an organisation but the person who will cause the work to be done?

The same comments made in the previous section about paralleling of tasks also apply here. Are tasks which actually have a dependency between them, being run in parallel?

All of these tests applied to each job will generate review comments of the Plan.

Finally, if you wanted to, you could do a simple risk analysis using the four parameters from the First Law of Project Management:

- Elapsed Time (when the job must be done)
- Effort (how much work is involved)
- Functionality (i.e. what is to be done)
- Quality (how well it is done)

You would do this by asking questions like:

- What happens if the job runs over? [Elapsed Time]
- Can the job be shortened? [Elapsed Time]
- What happens if the job is bigger than we estimated? [Effort]
- What would be the effect of adding more people? [Effort]
- Is this job doing something which is crucial to the project? If not, could it be put into a later delivery? [Functionality]
- What happens if this job isn't done perfectly? [Quality]

Case studies

Case Study #1 - Scenario

You receive a project plan to review. It is a document of about 15 pages in length. The pages are unnumbered and there is no table of contents. Looking through it you find it has three sections with the following titles:

- Introduction
- Technical requirements
- A hand drawn Gantt chart

The section entitled 'Technical requirements' is quite detailed. As you read it, you come to understand that the plan is to implement a system that will interface to some of the organisation's other systems. The system will be bought in, having been tailored by the supplier. Some development work will also be required on the organisation's side. The new system will replace an existing system. The plan shows the project beginning on 12 December 1995 and being declared live by 30 June 1996.

The section called 'Technical requirements' describes:

- The system that the project will deliver to the users
- The software, documentation, training and support services that form part of the project
- A period of parallel running and conditions that must be satisfied before the system can be declared live
- The hardware and software environment in which the system will be developed and run

This section also lays heavy emphasis on the users being involved at all stages of the system specification, design and development.

The Gantt chart is partially shown in figure 14.7. The horizontal bars indicate detailed breakdowns of each of the high level tasks. The breakdowns are very detailed for December and January and less so thereafter, but the Gantt chart gives the impression of being rich in detail. When you assess it using the WBS analysis, little or nothing seems to have been forgotten. Each task in the Work Breakdown Structure has initials against it, showing who will carry out the task. Each task also has amounts of effort shown against it. Notes to the Gantt chart explain how these estimates were arrived at and also explain the basis that each individual is involved in the project, e.g. 'full-time', 'two days per week', 'required only for reviews' etc.

What would be your assessment of this plan?

Case Study #1 - Analysis

Contents analysis
The plan contains three sections, whereas our proposed ideal table of contents contained thirteen! On the face of it, this doesn't seem like a very promising start, but we decide to persevere just a little to see what else we can find out.

1. Statement of what is to be done. This turns out to be covered adequately in the 'Technical requirements'.

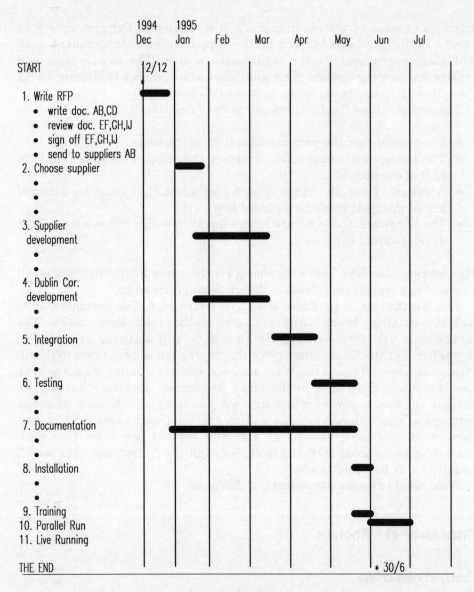

Figure 14-7

2. Deliverables. Covered in the 'Technical requirements'.
3. Completion criteria. Covered in the 'Technical requirements'.
4. Acceptance criteria. Covered in the 'Technical requirements'.
5. Work Breakdown Structure. The tasks down the left hand side of the

Gantt chart turn out to give as much as is known about the project at this point in time.

6.   Gantt chart. Present.
7.   Milestones. Can be deduced from the Gantt chart.
8.   Resources required. Human resources are present in the notes to the Gantt chart. Other resources - computers, software, etc., are covered in the 'Technical requirements'.
9.   Not stated explicitly but could be deduced from the previous section.
10. Project budget. Not stated.
11. Project organisation chart. Not stated. The implication from the plan is that the author is the Project Manager.
12. Backup plan / margin for error. If, on 30 June, the system isn't ready, then the existing manual system can carry on as before. It may not be a very elegant backup plan, but it'll work!

WBS analysis
See (5) above. Looks OK.

Gantt Chart analysis - High level overview
Looking at the Gantt chart we see exactly the kind of high level overview we are looking for. We can see:

- The main phases of the project and exactly when each phase starts and ends
- Which phases depend on one another and which can proceed in parallel
- The amount of work in each phase

Resourcing analysis #1 and #2
A quick look at the Gantt chart shows that the project is due to start the week before Christmas, and a high level of activity is assumed between then and the end of the year. Cultures vary, as do organisations. However, in Europe, it would be unlikely for such a schedule to hold true, and so this part of the schedule would probably have to be amended. This might have serious implications for the June 30 deadline. Analysing the Critical Path on the Gantt chart would determine (a) whether or not this was the case, and (b) what could be done about it. As for check #2, all jobs have people's names against them.

PSI analysis
Finally, let us calculate the PSI of the project.
1. Goal clearly defined [20]

Yes, but the detail needs to be filled out. This will be done during the RFP and ultimately the development process. Score say, 6. Remember, a low score can either be a reflection of (a) a trouble spot, or (b) a result of where you are in the project's life. In this case, it is the latter.

2. List of jobs [20]

Yes, but the list is necessarily incomplete given where we are in the project. Say 6 again.

3. One leader [10]

Yes, assuming the author of the plan acts as the kind of leader we require, i.e. the trail boss. Score 10.

4. People assigned to jobs [10]

Yes, though because the job list is incomplete (see 2 above), this is as well. Score 3 at this stage in the project.

5. Backup plan / margin for error [10]

Yes, albeit an inelegant one. Score 7, say.

Total from the planning phase is 32. As we already noted 40 is the threshold for a successful project, so we're not there yet. However, once the project has proceeded through the RFP stage we should be in good shape to go forward.

So, based on our initial quick assessment, despite an unpromising appearance, and some omissions, this plan appears to be in good shape. The main problem in it at the moment is the one with Christmas.

We could now go on to do:

- Schedule and effort analysis
- Critical Path analysis of the Gantt chart
- Resource loading analysis (checks 3 and 4)

and amongst other things, this would tackle the Christmas problem.

Finally, if we chose to, we could do a Gantt chart analysis of the entire project.

Case Study #2 - Scenario

You receive a project plan to review. It is about 30 pages long. The plan is for a project to develop a piece of software, deliver it to a user site, install it and load user data on it by 31 March 1996.

Checking the contents you find that it has sections corresponding to *all* of the items on our table of contents checklist. Each of these sections looks fairly substantial and contains the kinds of things we talked about. In particular, a leader for the project is named.

The Gantt chart - which contains the WBS under the heading 'Name' - for the project is shown in figure 14.8.

What is your assessment of this plan?

Case Study #2 - Analysis

Contents analysis
As described in the scenario, it appears to be OK.

WBS analysis
The following appear to be missing from this WBS:

- Any kind of requirements analysis or definition
- Any kind of high level design
- Software integration
- Development of tests (as opposed to carrying out the testing)
- Project management
- Configuration management and other project support activities
- Production of documentation
- Anything significant on Installation or Training

Gantt chart analysis - High level overview
Non-existent.

Resource loading analyses #1 and #2
The problem with the Christmas holiday season also seems to be hitting this project. All the jobs do have people's names against them.

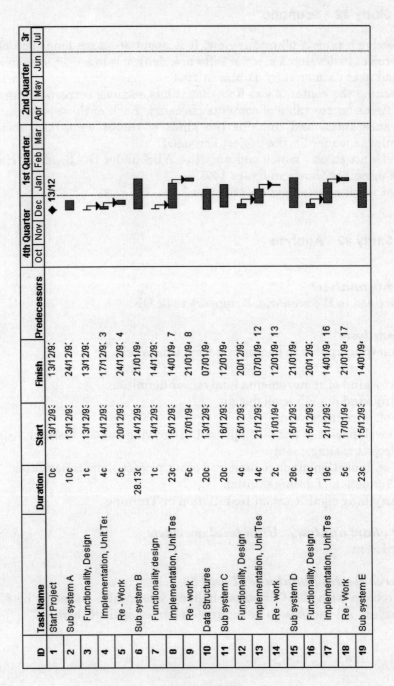

ID	Task Name	Duration	Start	Finish	Predecessors
1	Start Project	0c	13/12/9;	13/12/9;	
2	Sub system A	10c	13/12/9;	24/12/9;	
3	Functionality, Design	1c	13/12/9;	13/12/9;	
4	Implementation, Unit Tes	4c	14/12/9;	17/12/9;	3
5	Re - Work	5c	20/12/9;	24/12/9;	4
6	Sub system B	28.13c	14/12/9;	21/01/9;	
7	Functionality design	1c	14/12/9;	14/12/9;	
8	Implementation, Unit Tes	23c	15/12/9;	14/01/9;	7
9	Re - work	5c	17/01/9;	21/01/9;	8
10	Data Structures	20c	13/12/9;	07/01/9;	
11	Sub system C	20c	16/12/9;	12/01/9;	
12	Functionality, Design	4c	15/12/9;	20/12/9;	
13	Implementation, Unit Tes	14c	21/12/9;	07/01/9;	12
14	Re - work	2c	11/01/9;	12/01/9;	13
15	Sub system D	28c	15/12/9;	21/01/9;	
16	Functionality, Design	4c	15/12/9;	20/12/9;	
17	Implementation, Unit Tes	19c	21/12/9;	14/01/9;	16
18	Re - Work	5c	17/01/9;	21/01/9;	17
19	Sub system E	23c	15/12/9;	14/01/9;	

Figure 14-8(a)

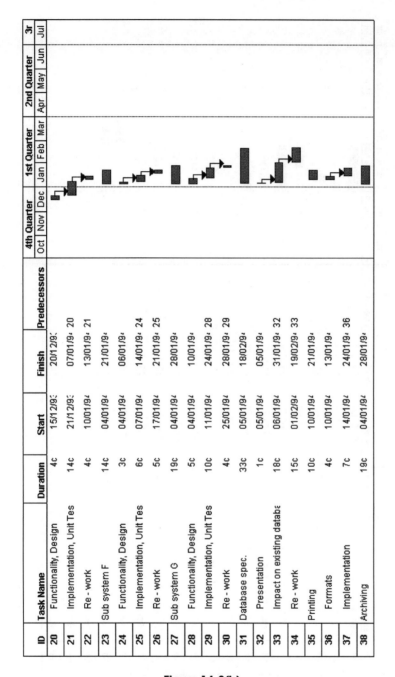

ID	Task Name	Duration	Start	Finish	Predecessors
20	Functionality, Design	4c	15/12/9:	20/12/9:	
21	Implementation, Unit Tes	14c	21/12/9:	07/01/9<	20
22	Re - work	4c	10/01/9<	13/01/9<	21
23	Sub system F	14c	04/01/9<	21/01/9<	
24	Functionality, Design	3c	04/01/9<	06/01/9<	
25	Implementation, Unit Tes	6c	07/01/9<	14/01/9<	24
26	Re - work	5c	17/01/9<	21/01/9<	25
27	Sub system G	19c	04/01/9<	28/01/9<	
28	Functionality, Design	5c	04/01/9<	10/01/9<	
29	Implementation, Unit Tes	10c	11/01/9<	24/01/9<	28
30	Re - work	4c	25/01/9<	28/01/9<	29
31	Database spec.	33c	05/01/9<	18/02/9<	
32	Presentation	1c	05/01/9<	05/01/9<	
33	Impact on existing databe	18c	06/01/9<	31/01/9<	32
34	Re - work	15c	01/02/9<	19/02/9<	33
35	Printing	10c	10/01/9<	21/01/9<	
36	Formats	4c	10/01/9<	13/01/9<	
37	Implementation	7c	14/01/9<	24/01/9<	36
38	Archiving	19c	04/01/9<	28/01/9<	

Figure 14-8(b)

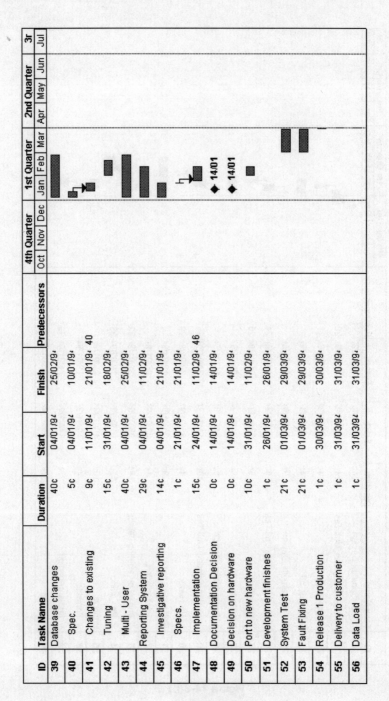

ID	Task Name	Duration	Start	Finish	Predecessors
39	Database changes	40c	04/01/9·	25/02/9·	
40	Spec.	5c	04/01/9·	10/01/9·	
41	Changes to existing	9c	11/01/9·	21/01/9·	40
42	Tuning	15c	31/01/9·	18/02/9·	
43	Multi - User	40c	04/01/9·	25/02/9·	
44	Reporting System	29c	04/01/9·	11/02/9·	
45	Investigative reporting	14c	04/01/9·	21/01/9·	
46	Specs.	1c	21/01/9·	21/01/9·	
47	Implementation	15c	24/01/9·	11/02/9·	46
48	Documentation Decision	0c	14/01/9·	14/01/9·	
49	Decision on hardware	0c	14/01/9·	14/01/9·	
50	Port to new hardware	10c	31/01/9·	11/02/9·	
51	Development finishes	1c	26/01/9·	26/01/9·	
52	System Test	21c	01/03/9·	29/03/9·	
53	Fault Fixing	21c	01/03/9·	29/03/9·	
54	Release 1 Production	1c	30/03/9·	30/03/9·	
55	Delivery to customer	1c	31/03/9·	31/03/9·	
56	Data Load	1c	31/03/9·	31/03/9·	

Figure 14-8(c)

PSI analysis

1. Goal clearly defined [20]

The goal of the project really cannot be defined clearly if there are no activities - requirements analysis or high level design - to define it! Assuming there is some requirements definition in the text of the document we will give them 10.

2. List of jobs [20]

The list of jobs, i.e. the WBS, is - to put it charitably - not very good. Say 10 again.

3. One leader [10]

The plan says that there is, so let's accept that. Score 10.

4. People assigned to jobs [10]

Yes, they have been. But because the job list is a mess, this assignation will be flawed too. Score half marks, as we did for point 2 above - 5.

5. Backup plan / margin for error [10]

Doesn't look good. The plan shows the system delivered and Data Load (job 56) taking place on 31 March 19964. If everything doesn't happen exactly on schedule, then the 31 March date will pass with nothing happening at the user site. Score -15.

Total here is 20. With 40 as the threshold and with no jobs in the plan which might increase the *Goal* and *Job list* scores, this project would look as though it has very depressing prospects indeed.

Case Study #3 - Scenario

You receive a project plan to review. It is about 30 pages long. The plan is for a project to develop and release a system. The document makes it clear that the plan is a very aggressive one, that the project will start on May 1 and must finish at 31 August at the latest. The plan is based on a requirements document which has already been signed off.

Checking the contents you find that it has sections corresponding to *all* of the items on our table of contents checklist. Each of these sections looks fairly substantial and contains the kinds of things we talked about. A leader for the project is named.

Checking the WBS you find that there are lots of omissions and inaccuracies and you note these down.

You look for a high level overview Gantt chart and find it (reproduced in figure 14.9). It is hand drawn but nonetheless appears to have the major blocks in it. A more detailed Gantt chart - not reproduced here, but containing all the kinds of things we expect - accompanies the high level overview.

A schedule and effort analysis, resource loading histogram showing everyone scheduled at or less than 100% and assumptions on people's availability are all included amongst the pages of the plan. There is also a note in the plan to the effect that all of the project team members' summer holidays have been accounted for in the estimates and schedules.

What is your assessment of this plan?

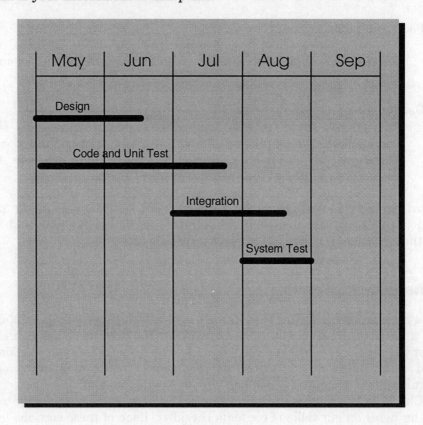

Figure 14-9

Case Study #3 - Analysis

Level one checks

Contents analysis
As described in the scenario, it appears to be OK.

WBS analysis
The results of the WBS analysis are already noted in the scenario.

Gantt chart analysis - High level overview
There is certainly a high level overview with a more detailed Gantt chart backing it up. However, there is a major flaw in the high level overview. The four activities in it overlap one another to a highly suspect degree:

- Software is being written while the system is being designed. This is always a dangerous thing to do.
- Integration of the software begins before all of the software has been written. While this could indicate good forward planning on the part of the Project Manager, it can sometimes be an indication that somebody is merely trying to squeeze everything into the allotted time. This would merit further investigation at a lower level of detail, i.e. at the Critical Path level.
- The System Test isn't entirely what it seems. A System Test should do exactly that - it should test the entire system. Yet, in this plan, System Test begins before the system is fully available. Again this might imply great foresight on the part of the Project Manager. Unfortunately it more often implies the presence of Parkinson's Law - 'Work expands (or contracts!) to fill the time allotted'.

Resource loading analysis #1 and #2
As we noted in the scenario, the summer holiday season has been allowed for. Also the who's doing what is contained in the more detailed Gantt chart.

PSI analysis
1. Goal clearly defined [20]
> By paralleling the design and writing of the software, there is a fair chance that the goal of the project will never be clear - that what the software people write will not be what the designers wanted. Give it say, 12.

2. List of jobs [20]

>   The list of jobs i.e. the WBS is, as stated in the scenario, not very good. Say 12 again.

3. One leader [10]

>   The plan says that there is, so let's accept that. Score 10.

4. People assigned to jobs [10]

>   If the job list is flawed, this will be too. Score in the same proportion to point 2 above - 6.

5 Backup plan / margin for error [10]

>   Doesn't look good. The plan shows every sign of Parkinsonian planning. Not only is there probably no margin for error, but the plan as it stands is probably not based on reality to begin with. Score -15.

Total here is 25. With 40 as the threshold and with no jobs in the plan which might increase the *Goal* and *Job list* scores, this project would look as though it has very depressing prospects indeed.

Level two checks

As we have seen in all three of these case studies, you can often - but not always - find out all you need to know about the plan by applying the five small checks that we talked about earlier, i.e. the ones that take 30 or so minutes. Just to remind you, these are:

Check	Effort involved
Contents	Small
WBS	Small
Gantt - Overview	Small
Resourcing #1 and #2	Small
PSI	Small

In this case, just for interest, we will look at what we can find out by applying one of the tests at the next level down. Thus, out of the four tests at this level, i.e.

Check	Effort involved
Schedule and Effort	Medium
Gantt - Critical Path	Medium
Resource loading #2 and #3	Medium

we will apply Schedule and Effort analysis.

Schedule and Effort analysis

The schedule and effort analysis, given in the plan, is shown in figure 14.10. Adding our comparison figures is shown in figure 14.11. An interpretation of the differences between these two sets of figures is as follows:

1. The amount of effort going into design would appear to be too low. On top of the paralleling going on between *Design* and *Code and Unit Test*, this further evidence is very disturbing.
2. This figure of 75% in *Code and Unit Test* is bordering on the insane!
3. So is the 3% in Integration.
4. As is the 10% in System Test.

This check only adds weight, if it were needed, to the evidence we already have.

Estimating Score Card

Project	Case Study 3
Author	
Revision No.	
Date	

Phase	Schedule (months)	%	Efffort (MM)	%	Schedule (months)	%	Effort (MM)	%	Schedule (months)	%	Effort (MM)	%
Design	25		12									
Code & Unit test	41		75									
Integration	17		3									
System test	17		10									

Figure 14-10

Estimating Score Card

Project   Case Study 3

Author

Revision No.

Date

Phase	Schedule (months)	%	Efffort (MM)	%	Schedule (months)	%	Effort (MM)	%	Schedule (months)	%	Effort (MM)	%
Design	25			12	A	26		18				
Code & Unit test	41			75	B	36		36				
Integration	17			3	C	18		9				
System test	17			10	D	18		20				

Figure 14-11

Guidelines for Writing Project Plans

If you are charged with writing a Project Plan then the following should help to ensure that you make the best possible job of it. (This is presented as an *alternative* to the one in the Introduction to Part Two.) Your plan should contain the following elements:

1. Table of Contents
2. Management summary
3. Statement of what is to be done (The goal of the project)
4. Deliverables (Also part of the goal). These may come under a number of headings:
    *   Software
    *   Hardware
    *   Documentation
    *   Services
5. Completion criteria - how do we know when the project is over? (A key part of the goal)
6. Acceptance criteria - how does our customer decide the project is over? (Also a key part of the goal)

The next six items are all part of the plan and the backup plan.

7. Work Breakdown Structure - a list of all the jobs that have to be done to complete the project together with estimates of their associated effort and any assumptions made
8. A Gantt chart - showing the Work Breakdown Structure phased over time, and stating any assumptions made. The Gantt chart should also show clearly the Critical Path of the project.
9. A breakdown of the effort and schedule in the project by project phase.
10. Milestones - a list of key dates extracted from the Gantt chart
11. Resources required - human and otherwise
12. Resource loading - how the resources are phased over time and how the availability of people's time has been calculated
13. Project budget [OPTIONAL] - derived from the effort in the Work Breakdown Structure and the section on Resources
14. Project organisation chart - amongst other things, this serves to identify the project leader.

15. Backup plan / margin for error. Sometimes called Risk Analysis. The Project Plan represents a prediction of how things will go in the future with regard to this project. The intention of this section is to show that the author of the plan has given some thought to what she will do when what happens in reality differs from the Project Plan.

Part Five

The rest of the wherewithal

Chapter 15

Resolving issues - problem solving/decision making

Introduction

In Parts One and Two of this book we have presented a general method for leading a project. We have talked about how to plan it, what things to do during the execution of the plan, and how to bring the project to a successful conclusion. The method we presented was conceptually very simple and pretty much common sense.

However, life is never that simple. Countless issues, large and small, will arise during your project. Not a day will go by when there won't be problems requiring solutions; every day, you will make decisions which will effect the outcome of the project.

This part of the book presents a general method and a toolbox of techniques that you can use to help resolve these issues, to solve problems and to make decisions. Armed with your common sense method in one hand, and your problem solving method in the other you should be the equal of any issue which arises to confront you.

In this chapter I will list these problem solving techniques and, where useful, give examples of their application. There are no right and wrong situations when one or other technique should be applied. As we have seen, projects are complex organisms, and any issue is likely to be complicated, with numerous factors to be balanced. Several of the techniques which follow may all resolve the issue. Only you can decide which resolution is right for your project. If this chapter had a subtitle it would be 'There's more than one way to skin a cat'.

Problem solving method

The general problem solving method we will use contains the following four steps:

- What's the problem?
- What's the ideal solution?
- Identify a range of solutions
- Implement one or more of the solutions identified

We will now look at ways to carry out each of these steps.

What's the problem?

The first thing you have to do is to know what the issue is. Sometimes you can set off trying to resolve an issue, before you have really understood it. Therefore you need to be aware that the following can happen:

- Sometimes the stated issue is not the real issue
- Sometimes a problem is stated by stating its solution
- Sometimes, even if an issue is stated correctly, you need to pull back and look at the bigger picture in order to arrive at a resolution

Often, a good way to identify an issue is to state it. Simply stating the issue - committing it to paper, or talking through it aloud - can both crystallise the issue, and - sometimes - throw up pointers as to how to move forward.

What's the ideal solution?

You may never be able to achieve it, but it's an invaluable thing to know. What would be the best outcome? It's related to our old hoary question - what do you want to do? What's the ideal solution? If there were no restrictions or constraints, what would you do? You'd be surprised how many times you can come out of the issue with a resolution which is not far off the ideal one.

Identify a range of solutions

The following are all designed to assist you in identifying possible solutions to your problem or issue.

Chess

We are told that world class chess players can see a game many moves ahead. They know that if they make a certain move, their opponent will probably do A, then they will do B, their opponent will do C, and so on. Often you can resolve something just by exploring your choices, thinking things through and looking at what is likely to happen.

If you do go one way, then here are the alternatives, and depending on what happens here then further alternatives present themselves. I regularly draw charts on the board showing the decision to be made, the options emanating from that decision, and the subsequent scenarios that become possible. These can end up looking like a large tree in winter, there are so many branches, but it gives you a very clear picture of what's facing you. Two other points to note are:

- If one particular path is more advantageous to you, you can see it very quickly and start to move things down that path by making the other paths seems less attractive to other people.
- You can save yourself a lot of time, because moves may become redundant, i.e. irrespective what happens as a result of the next decision(s), you will still end up in the same place further down the line.

The Brownie Points Game

Brownie points represent your popularity ratings with other people. Each person connected with the project will have given you a brownie point rating, either consciously or sub-consciously. At any given time, some ratings will be high and some not so. The Brownie Points Game says that you will choose to resolve an issue by doing it in such a way as to maximise your brownie points rating with a person or persons.

Shortly before the Gulf War started, Saddam Hussein gave all his soldiers salary increases. We don't know if he had a morale problem, but if that was the problem he was addressing, he chose to address it by playing the Brownie Points Game.

People who suck up to their bosses are constantly playing the Brownie Points Game with them. I once had a boss who told me, at my appraisal, that he was giving me a 10% rise. None of my peers were getting such an enormous rise, he told me - only me - and mine was for a performance above and beyond the call of duty. As it turned out, at least two of my peers also got 10% rises. My boss was playing the Brownie Points Game.

It is a feature of the Brownie Points Game that it can often achieve spectacularly good results. It is also a feature that those results can be very short term and have negative effects in the long run.

Brainstorming

Brainstorming is a wonderful technique. The idea is to get a bunch of people together and then write down all the possible ways of resolving an issue.

There are two phases. In the first phase all ideas, no matter how far-fetched, are acceptable. Nothing is ruled out. Any idea which appears to resolve the issue is added to the list. Note that you can use all the techniques in this section to come up with ideas. In the second phase, you run back down the list and try to extract the best idea or set of ideas.

Do nothing

When we think of projects we think of frenzied levels of activity while we work to get the project done. What if an issue could be resolved by doing nothing? Got its attractions? You bet it has. Strange as it may seem, I have identified five variants of the do nothing approach. They are:

- Literally do nothing. Whether you genuinely believe the issue will go away, or whether you just wish it would, isn't the point; you decide to take no action.
- Take another reading. You resolve to do nothing, and look at the issue again some short time in the future. Depending on this next reading, you may decide to take action or if things appear to be going the way you wanted, to wait and read again.
- Chaff. Chaff is strips of aluminium dropped by war planes to confuse enemy radar into thinking there are lots of your side's planes. In our context it implies that you give the impression of doing something about an issue when in fact you're doing nothing. For example: You may have inside information that an issue which is causing your team major grief, is about to be resolved. You don't want them to see you doing nothing because it's such a hot thing with them, but at the same time you don't want to waste any time on it because you know resolution is in the pipeline. You therefore send forth signals implying a major level of activity on the issue, when in fact you're doing absolutely nothing. This is chaff.
- Recce (reconnaissance). You need to get more information. While you are gathering this information, you do nothing about the issue itself.

- Stonewalling. This is where you decide to do nothing and want it known that you're doing nothing. The classic has to be when someone asks you for a rise, and you have decided they're not getting one. Stonewalling basically involves saying no until they go away!

Truth tables

Truth tables are a technique taken from Computer Science and are very useful in analysing a problem. Here is a somewhat contrived example. I would like to give up my job and become an organic farmer. Is there a way I can do this without taking a hefty drop in my standard of living? The issue is composed of two factors here - becoming an organic farmer and not taking a drop in income - but any number of factors can be considered; the truth table just gets bigger. Each factor has 2 possibilities, either it happens (yes - 'Y') or it doesn't (no - 'N'). The truth table is then drawn as follows:

Option:	1	2	3	4
Become an organic farmer	Y	Y	N	N
Take a drop in income	Y	N	Y	N

I then have four choices.

- Option 1 means that I become an organic farmer, but I take a drop in income. Doesn't solve the problem.
- Option 2 means that I become an organic farmer and take no drop in income - the ideal solution.
- Option 3 is not to become an organic farmer, but to take a drop in income. This is clearly the worst scenario, as it takes me further away from my defined goal - to be an organic farmer and suffer no loss in income.
- Option 4 is where I am at the moment: I'm not an organic farmer but my income is reasonable.

This analysis tells me that in terms of my defined goal, I have not reached it, but neither am I as far away from it as I could be. As I said, it's a somewhat contrived example, but still the insight is interesting.

The Ronald Reagan Method

Sometimes, in your projects, an issue will come along and you don't really care how it is resolved; all that is important to you is that it *is* resolved, i.e. that some decision gets made. For example, it might be that until a decision is made, your project is held up. Some years ago there were stories circulating that Ronald Reagan made all his decisions, large or small, in the following way:

One sheet of paper was handed to him; an issue was described briefly, in simple sentences with short words. The decision to be made was stated at the bottom; and two boxes, one marked 'YES' and one marked 'NO', were drawn. A note said 'Please tick one'. The word 'one' was underlined.

I have often used this box method at meetings. It is useful in cases where the meeting is snarled up on an issue and you want to push the meeting forward. State the decision to be made, and get people to choose.

Gradually warm up an issue

This is a very effective technique and one which really proves the truth of the saying that there's more than one way to skin a cat. Most of the methods so far, have one thing in common: they attempt to resolve the issue there and then. Gradually warming it up resolves it over a longer timeframe.

You have an issue, you know it's going to be a thorny one, and you're fairly sure that if you went at it head-on, you'd be shot down. The first thing then is to just get it on the table. You say perhaps, 'I don't want to talk about this today, but I'd like to deal with it some time in the future'. This gets the other side thinking about it. You then take it a stage further: maybe you have an informal discussion about it over lunch or coffee. Following this perhaps you write a proposal and see how that flies. This process is continued until you get what you want. If, at any stage, you find it's not going the way you want it to go, you back off, wait and then move forward again gradually.

I have used this method over short (1-2 week) and long (1 year) periods. It is highly effective.

'What would you do in my position?'

If nothing else, it provides you with another option for resolving the issue. Note that it is another way of asking what the other person's ideal solution is.

Put yourself in the other person's position

See things from the other person's point of view. Any good salesman will tell you that if you can do this; see your customer's point of view, his problem, his concerns, his fears, his objective, his motivation, then you're well on the way to closing the sale.

Treat it as a project

Apply Structured Project Management!

Do a deal
'I'll do this if you do that'. 'Here's what I'll do for you; now, what'll you do for me?'

Lose your temper
Can often be disastrous, but can sometimes be highly effective, particularly if, like me, you're a person who doesn't often lose it. Several times, I have had to pretend I was losing my temper, and have wondered whether I should be considering a career as an actor!

Pep talk
Sometimes all the person needs is a bit of a lift. A pep talk is what the coach gives the team at half-time. It is usually very obvious if someone is doing it to you, but depending on your state of mind, it may be enough. It is a very simplistic approach and you need to be sure that it has worked, because if not, you have not resolved the issue.

Selling something unpleasant
For the particular case where you have to sell something unpleasant to somebody - a nasty or boring assignment, for example - you can use a technique from selling. This is the idea that you don't offer your customer a choice whether or not to buy; what you offer him is a choice of ways to buy. Thus you might offer a person a number of different ways he can carry out the particular assignment.

Grovel
This may be a hard one to swallow, but there are times, particularly when you've cocked something up, that an apology is the only way. Many people have problems apologising to subordinates, and apologies aren't easy at the best of times. Sometimes, unfortunately, it's the best way.

I have saved two really fancy ways of identifying possible solutions until the end. They are very complicated, risky in that they can backfire, but hugely enjoyable if you can pull them off. You might use them just for the hell of it, to test your skills; or to show off your power to other people - peers, staff, the opposition. Don't use them too often - save them for a special treat for yourself.

Feigned retreat
Feigned retreat, as you might imagine, is a military term. The classic example of its use is the Battle of Hastings in 1066 [Ref. 37]. It is an example of what Clausewitz [Ref. 14] calls a 'stratagem'. What this means

is that by your actions you mislead the other side into thinking you're going to do something different from what you actually plan to do.

Feigned retreat is beautiful when it works, as in the following example. (Some of the details have been changed to ensure anonymity, but you'll get the gist.)

I once worked for a company, and my division bid for a large project from another company. We wanted that project really badly. The other company messed around for a long time - they were going to do it themselves, they were going to sub-contract it elsewhere. Our proposal was totally unacceptable - they couldn't believe it was going to take as long as we said, or that it would need so many people.

There was to be one last crunch meeting. It began with the same old stuff - they had to have the product sooner, they could easily do it themselves, did we have anything new to offer? Yes, we said, you guys take it, we don't want it. We can help if you like, perhaps sell you the odd piece of consultancy. And we've done a lot of work in estimating this, so we could give you some help there, because we think some of your estimates may be a little bit out (they were wildly out!). So why don't you guys go away, and come back to us if we can help. This was all said in the most civil of terms. Inside, we were squirming; if we lost the job, we had major problems. However, we didn't. After a hurried conference, the other guys came back and awarded us the contract.

Here's another example of what can happen when you try to execute a feigned retreat. In military situations, feigned retreats are considered very difficult manoeuvres to carry out. This is because a feigned retreat can, all too quickly, become a real one.

A guy I knew - let's call him Albert - was the king-pin in an organisation for a long time. His boss was ineffectual, and Albert did pretty much as he wanted. Then a new boss arrived, and things started to change; a lot of Albert's power started to be eroded by his new boss. Albert was totally cheesed off, and chose the following course of action. He knew he was crucial to the running of the place, and in this he was quite correct - he was the most skilled technical person there, and extremely difficult to replace. He would get another job offer, and then attempt a feigned retreat on his boss - let's say he's Bert.

Having secured the job offer, Albert went in for the meeting. 'I really like working here, Bert, and I like working with you, but I'm unhappy with some things and I'd like to discuss what can we do about them.' Albert went through the various things - responsibilities, position in relation to his peers, grading, salary. Bert pretty much stonewalled - a few minor concessions, but nothing of any substance.

Albert repeated his position - this time somewhat more forcefully - how he really liked so many things about the place, but unless his perfectly reasonable demands could be sorted out, he would be forced to leave, and he didn't want to. Bert continued to stonewall. OK, Albert said, he hadn't wanted to do this, but Bert was leaving him no option.

Albert explained that he had another job - much more responsibility, better salary, more prospects - and that he would be forced to take it unless he and Bert could settle their differences. Bert rose, extended a hand across the table, and said: 'Why, Albert, congratulations. You know we'll be sorry to lose you, but it sounds like a wonderful opportunity that will really advance your career ... '. Albert left. He had never wanted to, and ended up having to relocate his family 3,000 miles.

Double envelopment (the pincer movement)

Double envelopment involves coming round an opponent from both sides so as to surround him; the phrase 'pincer movement' describes it graphically. Again, it is a military term, and the classic example is the Battle of Cannae in 216 BC Ref. 33 when Hannibal defeated a Roman Army in Italy. A more recent example from our own times was the series of manoeuvres carried out by the Allies which brought the Gulf War to a conclusion.

In a pincer movement as we're applying it, you decide to resolve the issue by identifying a number of solutions, and then applying two or more of them simultaneously. The thinking is that at least one of your attacks should work, and if they all work it provides a dazzling display of your powers. The downside is that if none of them works, you end up kinda naked and unarmed, i.e. you've used up all your ammunition.

You can contrive a pincer movement by taking your plan and fallback plan, and applying them simultaneously. The trouble with this is that you then have no fallback plan. You could live your whole life and never do a pincer movement and still be highly successful in resolving issues. I mention pincer movements here mainly because they're great fun, and a good test of your skills.

Implement one or more solutions

Here are three methods to help you to pick a solution from the group of solutions you have generated.

Write down the pros and cons

Take a piece of paper, write down the problem, write down the action you intend to take. Then draw a vertical line down the centre of the page and note the advantages on one side and the disadvantages on the other.

Betting
It is not the intention of this book to turn anyone into a compulsive gambler, but betting is a technique I have found very useful when dealing with issues. You can bet on anything - the chances of a milestone being met, the project completing successfully, a key person leaving the team - you name it and you can bet on it. Generally it is best if the bets are small (less than £5) and short term, i.e. they can be resolved within a matter of weeks. Having to bet does three things:

- it causes both parties to think very seriously about any situation, and the odds each attaches to a particular thing happening
- if the thing is within our control it causes us to make a major effort to ensure that it goes the way we wish it to go
- it establishes a level of confidence about the issue

Give yourself a present
Promise yourself a little present if the solution(s) you selected works out as you intended.

Finally, here are a few other rules of thumb that you should also bear in mind when resolving issues.

Don't dump on them at least until they dump on you
If one of the methods you have identified to resolve an issue involves taking a dump on another person, don't choose that method unless they have first dumped on you. (Statesmen of the world take note.) Thus the issue remains at a civil level unless the other side opens hostilities.

Choose the right moment/timing is everything
One of my customers can be quite grumpy to be back in work after the weekend. I never call him on Monday mornings!

Get the monkey off your back
However you choose to resolve an issue, it is nice if you can end up with a resolution where the issue is no longer your problem. This is what is called 'getting the monkey off your back'. All other things being equal, a method which moves the monkey off you is the one to go for.

If one technique doesn't work try another one
Any issue can be resolved. If you find one technique isn't cutting it for you, try a different one.

If it's potentially harmful sleep on it

Maybe you're going to fire someone, or take a giant dump on somebody, or do something for which you might get into trouble. Whatever it is, if the thing has serious negative consequences, mull it over during the drive or train ride home. Sleep on it. Then, in the morning, if you still think it is the best thing to do, do it.

Don't let things fester

Don't let things fester. By all means wait and choose the right moment, but don't procrastinate and let a thing run on. The chances are it will only get worse. Resolve the issue as quickly as is practicable.

Chapter 16

Coping with stress

Introduction

Stress occurs when you're not in control, when outside events are driving you instead of you driving events.

Much of this book so far has been about trying to get to a situation where you are in control; where the uncertainty and guesswork surrounding your project have been reduced to a minimum, and where you know you have done all that can be done at any particular point. In chapter 15 we looked at ways of overcoming problems and difficulties that might be causing you stress. All of these things should cause a significant reduction in your stress levels.

However, even the bravest of us are still prone to anxiety, worry, stress, and so this chapter talks about some other things you can do. In general these things won't remove the cause of the stress - it is up to other parts of this book to do that for you. What the methods in this chapter will do will be to change your attitude to the issue in question, and hopefully reduce your anxiety about it. Here's a quote to set the tone of this chapter.

> You can think about your problems or you can worry about them, and there is a vast difference between the two. Worry is thinking that has turned toxic. It is jarring music that goes round and round and never comes to either a climax or conclusion. Thinking works its way through problems to conclusions and decisions; worry leaves you in a state of tensely suspended animation. When you worry you go over the same ground endlessly and come out the same place you started. Thinking makes you progress from one place to another; worry remains static. The problem of life is to change worry into thinking and anxiety into a creative action.
> **Harold B. Walker**

With this idea in our back pocket, let's look at twelve ways of reducing and controlling stress.

Ways to reduce stress

Who has the ball?

If you are stressed on a project, then you need to locate the thing that is causing the stress. Having located it, there are only two possibilities - either you can do something about it or you can't. If you can, then you have the ball and you run with it. Note that this may involve starting another project.

If you can't do anything about it - and by this I mean you have tried all the techniques in chapter 15 on problem solving - if you really can't do anything about it, then somebody else has the ball. Having identified who this is, and note that it may be Fate (or God, whichever you prefer), and if you still can't see anything you can do to influence the outcome, then THERE IS NOTHING YOU CAN DO. And by nothing I mean nothing. In particular, don't worry about it. Identify the event(s) that will cause the ball to come back to you. Wait until it comes, as sooner or later it will, and then off you go, back into action.

Keep a sense of proportion, or, there's always someone worse off than you

Before I finish this chapter thousands of innocent people will have died throughout the world. They will die of hunger, disease, torture, execution, neglect, abuse, loneliness. It's important to keep a sense of proportion. In general, unless you are involved in certain types of projects, e.g. military, medical, you almost certainly won't be doing life-threatening things.

Many of the things that face you in your projects don't add up to a hill of beans (as Humphrey Bogart said) in the context of some of the real problems in the world. The next time you're feeling stressed pick up the paper and read the world news. Alternatively, you could turn (as promised) to Winnie the Pooh. This is our friend Eeyore again, in conversation with Christopher Robin.

> 'Hallo, Eeyore,' said Christopher Robin, as he opened the door and came out.
> 'How are you?'
> 'It's snowing still,' said Eeyore gloomily.

'So it is.'
'And freezing.'
'Is it?'
'Yes,' said Eeyore. 'However,' he said, brightening up a little, 'we
haven't had an earthquake lately'.

Try treating it as a game

If you are stressed it means you feel that something you hold dear is under
threat. It could be your life, your job, your marriage, your career, your
reputation, your home, your family. One way to behave is to try treating it
as a game. Suppose the stakes weren't so high. Suppose it were just a game
and in a couple of hours time, the game will be over and reality will return.
Now, with this different viewpoint, do you get any new insights into how to
move forward?

Exercise

I didn't think this one up. Doctors recommend exercise, particularly aerobic
ones - swimming, cycling, running, rowing, and so on - the very rhythmic
exercises as a cure for stress. Yoga and any kind of meditation are also
very good.

See it a year from now

Take the thing that is causing you stress and imagine how it will look a
week, a month, a year from now. Will it really seem that important? Do
you think you will actually be able to remember it? Pretend it is some time
in the future and see how the picture looks.

Has it bottomed out?

In calculus there's this idea of taking a point on a curve and comparing it
against a closely neighbouring point. From this you can determine whether
the curve is ascending or descending. (I'm being fairly loose in explaining
the mathematics of all of this!) You can use this idea by taking a reading,
as it were, each day, and determining whether your situation is improving
or not.

Compare today to yesterday. If things seem even infinitesimally better
then maybe the situation has reached rock bottom and is now starting to

improve. This one is particularly good for debts ! and, if the curve is going the wrong way, try another method.

Get gates to your house

My house has gates and a short drive leading up to it. Often when I come home in the evening and close the gates, I have the feeling of locking the problems of the world out. Tomorrow, when I go through the gates, the problems will still be there, but tonight, I'm alive, I've got my family. I have a little oasis in the desert. Tomorrow is still there, but it is in the future, somewhere out there. In the meantime I can enjoy what I've got.

The Marathon runner

I used to run Marathons. Because the thought of running 26 miles is so outrageous, there's this idea in Marathon running that you forget about how far the distance is, and just focus on the next tree or house or telegraph pole. Sure, the rest of the race still remains to be run, but by taking a very short horizon, focusing on it and blocking out all the other, future stuff, you can reduce enormously the pressure on yourself.

Write down what the problem is

A bit like 'Stating the issue' in chapter 18. Write the problem down, study it and see if that in itself is not therapy and gives you a fresh insight.

The world closes down at the weekend

Many of the institutions that cause us stress - banks, businesses, the government - close down at the weekend. In many countries, postal deliveries, which might bring further stress, stop sometime on Friday afternoon. This means you have a whole two and a bit days respite before having to go back into the fray.

Talk to somebody

As the old saying goes 'A problem shared is a problem halved'.

Keep a diary

Some novelist - and I can't remember who it was to save my life, or even find the reference (if someone can help, I'd appreciate it) - said 'I write to see what I think' (or words to that effect). Write, or more specifically keep a diary, to see what *you* think. Use it to analyse, to comment, to understand, to suggest ways forward. You may find it a help.

Chapter 17

Picking the right people

Introduction

For many projects you will need to pick people and the question we discuss here is how to pick the right ones. This book talks about taking a project-oriented view of an endeavour. Some people do this instinctively. I believe that most others can be taught to do it without a great deal of difficulty. Indeed, that is what this book is trying to get the reader to do. In this chapter we will talk about 'interviewing', but you should think of this in the sense of finding people for your project, as opposed to simply hiring people.

Method of interviewing

In my last regular job, I was General Manager of a US multinational's European Software Development and Support centre. There we adopted a two-stage approach to interviewing people. In the first stage I screened all the resumes and did preliminary interviews. (Given that we were over 60 people, and that we were very choosy about whom we picked, you can see that this would have made for a hell of a lot of interviews in a year. The rationale was that I was the Project Leader and I needed to have a large say in who worked on my project.)

Companies all say that 'people are our most important resource', but how many of them see hiring and people-related issues as belonging to the Personnel or Human Resources departments? People are how we get our projects done. That is why they are our most important resource.

The interviews were generally short (half an hour), and really only asked three questions:

- what have you done?
- what do you want to do?
- what are you like?

A result of the same person doing all the screening is that over a period of time, such a screening process guarantees a consistent type or types of person getting through to the second interviews. It may result in people who would have been right, being excluded. On the other hand, if you've found a type or types that work for you, why change?

In the second interview, which could last 3 or 4 hours, the person got to meet as many of the other team members as possible, peers, subordinates, managers. We encouraged the person to walk around and talk to people, particularly to people doing a job similar to the one this person would be doing. The person did this in a totally uncensored way, i.e. he could talk to whoever he chose and the person to whom he talked could say whatever he liked. There was no rehearsal or 'party line'. We took the view that we had nothing to hide, that people needed to see us warts and all. We wanted people to feel what it would be like to work in our team, and that was why the interview lasted so long and the candidate saw so many people: It was the closest they could get to us short of actually coming to work there.

Interview questions

Here is how we went about getting answers to our three basic questions:

- what have you done?
- what do you want to do?
- what are you like?

What have you done?

It is at this stage you find out what experience and qualifications the person has. For a very technical area there are certain technical skills that are essential. We look for people who describe their career in terms of milestones or achievements, i.e. project-oriented people. Typical questions are:

- What was the greatest moment of your life?
- Tell me the three things you've enjoyed doing most in your life?
- What was your biggest setback?

Things we look for are:

- Punchy replies - the person tells you the answer, gives you what you asked for and shuts up. Rambling replies make me very edgy, as they seem to me to be indicative of a jumbled or unstructured sort of mind.
- A feeling that the person has pushed through difficulties to get a job done.

What do you want to do?

THE KEY QUESTION. All along we have talked of harnessing people's personal objectives to enable us to make our project happen. If the person doesn't know what he wants, then I will almost always not hire them. If they don't know what they want, then how can you use them in your project - it may not be what they want.

Obviously, I won't just ask the bald question and if they can't answer kick them out. I'm prepared to probe, and have done so to an excruciating degree on occasions. However, at the end of the day, you have to winkle it out of them. Incredibly, this can sometimes be the first time they realised what they wanted to do. We ask questions like:

- What do you definitely not want?
- If you could pick any job in the world what would it be?
- How would you like your career to go?
- What drives you?
- Where are you on task-oriented vs. people-oriented?
- What do you do in your leisure time?
- What would someone else say about you - a former boss, your girlfriend? It almost doesn't matter who it is - it's just that if the person is hanging tough on this question, you need to get an answer.
- How hungry are you for the job?

You need to know what the person will be like when they show up on your team: You know what you want to do with your project, and what part you want him to play. The question is what does this geezer want to do?

What are you like?

Finally, you need to get a feel for the person's personality. Do you feel that they'll fit in with the general chemistry of your group?

- Describe your personality.
- Are you the kind of person that if I ask you to do a job I can regard it as done?
- What strengths and weaknesses would you be bringing to the table?
- Say something negative about yourself.
- What do you like to read?

Chapter 18

Negotiation

Introduction

Every one of us, in all aspects of our lives, has to negotiate. We do it over salary, when we buy things, in our personal lives, as part of our jobs; and we see it going on in world affairs where the stakes can sometimes be scarily high. We are familiar with what happens in negotiation: We take a position, the other side takes one and then both sides argue until a compromise is reached.

There is a wonderful little book called *Getting to Yes* by Roger Fisher and William Ury [Ref. 22]. Based on work done at Harvard, this short book presents a method called *principled negotiation* or *negotiation on the merits*. The method has as its objective to produce a wise agreement. A wise agreement is defined as 'one which meets the legitimate interests of each side to the extent possible, resolves conflicting interests fairly, is durable, and takes community interests into account'.

Principled negotiation

The principled negotiation method has four steps:

1. Separate the people from the problem.
2. Focus on interests, not positions.
3. Generate a variety of possibilities before deciding what to do.
4. Insist that the result be based on some objective standard.

Let us look at each of these in turn.

1.   Separate the people from the problem

Often negotiations can end up as personal battles between the participants, where strong emotions and people's personalities obscure the real issues. Principled negotiation tells us to disentangle the people from the issues; and to move from a confrontational situation to one in which the participants are working together to attack the problem as opposed to attacking each other. Some of our techniques from chapter 15 can be useful here, particularly the following:

- Exactly what is the issue?
- State the issue
- Truth tables
- What's the ideal solution (very useful)
- 'What would you do in my position?'
- Put yourself in the other person's position
- Treat it as a project. Apply step 1 of Structured Project Management - visualise what the goal is; set your eyes on the prize

2.   Focus on interests, not positions

Most often we take up 'negotiating positions' based on a number of factors ('interests') which are important to us. In a conventional negotiation, the position can quickly come to obscure the interests. Principled negotiation says to focus on the interests and not the positions. Again the techniques mentioned above can be used to help to do this.

3.   Generate a variety of possibilities before deciding what to do

In other words, brainstorm.

4.   Insist that the result be based on some objective standard

In a conventional negotiation results are often arrived at by one side giving in, or the other side being intransigent. A different way is to agree in advance an objective standard or set of criteria by which the outcome will be judged. Once this is done, nobody has to give in - both sides can use the standard as the definitive reference point. Examples of an objective standard are market value, precedent, equal treatment or expert opinion.

   In this chapter I have tried to give you a feel for the method of

principled negotiation. Like many of the other things in this book it smacks
of just plain common sense: Instead of arguing the toss about something,
we say instead 'look we have this problem, how can we solve it to our
mutual satisfaction?' It is a way that we know instinctively is

- more effective
- more likely to be successful
- more likely to produce the best solution
- a damn sight more pleasant

than traditional negotiation. *Getting to Yes* won't take you long to read -
it's about half the length of this book. I urge you to get your hands on a
copy.

Chapter 19

Meetings

Introduction

A meeting can be an incredibly useful arena on a project. In a well-conducted meeting you can smash through obstacles, resolve issues and make decisions, and come out feeling like you really moved the project forward and that in paying today's salary, your employer really got value for his money. How many of us, though, attend meetings which:

- drift along
- appear to have no purpose
- have no agenda so you have no idea whether or not you're making progress
- appear as if you didn't need to be there at all

This chapter contains, a quick way to find out if the meeting you're being asked to attend will be such a meeting, and some hints about how meetings should be run so as to be of the effective kind described in the opening paragraph.

The Meeting Alarm

If somebody asks you to a meeting you should find out:

- What is the objective?
- What preparation is required?
- Why do you need to go? (the first two questions should make this clear. If you have to ask this question, it is in itself a danger sign.)
- How long will it last?
- Who is the chairman?

If you cannot get straightforward, punchy answers to these questions, then I suggest the meeting is likely to be a total waste of time, and you should refuse to go. (Clearly it is up to you to decide if internal politics require that you should attend anyway!)

Organising and running meetings

Here are nine steps towards better meetings:

1. Identify the objective(s) of the meeting
2. Identify the participants you need, and the chairman
3. Based on (1) and (2) build the agenda
4. Set a time constraint on each agenda item and on the meeting as whole
5. Publish the objective(s), agenda, time constraints and indicate to each participant what preparation is required
6. Hold the meeting
7. The chairman drives the meeting towards the objective(s)
8. Prepare an action list arising out of the meeting
9. Leave when the objective(s) has/have been met and the action list completed

Chapter 20

Presentations

Introduction

Your projects will invariably require you to give presentations - to your customer, to the project team, to your peers and to your superiors.

Some people are born presenters - one could almost call them actors. We have all seen them. They are totally authoritative on their subject. They come across as humorous, dramatic, somewhat informal, relaxed, honest, caring, believing intensely in what they are saying. They tell their story in a punchy, effective way that is never boring, but instead grabs and holds our interest. They use plenty of eye-contact, and often employ audio-visual aids and props.

Others are less convincing. Perhaps they are smug, patronising, over-aggressive, too verbose and run on too long, too rehearsed, boring, too casual, dishonest or just unsure of their subject matter. Others still find presentations the most terrifying ordeal imaginable; something which becomes apparent the minute they stand up and open their mouths.

It is not the intention of this chapter to teach presentation skills, i.e. how to present your material. There are enough media companies around today who can do that sort of thing, and who can give valuable advice on how to improve our effectiveness when speaking to an audience.

Our aim here is to consider how best to structure your material - i.e. what we present - for a presentation. Anybody, no matter how good or bad a speaker, can do what we recommend here; and the approach described will compensate for many speakers' shortcomings. Aside from this, it is up to the media companies to turn us all into Laurence Oliviers. Probably the best injunction ever on giving a presentation is:

- Tell 'em what you're gonna tell 'em
- Tell 'em
- Tell 'em what you told 'em

While it is hard to improve on this for the presentation itself, there is a lot you can do by way of preparation beforehand. Here are some guidelines I use:

- Identify the main messages you want to get across. There should be only a handful of these and they should be crystal clear. Also, you need to know whether you are merely trying to explain and describe something or to persuade your audience about something.
- The trouble with crystal clear messages is that they are also blunt. You may want to soften the messages a little by putting what I call 'shading' on them. By this I mean putting some colour into the black and white messages so that they appear happy/sad, optimistic/pessimistic, the start of something big/the harbinger of doom, threatening/benevolent, light-hearted/serious, no problem/big problem, or any one of a million other things. Blunt messages are just that. Shading means you anticipate the mood of your audience and deliver the blunt messages to maximum effect.
- If you are doing some kind of handout, structure it around these messages and their shadings.
- Rehearse your speech with a person or persons other than the intended audience. Explain the messages and shadings you are trying to put across and see if your presentation achieves those. Do this several times if necessary.
- Anticipate questions, both on your own and in rehearsal, and prepare answers which support your messages and shading.
- Questions can often take you down paths you hadn't intended to go, and this side-tracking can cause you inadvertently to deliver messages and shadings you hadn't intended. Try to spot these potential side-tracks in rehearsal and anticipate how you will use them to reinforce your messages and shading.
- Give the presentation by following the adage above:

  ➢ Describe the layout of your presentation
  ➢ Give the presentation, referring constantly to the layout, so that the audience can follow where you are; and deliver your messages with their shadings
  ➢ Re-cap on the messages and shadings you delivered

Chapter 21

Shortening projects using accelerated analysis and design

Introduction

In the 1970s there was a great swing towards the idea that more time spent getting the requirements and design right would result in:

- shorter time spent coding and testing
- fewer bugs
- an all-round better product

At the same time, tools started to appear which automated parts of the coding and testing process. Thus it seemed we had the best of all worlds - put the time and effort into the fun bit - Requirements and Design - and automate as much as possible of the time and labour-intensive stuff. As a result, conventional wisdom now has it that it is impossible to shorten the Requirements and Design phases of a project without seriously compromising the quality of the final product.

I believe this wisdom to be fundamentally untrue; and the rest of this chapter shows a way of significantly shortening a project and, if anything, improving the quality of the finished product. The next section talks about what really consumes the time during the Requirements and Design phases of projects. The following section describes how to carry out an Accelerated Analysis & Design (AAD) session. The fourth section talks about the risks involved and how to deal with them. The fifth section talks about some of the practical considerations involved in carrying out AADs.

What takes the time?

Requirements and Design phases are a bit like adultery. They typically consist of bouts of intense activity interspersed with periods of quite low levels of activity. It is not the intense activity that causes traditional Requirements and Design phases to be as long as they are. Instead it is things like:

- Large amounts of documentation to be produced; much of it caused by the write/review/revise nature of traditional Requirements and Design approaches
- Loss of continuity due to the put-down / pick-up nature of the traditional approach
- Delay in getting responses and/or decisions
- Sometimes somewhat unfocused effort either resulting in, or because of, low team spirit
- Difficulty in getting the right people at the right time
- Interruptions
- People having other responsibilities ('Hey, I've got my own job to do!')
- The long time between reviews, walkthroughs or meetings means that it is possible for things to go a long way wrong before they are spotted
- The natural overhead in traditional project management methods and structures
- Meetings (and the difficulties of coordinating peoples' diaries)
- Getting things (decisions, documents) responded to, reviewed and approved
- Reworking and refining (of documents, ideas etc.)

How to carry out an AAD

Accelerated Analysis and Design (AAD) addresses these problems in the following way. A one week or two week long meeting - an AAD session - is arranged. Ideally it will be held offsite. Invited to the meeting are all the decision makers on a project, be they users and DP people, in the case of an in-house development, or engineering and marketing people in the case of developing a commercial product. All the people who have a say have to attend.

A useful thing to do in advance of the AAD process is to have a sort of mini-seminar whose objective is to set both the AAD team's and upper management's expectations. This seminar would explain what the process is and what results can be expected. Having done this, there is preparation that needs to be done by each of the AAD team members. Each participant must independently write down:

- the name of the system/product being built/project
- a one sentence description of what the system/product will do
- three or four, either benefits of the system/product, or else three or four problems that it will solve

Apart from the attendees - and, by the way, 8 is about the maximum number you can usefully have on an AAD - two more people are required. The AAD session needs a leader, and it also needs what we call a technical scribe. The leader works from 'eight till late'; the technical scribe works from after lunch until late. This is what they do.

On day one, the leader starts the AAD session with the group. The scribe may or may not be there - it doesn't really matter one way or the other. The group begins to put down the main requirements for the system / product. Typically this is done at a board, flip-chart, or - if your budget can rise to it - a photocopying whiteboard, one of the most wonderful inventions known to man. As the main requirements are hammered out, these are then further broken down, and this process will continue until the required level of detail is achieved.

I'm assuming here that you're doing your Requirements and Designs in English language documents, on the basis that this would be the lowest common denominator for all software development organisations. Thus, what you are doing during the AAD is taking a table of contents or template for a Requirements or Design document and filling in the blanks. If you've progressed from this and are using some one of the structured methodologies or CASE, then AAD is even more effective when used with these approaches.

To continue with our AAD. The technical scribe shows up in the afternoon. Typically, this person is a senior designer level person. The AAD session ends at say 5 p.m., and the scribe and the group leader take all the notes from the day and write as much of the Requirements Spec. as has been created. This document is then on each group member's desk when they arrive next morning.

The process begins again, using the fresh document as a starting point. Typically one would hope to have 95% of the Requirements nailed down by the end of the second day, but it might take much longer than that. AAD sessions are completely time-driven, and so you plan to do as much as you can in the time allowed, as opposed to having a fixed amount of work to do, and a variable amount of time in which to do it.

The days continue in this way with updated documentation being created each evening, and used as a starting point next morning. Results vary, but at the end of a two-week AAD session, you could expect to have a Requirements Spec. that was almost 100% correct (only small items of detail should be in doubt, if any); and some proportion of the design of the system/product in place.

Risks in holding an AAD

In this section we talk about the risks involved in holding an AAD, and what, if anything, can be done to minimise them. Each risk is listed and then a possible action that could be taken:

- You end up with the wrong people. Say, for example, there's a senior decision maker missing. Probably the most serious thing that can happen. If this does happen to you, you need to kill the AAD session immediately. Careful preparation should reduce the risk of it happening.
- Group think. This is where the group gets so caught up in the AAD that ideas which aren't very good or even downright wrong are accepted and used. Try to pick attendees whose personalities are such that this probably wouldn't happen.
- Foul up previously good relationship with users or marketing if the AAD doesn't deliver. No solution!
- Risk to one's own career if the AAD doesn't deliver. No solution! Good luck!!
- Insufficient time in an AAD for subconscious problem solving. Sometimes we do our best work away from the office where we can often come up with highly creative solutions to problems. An AAD doesn't really give us this luxury. This risk is offset to some extent by the synergistic effect of the AAD.
- Expectations not satisfied; particularly those of upper management. Clearly, these need to be set correctly. That's where the idea of the mini-seminar is very useful.
- The standards or quality assurance or quality control department view the procedure with suspicion, and slow down the procedure by insisting that all their standard stuff be done in addition to the output from the AAD.
- Some standards (e.g. document signoffs) are there because they assume a traditional Requirements and Design life cycle. That is to say, many of them are based on a put-down / pick- up approach. For an AAD type approach, the standards should probably be revisited

and altered to reflect the AAD way of working.

- Corporate or country culture. The hours and / or emotional intensity involved in an AAD may not suit every company. No solution!
- Part way into the AAD, the project is found to be too big so that the expected results cannot now be achieved in the timeframe. Produce less of the deliverables or else take one chunk of the system down to the promised level of detail.
- Can't come to a consensus. A problem. Your best bet is that this effect can be offset by the feeling of people working together towards a common goal.
- Not much time in an AAD for tact. Yes, there isn't!
- Anti-climax / let-down after the AAD is over. Create a post AAD session job list so that there is natural follow-on from it.
- Requirements get missed. Yes, but this risk also exists in the traditional approach.

Practical considerations

This section talks about some of the practical considerations involved in running an AAD. It does so under three headings:

- Who should come
- What you will need
- Productivity

Who should come

The leader. Should be from outside the project, if not the organisation.
Up to four analysts / designers. These would be from the DP department or software engineering organisation as appropriate.
Up to four 'clients'. Generally one would expect to see more of these than analysts / designers. For the development of a DP system, they would ideally represent different levels of potential user from operational personnel up to management. For the development of a commercial product a mixture of marketing, sales and potential target customers would probably make sense.
The *project* leader - if he is not already included among the group of analysts/designers or clients.
The technical scribe. A person with a good knowledge of analysis and design. Also should be able to use a word processor!

What you will need

The room
- Ideally offsite
- Windows - really important
- Walls to tape or pin to
- 24 hour availability
- No telephones
- Big tables to work at
- Comfortable chairs
- Refreshments. Away from the room is probably better. Light lunches and no wine

Equipment
- White or black boards. (A whiteboard that photocopies would be perfect.)
- 2-3 flipcharts and plenty of pens
- Overhead projector and screen
- Photocopier
- PC
- Laser printer
- Word Processor
- Spreadsheet
- Project Planning tool
- Software for producing slides/overheads
- (possibly) a fax machine

Miscellaneous
- Stapler
- Highlighters
- Paper clips
- Scissors
- Hole punch
- Pads and pens/pencils
- Sellotape

Afterword

Delegation (or the real joy of management)

We only pass through this world once and we are limited in what we can do by the amount of waking hours available to us. We as project managers are in a unique and privileged position: We can use other people's time to accomplish what we want, thereby dramatically increasing the amount of time available to us, and as a result, the things we can achieve.

Think about it. For each person on our team, we have that person's time to harness to our ends. It's like having our own lifetimes extended or even being given multiple lifetimes. We can only make truly effective use of this power if we delegate, passing down as much stuff as we can to our team members.

- Use the guidelines in chapter 17 to surround yourself with the right people
- Delegate as much stuff as you can away to them, following the guidelines in chapter 7.

Do this as fast as you can trust people to take it. If you do both of these things, you will find your days opening up with time that you can use for all those new things you always wanted to do. Then, and only then, will you experience the *real* joy of management.

Appendices

Appendix 1

ISO9000 estimating procedure

Introduction

This document describes an estimating procedure, based around steps 1-5 of the Ten Steps, which could be used *by all personnel, not just Project Managers,* when making estimates. This procedure could form part of a series of project management procedures which could, in turn, go into a software development organisation's Quality Manual. The procedure has seven remaining sections.

Section 1 shows how to develop a Work Breakdown Structure (WBS) and to use this to make estimates of effort. This is the 'demand' side of the project equation.
Section 2 shows how to calculate the 'supply' side, i.e. the availability of resources.
Section 3 shows how to match the demand to the supply, thereby building a model of how your project might unfold.
Section 4 shows you how to build in some contingency to your plan.
Section 5 shows you how to use this model to identify options and make sensible decisions about what can and cannot be achieved.
Section 6 shows you what to do once a preferred option has been chosen.
Section 7 contains a sample Work Breakdown Structure.

Section 1
Work breakdown structure, effort, task dependencies

Produce a work breakdown structure (WBS) for the project

This is essentially a structured list of all the jobs that must be done to complete the project. The list should have a 'folded map' format, i.e.:

- All the major milestones shown - you can get these immediately from step 1 in the following section
- As much detail as possible (i.e. down to the man-day level) in the upcoming phase
- As detailed as it can be thereafter

Make the WBS as excruciatingly detailed as possible by milking every scrap of information you have for all that it's worth.

To help you to do this, a sample WBS is provided in section 8 of this document. This WBS follows a general purpose software development lifecycle. The WBS is presented in such a way that you could add in your own lifecycle elements and WBS checklist elements, gathered from your own experiences over time.

Steps to take ...
1. Write down all the jobs in your project and for each job identify:

> ➤ Which jobs it depends on
> ➤ Which jobs depend on it.

2. Present this list in a top-down way with:

> ➤ Clear start and end points
> ➤ A high level overview, i.e. the (less than a dozen or so) top level jobs that have to be done to complete the project
> ➤ The milestones associated with these jobs
> ➤ Wherever possible, these jobs broken down repeatedly until the lowest level of detail (i.e. the man-day level of detail) is achieved
> ➤ For the next 4-6 weeks, no job should be more than 5 man-days in size

You can do this with whatever you normally use for writing, or alternatively - and far better - use a PC-based project planning tool.

3. Guess and document the amount of effort (sometimes also called work) in each job. Note that it is *effort*, not elapsed time that we are looking for here. Nor is it the quantity called *Duration* that PC-based project planning tools are so fond of. For each element write down the basis on which the guess was made, e.g. the document has 12 sections, allow 1 hour per section, therefore 1.5 man-days; or 'This is what one of these normally takes me' etc. If any data are available from previous projects, use them.

If you feel that you simply cannot guess certain jobs - because they are unclear or unknown - try first to break them down to lower levels of detail.

When you eventually feel you can go no further in this process, and if certain jobs are still unclear or unknown - which they will be - then make and document an assumption. Finally, involve the people who will do the work in the estimating process. For that matter involve anyone whom you think might have a valid input.

Enter the guesses of effort for each job onto your list. Document the way each guess was arrived at. Note that this includes documenting all the assumptions you made.

When producing estimates with an individual the individual's normal working day should be used - no productivity factor should be used. Where it is not known who will work on a particular job, a productivity factor of 20% should be used. Thus a 10 man-day task actually becomes 12 days.

4. Add up all the effort in all the jobs. This gives you the total amount of work in the project. Using manpower rates, it also gives you the project budget, if you need it. This is the 'demand' side of your project. All of this should be documented in the Project Plan.

Section 2
Availability of resources

Staffing Plan

Generate a staffing plan showing:

- Types of people required
- Number of each type required
- When the different people will be required

Calculate the manpower available to the project

Typically, apart from your project, the members of your team will spend their time in a number of other areas:

(a) Definite other projects in which they are involved.
(b) Vaguer, support / maintenance / quality / other request sorts of things which take up a definite chunk of time every week.

(c) Annual leave, public holidays.
(d) Unpredictable things which can't be anticipated. Sick leave comes under this heading.

Areas *(a)*, *(b)* and *(c)* can all be quantified, while some assumption can be made about *(d)* thereby quantifying it.

Steps to take ...

1. Work out for each person how much of their time (measured in days per week, hours per day or any other measure that means something to you) is being spent on these activities and hence how much time (measured in the same units) is available for your project.

2. Document each person's availability in your project plan and your PC-based project planning tool if you are using one.

Section 3
The Project Model

Use the WBS and manpower availability to build a project model

Steps to take ...

1. Now match people to jobs. Wherever possible try to ensure that there is only one resource per task. Ensure that, as far as possible, every job has a human being's name - as opposed to an organisation or a 'TBD' or 'ANO' - against it.

   ➢ Ensure that, as far as is possible, you have used exactly each person's time available to the project - no more, no less.
   ➢ If you are using a PC-based tool, use it to assign people to jobs. The tool will now draw for you a Gantt chart of your project. Amongst dozens, if not hundreds of useful things, the tool will show you your project's Critical Path.
   ➢ Failing this you will have to draw the Gantt chart yourself manually. If you are doing this, be warned that the manual approach will almost certainly introduce errors. The Gantt chart is a model of how your project may unfold over time.

Section 4
Build in contingency

Use the First Law of Project Management to build in a margin for error

You have built a model of your project, either on your PC or on paper, and this model tells you how you believe your project will unfold once it gets on the road.

You could imagine, at this point, that you know things like the end date, the amount of people required, the budget, and so on. However, you don't. The model you have created is exactly that - a model. It is a prediction of how the future may turn out.

Before you start making commitments based on the model you need to ask yourself one vital question. 'What will I do if the model is wrong - what will I do if it doesn't work out like I thought?'

A margin for error can be achieved by looking at the four parameters upon which the First Law of Project Management is based.

Just to remind ourselves, these are:

- What is to be delivered (Functionality)
- When it is to be delivered (Delivery Date)
- The amount of work involved in delivering it (Effort)
- The quality of what is delivered (Quality)

The First Law of Project Management states that there is a function which connects these four variables, and that this function is a constant, i.e.

$$f \text{ (Functionality, Delivery Date, Effort, Quality)} = c.$$

Thus, if one of these variables changes, the others change so that the overall equation remains the same.

We are all familiar with this effect. Shorten the delivery date, for example, and (a) Functionality must decrease, (b) Effort must increase, or (c) Quality must decrease.

Steps to take ...
1. To achieve a margin for error and a fallback position, examine your project using these four parameters as a basis. You can examine your project at three different levels, each requiring progressively more effort on your part. These levels are:

> Overall (i.e. treating the entire project as one large job)
> Critical Path jobs
> All jobs.

At each level, you examine the relevant job(s) and ask yourself the following questions:

> What happens if the job runs over? (Elapsed Time)
> Can the job be shortened? (Elapsed Time)
> What happens if the job is bigger than we estimated? (Effort)
> What would be the effect of adding more people? (Effort)
> Is this job doing something which is crucial to the project? If not could it be put into a later delivery? (Functionality)
> What happens if this job isn't done perfectly? (Quality)

Based on the answers you should modify the estimates of effort and/or elapsed time for some or all jobs.

2. Alternatively, you could add in a figure of, say, 15% to cover contingency. Add this to all effort estimates and this will automatically be reflected in extended deadlines and delivery dates.

Section 5
Identify options

Identify a number of different ways the project could be done

At this point it is quite likely that the end date and/or resources required and/or functionality which your project model is telling you is achievable, are not in line with what management or customers require.

If this is so, then you can use the model to see what is and what is not achievable.

1. Identify a number of options using the four parameters mentioned in section 4:

> What is to be delivered (Functionality)
> When it is to be delivered (Delivery Date)
> The amount of work involved in delivering it (Effort)
> The quality of what is delivered (Quality)

A review of the model will answer questions like:

> ➤ Can the job be shortened? (Elapsed Time)
> ➤ What would be the effect of adding more people? (Effort)
> ➤ Is this job doing something which is crucial to the project? If not, could it be put into a later delivery? (Functionality)
> ➤ What happens if this job isn't done perfectly? (Quality)

to make creative decisions and identify options about how best to take the project forward.

2. Again, having the model of your project on a PC enables you to do the 'what-if' analyses described above very quickly. Based on what you discover, document the different versions of your project model.

    Similarly, if you are doing this manually, modify your documentation to produce different versions.

Section 6
The Preferred Option

Introduction

The process of reaching a preferred option should be documented and the preferred option formally approved. Once this is done, a number of simple procedures should be carried out. The aim of these is to enable the project model to be used as 'instrumentation' with which to guide the project.

Baseline the project model of your preferred option

Basically, this means taking a snapshot of your project model. Actuals will then be recorded against this so that the accuracy or otherwise of the model can be determined, and the model can be recalibrated where necessary.
  All PC-based tools provide a facility for doing this. Alternatively you can merely lay out your plan with:

*   Two columns for Estimated Schedule and Effort - these will have values in them
*   Two columns for Actual Schedule and Effort - these can be filled in as the project proceeds

Extract major milestones

The major project milestones should be extracted from the project model and explicitly stated in the Project Plan. These will serve:

- As useful intermediate targets to be met
- As an early warning system if the milestones aren't met

Section 8
Sample WBS

1.   Product Requirements Phase

1.1 *Product Requirements document*

- Research
- Write
- Circulate
- Individual review
- Review meeting
- Updates/changes to document
- Circulate again
- Second review
- Signoff

1.2 *End Product Requirements Phase*

2.   Software Requirements Phase

2.1 *Software Requirements document*

- Research
- Write
- Circulate
- Individual review
- Review meeting
- Updates/changes to document
- Circulate again
- Second review
- Signoff

2.2 *Software Acceptance Test Plan*

- Research
- Write
- Circulate
- Individual review
- Review meeting
- Updates/changes to document
- Circulate again
- Second review
- Signoff

2.3 *End Software Requirements Phase*

3.   Architectural Design Phase

3.1 *Architectural Design document*

- Research
- Write
- Circulate
- Individual review
- Review meeting
- Updates/changes to document
- Circulate again
- Second review
- Signoff

3.2 *Software Integration Test Plan*

- Research
- Write
- Circulate
- Individual review
- Review meeting
- Updates/changes to document
- Circulate again
- Second review
- Signoff

3.3 *End Architectural Design Phase*

4.   Detailed Design Phase

4.1 *Detailed Design document*

- Research
- Write
- Circulate
- Individual review
- Review meeting
- Updates/changes to document
- Circulate again
- Second review
- Signoff

4.2 *Software Unit Test Plan*

- Research
- Write
- Circulate
- Individual review
- Review meeting
- Updates/changes to document
- Circulate again
- Second review
- Signoff

4.3 *End Detailed Design Phase*

Notes:
1. During the first four phases, the cycle (Circulate - Individual review - Review meeting - Updates/changes to document) could be repeated more than once. You should state in your estimates how many iterations of this cycle you are assuming.
2. Research could be a significant project in its own right requiring much further detailed breakdown.

5.   Coding Phase

5.1 *Produce code element*

- Write code element
- Clean compile code element
- Lint code element
- Walkthrough code element

  - ➤ Prepare for walkthrough
  - ➤ Attend walkthrough
  - ➤ Updates/changes to code
  - ➤ Signoff on walkthrough

- Code element documentation

5.2 *End Coding Phase*

6.   Unit Test Phase

6.1 *Unit test code*

- Prepare Test Plan and test set
- Test code
- Make corrections to code
- Test code again
- Prepare Unit Test Document

6.2 *End Unit Test Phase*

Notes:
1. The cycle (Test code - Make corrections to code) could be repeated more than once. You should state in your estimates how many iterations of this cycle you are assuming.

7.   Integration Testing Phase

7.1 Integration testing of code

- Any remaining preparation of Test Plan and test set, not already covered by System Integration Test Plan
- Test code
- Make corrections to code
- Test code again
- Prepare Integration Test Document

7.2 End Integration Testing Phase

Notes:
1. The cycle (Test code - Make corrections to code) could be repeated more than once. You should state in your estimates how many iterations of this cycle you are assuming.
2. Both 'Test code' and 'Make corrections to code' could be significant projects in their own right requiring much further detailed breakdown.

8.   System Test Phase

8.1 Execution of internal Software Acceptance Test Plan

8.2 End System Test Phase

9.   Release Phase

9.1 Installation

- Plans
- Activities
- Test
- Record results

9.2 Data conversion

- Plans
- Activities
- Test
- Record results

9.3   Reviews

9.4   Software Release

9.5   End Release Phase

10.   Operation and Maintenance Phase

10.1 Evaluation

10.2 Design reviews

10.3 Support and Maintenance

10.4 Audit

10.5 End Operation and Maintenance Phase

11.   Other possible WBS elements in Lifecycle

11.1 Training

- Familiarisation by project personnel
- Training of project personnel
- User training

11.2 Recruitment

11.3 Test environment development

- Overhead in dealing with software development staff

11.4 Development support

- Database Administration
- Development environment
- System build

11.5 Project Management
See chapter 4 for a full breakdown of tasks. Allow 6-8% of total project effort, as described in chapter 4.

11.6 Configuration Management

- Reviews
- Ongoing Configuration Management

11.7 Documentation

- Reviews
- User (different types)
- Administrator
- Release Notes
- Technical manuals, i.e. manuals describing how the software works
- Help texts
- Overhead in dealing with software development staff

11.8 Quality Management / Quality Plans

Appendix 2

Structured Project Management (The Ten Steps) and PRINCE

Introduction

If you use no methodology at all in your project management, if all you use is your native cunning and survival skills, then over time it's possible that you will find yourself doing some of the things that make for successful projects. [I say it's possible, because you may not. Many people - especially in software - go their whole project management lives and never cotton on to what worked and didn't work for them in the past. As a result they never know - starting out on a project - whether or not it is likely to succeed. They live their lives in permanent suspense, agitation and worry. Sometimes things work out, sometimes they don't.]

If you go from this first situation to using a methodology you should probably see an improvement. Hopefully the methodology will force you to do some of the things that make for successful projects.

Ultimately, however, it's only by applying the Ten Steps that you will be doing all of the things that make projects successful. The Ten Steps are the 'best' way to run a project. Thus, the Ten Steps can serve as a benchmark against which to compare other approaches.

I mention all of this as a way of explaining where methodologies fit into the scheme of things. Methodologies cause you to do some of the things that make projects successful. A good methodology may cause you to do a lot of them. No methodology that I'm aware of guarantees success. The Ten Steps do solely because they were derived from observation of what makes other projects successful.

PRINCE (PRojects IN a Controlled Environment) is a particularly popular methodology in the UK, and to a lesser extent in Ireland; and it is to this we now turn. I do so, not so much because I think it's either a particularly good or bad methodology, but because it will serve to illustrate the relationship between a particular methodology and the Ten Steps. Or to put it another way - actually two other ways:

- What, if anything, do methodologies bring to the party?
- What, if anything, do the Ten Steps have that methodologies don't have.

I will try to answer these two questions with reference to PRINCE. If you happen to use some other methodology you might like to benchmark it against the Ten Steps in the way we do here.

PRINCE Components

As we would expect, PRINCE's project management components have direct analogues in the terminology of Structured Project Management.

PRINCE	Structured Project Management
Products	Deliverables
Activities	Jobs
Organisation	Project Manager; Team; Management; Customer
Plans	Plans generated through steps 1-5
Control	Steps 6-10

Let's look at each of these in turn.

Products

Step 1 of the Ten Steps, especially the First Law of Project Management, shows you why a project won't work unless you operate a change control system.

PRINCE will give you a Configuration Management (CM) approach which can be used on all project products or deliverables, i.e. it gives you a possible way of implementing a change control system.

Activities

PRINCE breaks down activities into three types - management, technical and quality. The intention behind this is to ensure that all work necessary for the success of the project gets done, not just the technical work. PRINCE supplies checklists that help project planners to catch all of these diverse activities. This is all useful stuff.

PRINCE does not make clear what our step 2 did, i.e. that DETAIL as early as possible in the project is the key to all of this. The concept of the folded map, of trying to think the project through and link all the little tasks that need to happen, of trying to get the estimates right, of building in contingency - PRINCE does not highlight how these are amongst the absolutely most important things for project success.

Organisation

PRINCE proposes organisation structures, roles and job descriptions for project participants. These are useful, even if this is one of the areas where PRINCE is perhaps regarded as being top-heavy.

Whatever organisation structure is put in place, ultimately the project will need a single 'trail boss' who is prepared to put in a certain level of work doing certain things to make the project happen. The Ten Steps make this clear and the PSI shows in a quantitative way exactly how important this is, and what its contribution to the overall project success is.

Plans

PRINCE specifies a whole series of plans that should be produced. These include:

- Project Technical Plans
- Stage Technical Plans
- Detailed Technical Plans
- Individual Work Plans

- Project Resource Plan
- Stage Resource Plan
- Detailed Resource Plan

- Quality Plan

- Exception Plan

In the Ten Steps this information is all contained in one document, the

Project Plan. Apart from the wisdom involved in generating such large amounts of paper - a typical Structured Project Management plan for say, a 10 man-year project, would not be expected to be more than about 40 pages - there are a couple of important philosophical differences between the two approaches:

- The Ten Steps place a much greater emphasis on up-front planning. In the Ten Steps, the equivalent of PRINCE Stage Plans are prepared very early on in the project. The importance of this in anticipating surprises before they become problems is one of the keys of Structured Project Management's success. PRINCE places no particular emphasis on this.
- PRINCE asks for the preparation of Exception plans - 'here's what we will do when things go wrong'. PRINCE assumes things will go wrong, slips are expected. Would it be going too far to say that such a philosophy creates a culture where slips are not regarded as big issues? Or perhaps, then, that only big slips are important. The Ten Steps don't pretend that things won't go wrong, but when they do the philosophy is to try to do everything possible to recover the slip. A positive culture versus a negative one.

Control

PRINCE has a number of management, quality and technical controls. Quality and technical controls are necessary in any project, and if these can be found in PRINCE, then that's a few less wheels to be re-invented.

PRINCE's management controls can all be easily provided by Structured Project Management's elements. Thus:

PRINCE	Structured Project Management
Project Initiation	Use steps 1-5, PSI and *How To Assess Project Plans*
End-Stage Assessment Mid-Stage Assessment,	Use steps 1-5, PSI and *How To Assess Project Plans*
Checkpoint Meeting	Use Monday morning meetings and Project Manager's Daily routine
Highlight report	Project Status Report.

Summary

Like any methodology, PRINCE provides useful methods, checklists and structures, and if any of these stop somebody from re-inventing a wheel they are valuable. The downside of methodologies is that they can often bring a top heaviness both in approach and philosophy that tends to reduce the amount of momentum in projects. This is the 'servicing-the-methodology-rather-than-getting-the-project-done' syndrome.

Using something like PRINCE won't guarantee a successful project. Using a method whose derivation is project success factors will.

Appendix 3

Probability of success indicator

Introduction

We have described the current status of the PSI and our research on it in chapters 1-10. While there is still a lot of subjectivity in the scoring, our confidence in it has improved significantly in the three years it has been in use.

The original work we did on the PSI was described in chapter 20 of the first edition of this book. For those of you who are interested in seeing how it has evolved, that material is retained here in this Appendix.

Calculating a project's PSI

The PSI is a number lying in the range 0-100, which is assigned to projects using the scoring scheme given below. The PSI can be calculated at any point in a project's life and gives a measure of how likely the project is to complete successfully. The PSI could be calculated in a variety of different ways. An individual (e.g. the project manager or an external consultant) could do an assessment of the project and calculate the PSI using the rules below. Alternatively, a number of people involved in the projects (Project leader, Team members, Management, Customers) could be polled for their opinions (say, using a questionnaire) and the results averaged.

Who calculates the PSI, who gives input and how the input is gathered - questionnaire, interview, show of hands (!) - are all factors that can be considered if you are going to use the PSI. Here I have chosen the quickest and simplest way, i.e. where one person (me!) does an analysis of a given project.

How to calculate the PSI

The PSI is calculated by applying a score to each of the Ten Steps as they relate to the particular project. The maximum possible scores are as follows:

Step	Score	Totals
1	20	
2	20	
3	10	
4	10	
5	10	total=70
6	10	
7	10	
8	10	
9	0	
10	0	total=30

Just as an aside, notice how critical the planning stage is. I am firmly convinced that the success or failure of projects is determined in the first 10% of their lifetime. OK, back to the PSI. Here's how you determine each of the scores.

1. Goal {20}
Write down:
- A one sentence description of the project [8]
- Three or four bulleted items on what constitutes project completion [6]
- A 2-3 page blurb which attempts to answer the questions on the visualisation checklist (see p.10) [6]

Having done this, score the project using the numbers in square brackets.

2. Job list {20}
- Is the job list up to date? [4]
- Is it complete? Does it cover at least all the items in the checklist on p.19? [4]
- Are all the major milestones indicated and well-defined? [6]
- Is it detailed to first milestone? [6]

Score using the numbers in square brackets.

3. One leader {10}
Questions like the following should help you to smoke out this one.
- Name the Project Leader.
- Is there a person who has the 'fire in the belly' to get the project done.
- How many other projects does he or she lead?

Score as follows:
> ➤ 1 leader   10
> ➤ 2 leaders   4
> ➤ 0 or more than 2   1

4. Assign people {10}
Use form #2 from Case Study 5 (Chapter 5) and the job list from 2 above to score all of the people-jobs in the job list. Add up all the scores and divide by the number of job-persons. Then depending on where the resulting number lies, score from 10 as follows:

1.00 - 1.25   10
1.25 - 4.49   4
4.50 - 5.00   1

You could do this in two cuts, first at the person level (divide by the number of people), then at the job-person level.

5. Margin for error {10}
Use form #3 (chapter 6) to:
- Write down the major risks
- Describe the fallback position
- Explain how, by differing from the final goal, this fallback position creates for you a margin for error.

You could do this at a number of levels:

- At the project level
- For the major milestones
- For those items on the critical path
- For each job-person

Lose 15 from your cumulative score if you have no margin for error.

6. Leadership style {10}
Do the analysis required by form #2 from Case Study 5 (Chapter 5). Compare with what's happening on the ground. Score out of 10.

7. Know what's going on {10}
Analyse the reporting and monitoring mechanisms in use, and score out of 10. Lose points for no monitoring and controlling against the plan.

8. Tell people what's going on {10}
Analyse information dissemination mechanisms e.g. does everyone have an up to date copy of the plan - do they get it each time it changes? Lose points for no progress meetings and no progress reports.

9. Repeat 1 through 8 {No score}

10. The Prize; The Reckoning {No score}

Examples

Let's look at some examples. Two, which we know well by now, are Scott's and Amundsen's expeditions to the South Pole. Let's score these as examples 1 and 2.

Scott
1. Goal clearly defined? Not really. Only after he'd set out for the Pole did it actually become an objective. Half marks. [10]
2. A list of jobs so that everybody knew their part. No. Hardly at all. People's roles were confused and kept changing. [6]
3. One leader. No problem here. [10]
4. Jobs assigned to people. As mentioned earlier, there was a problem with people's roles and what was expected of them. [4]
5. Fallback position. History proves there wasn't. [-15]
6. An appropriate leadership style? Scott had the one (autocratic) style that he used with everybody. I would score it low. [4]
7. Know what's going on. Given that most of the plan was in Scott's head he had to have a reasonable knowledge of what was going on. Where he would have fallen down would have been in understanding undercurrents and morale-type issues. [6]
8. Tell people what's going on? Hardly at all. [2]

This gives a profile as follows:

Step	Possible	Actual	Totals
1	20	10	
2	20	6	
3	10	10	
4	10	4	
5	10	-15	15
6	10	4	
7	10	6	
8	10	2	
9	0	0	
10	0	0	12
		Grand Total	27

Amundsen

1. Goal clearly defined? Absolutely. [20]
2. A list of jobs so that everybody knew their part. Completely. But let's say he could have done a little better. [18]
3. One leader. No problem here. [10]
4. Jobs assigned to people. Yes. See chapter 4, or better still read Ref. 26 if you doubt it. [9]
5. Fallback position. Yes - they put on weight, remember? [10]
6. An appropriate leadership style? Yes, Amundsen was very sensitive to his people. [9]
7. Know what's going on. Absolutely. [8]
8. Tell people what's going on? Yes. [8]

This gives a profile as follows:

Step	Possible	Actual	Totals
1	20	20	
2	20	18	
3	10	10	
4	10	9	
5	10	10	67
6	10	9	
7	10	8	
8	10	8	
9	0	0	
10	0	0	25
		Grand Total	92

Project X1
This is a project I worked on about ten years ago. It was the one I mentioned in chapter 3 where there were two leaders.

1. Goal clearly defined? Sort of. There were no real specifications, but there were people on the project who had a good knowledge of what the system was trying to deliver. Give it half marks - roughly. [9]
2. A list of jobs so that everybody knew their part. We knew what we had to do from day to day; but did we know how that fitted into the bigger picture, and whether we were making progress? Definitely not. [6]
3. One leader. No - there were two. [1]
4. Jobs assigned to people. People were certainly assigned to jobs. However, given that the job list may have been incomplete - see above - then we'd have to mark this low. [4]
5. Fallback position. Well, I suppose there was because when the excrement hit the ventilating device, management was able to re-configure the project to deliver decreased functionality. [4]
6. An appropriate leadership style? There were two leaders, one autocratic and opinionated, the other wishy-washy and a bit of a moan. [4]
7. Know what's going on. See the comments above on job list and assignment of people. [4]
8. Tell people what's going on? Somewhat. [4]

This gives a profile as follows:

Step	Possible	Actual	Totals
1	20	9	
2	20	6	
3	10	4	
4	10	1	
5	10	4	24
6	10	4	
7	10	4	
8	10	4	
9	0	0	
10	0	0	12
		Grand Total	*36*

The Battle of the Somme

Here's one we mentioned earlier in the text, the opening of the Battle of the Somme in the First World War.

1. Goal clearly defined? Yes, no doubt about it. [20]
2. A list of jobs so that everybody knew their part. Yes, dock 'em a couple of points on the basis that they might have done slightly better. [18]
3. One leader. Yes. [10]
4. Jobs assigned to people. Yes - done very well. [8]
5. Fallback position. Nope. [-15]
6. An appropriate leadership style? Leadership in the First World War has been the subject of much controversy and literature. The prevailing style in the military of the time was 'don't think - just do what you're told'. I'll give them 5 on the basis that more responsibility and initiative should have been passed down the line. [5]
7. Know what's going on. The technology of the time made communications on the battlefield very, very difficult. Half marks. [5]
8. Tell people what's going on? See earlier comments on 'do what you're told'. Half-marks. [5]

This gives a profile as follows:

Step	Possible	Actual	Totals
1	20	20	
2	20	18	
3	10	10	
4	10	8	
5	10	-15	41
6	10	5	
7	10	5	
8	10	5	
9	0	0	
10	0	0	15
		Grand Total	56

Project X2
This is another project I once worked on.

1. Goal clearly defined? Yes - pretty well. We had a detailed spec. and descriptions of the functionality that would be in each release. [16]
2. A list of jobs so that everybody knew their part. No, we never really managed to stabilise our lists. We would get lists written, and then a short while later we would be told that 'everything has changed', and the lists were no longer valid. [10]
3. One leader. No. We had horrifying problems - too numerous to mention - with leaders. Let me score it 1 on the basis that we were in the 0 or more than 2 category. [1]
4. Jobs assigned to people. Well, because the job lists were in flux, so too were the job assignments. [3]
5. Fallback position. Yes, we did. As the going got tough we were able to move functionality from the first release into subsequent ones - a standard trick amongst software developers. [7]
6. An appropriate leadership style? Because of the problems described earlier, I eventually had to take control of this project and drive it through to a conclusion. Let me (modestly!) score myself 7. [7]
7. Know what's going on. By and large, yes we did. [6]
8. Tell people what's going on? We tried. [6]

This gives a profile as follows:

Step	Possible	Actual	Totals
1	20	16	
2	20	10	
3	10	1	
4	10	3	
5	10	7	37
6	10	7	
7	10	6	
8	10	6	
9	0	0	
10	0	0	19
		Grand Total	56

Project X3
Here's another software project I worked on. The Project Manager is one of the best I know.

1. Goal clearly defined? Yes. [18]
2. A list of jobs so that everybody knew their part. Yes. [18]
3. One leader. Yes. [10]
   (Aside: There's a pleasure all of its own in thinking back over a well-run project. I can feel a warm glow all over as I remember this one.)
4. People assigned to jobs. Yes. [8]
5. Fallback position. Yes, even though it wasn't needed. [8]
6. An appropriate leadership style? Yes. [8]
7. Know what's going on. Yes. [8]
8. Tell people what's going on? Yes. [8]

This gives a profile as follows:

Step	Possible	Actual	Totals
1	20	18	
2	20	18	
3	10	10	
4	10	8	
5	10	8	62
6	10	8	
7	10	8	
8	10	8	
9	0	0	
10	0	0	24
		Grand Total	86

Operation Desert Storm
Clearly, I wasn't in on the planning of Operation Desert Storm. However, here's a man in the street's assessment of it.

1. Goal clearly defined? Yes, with clinical accuracy. [20]
2. A list of jobs so that everybody knew their part. Seems like. [18]
3. One leader. Yep - Mr Schwarzkopf. [10]
4. Jobs assigned to people. Seems to have been done well. [7]
5. Fallback position. My guess is that there was - can't know for sure, though. [7]
6. An appropriate leadership style? Don't seem to come much better. [9]

7. Know what's going on. We didn't, but presumably the powers that be did. [8]
8. Tell people what's going on? Again, we didn't, but I think those involved did. [8]

This gives a profile as follows:

Step	Possible	Actual		Totals
1	20	20		
2	20	18		
3	10	10		
4	10	7		
5	10	7		62
6	10	9		
7	10	8		
8	10	8		
9	0	0		
10	0	0		25
			Grand Total	87

Analysis

Trends
The projects described earlier are shown in tabular form in figure A3-1. From the limited sample presented here and/or studied by us, a few things have become apparent.

- Any project with a planning phase score below about 40 looks dodgy
- Any project with a total score below 60 looks dodgy
- If you get a low score from the planning phase, then putting it charitably, you have limited scope to improve things subsequently. Putting it less charitably, if you come out of the planning phase with a low score, then it would appear that you can do what you like and it won't really make a lot of difference to the eventual outcome.

This last observation gives rise to my corollary to the famous Brook's Law [Ref. 7]. Brook's Law states . . . 'Adding more people to a late project makes it later'. My corollary states . . . 'Projects succeed or fail in the first 10% of their lifetimes'.

Usage
What we have described here is a very simple risk analysis. It can be done at any point in a project's life. It is very much a garbage-in, garbage-out exercise; if you tell it lies, it will tell you lies in return.

Limitations
At the moment the limitations of 'taking the PSI challenge' (if I may call it that) include the following:

- It is based on a very small sample
- The scoring is somewhat coarse
- The scoring is somewhat subjective
- It has had limited application in real life
- Both the scale and scoring process need to be tuned and refined by reference to many other projects

That much having been said, we are now using the PSI on consultancy assignments and on training courses. Any projects we have studied to date have verified the accuracy of our PSI scoring scheme. We're looking forward to doing more work in this area.

Probability of Success Indicator - Analysis Table

	Marks available	Scott	X1	The Somme	X2	X3	Desert Storm	Amundsen
1. The Goal	20	10	9	20	16	18	20	20
2. Job list	20	6	6	18	10	18	18	18
3. One leader	10	10	1	10	1	10	10	10
4. Assign Jobs	10	4	4	8	3	8	7	9
5. Fallback position	10 (70%)	-15 15%	4 24%	-15 41%	7 37%	8 62%	7 62%	10 67%
6. Leadership	10	4	4	5	7	8	9	9
7. Know what's going on	10	6	4	5	6	8	8	8
8. Tell people what's going on	10	2	4	5	6	8	8	8
9. Repeat steps 1 through 8	0	-	-	-	-	-	-	-
10. Prize; the reckoning	0 (30%)	- 12%	- 12%	- 15%	- 19%	- 24%	- 25%	- 25%
Total	100%	27%	36%	56%	56%	86%	87%	92%

Figure A3-1 PSI analysis table

Comments:
- Scott - The worst project we have - ground zero on our scale
- X1 - Scores very poorly as you would expect
- The Somme - Illustrates that in certain circumstances a margin for error can be a dealbreaker
- X2 - Poor profile after Planning just about saved by a strong Implementation

- X3 - Profile similar to Amundsen - strong Plan, strong Implementation
- Desert Storm - Almost as good as Amundsen, the best project we have

Rules of thumb:

Anything coming out of the Planning stage below 45% is very dicey. Failures will probably end up with scores of below 60%.

Appendix 4

Basic precepts and glossary of terms

Introduction

Chapter 19 of the first edition of this book contained some basic information which I think is worth retaining here.

For something that is meant to be so complex, project management doesn't actually require much basic terminology. There are really four things you need to know about:

- Effort, also sometimes called Work
- Schedule, also sometimes called Elapsed Time
- Critical Path
- Milestones

In addition, there are a whole heap of additional terms that are bandied about from time to time and these are presented in a glossary of terms which follows.

The Four Big Ones

Let's look at the four big ones first.

Effort (Work)

Effort is, quite simply, the amount of work in something. Effort is measured in units such as man-days, man-weeks or man-years. If a person digs a hole and it takes 5 days then the amount of work is 5 man-days. If 5 people dig a hole and it takes them 1 day then that is also 5 man-days.

Schedule (Elapsed Time)

Schedule is the elapsed or calendar time that something is going to take. Schedule is measured in the ordinary calendar units of time - hour, day, month, year. In the previous example of digging the hole, the schedule in the first instance was 5 days; in the second it was 1 day.

Critical Path

Critical Path is a much misunderstood term. Critical Path is the shortest time (i.e. the shortest schedule or elapsed time) in which something can be completed). In the examples which follow, you will see the significance of critical path.

Milestones

Milestones, as originally placed on roads, showed a traveller how far she was from the start or end of her journey. Milestones in projects do exactly the same. They 'anchor' the project at particular points in time. They show how much of the project has been completed and how much is still to go.

Abbreviations and Rules of Thumb

You may also find the following of use:

8 man-hours [MH] = 1 man-day [MD]
5 man-days   = 1 man-week [MW]

Technically there are 4.3 man-days in a man-week, but 5 is easier to work with.

19 man-days   = 1 man-month [MM]
12 man-months   = 1 man-year [MY]
220 man-days   = 1 man-year.

Technically, there are 228 man-days in a man-year, and I think this may be true in the US. Certainly in Europe it's closer to 220.

Example 1

Pregnancy is an often used example of a project. For this, our four terms above are:

Effort:	9 woman-months
Schedule:	9 months approximately
Critical Path:	9 months (i.e. adding more women won't shorten the project)
Milestones:	Doctors can identify particular significant points in the growth of a child from conception to delivery.

Example 2

Here's another project. It has six jobs in it as follows:

- Write document
- Circulate document
- Review document
- Revise and update document
- Circulate document again
- Sign off document

The project ends when this particular document is signed off by the relevant parties.

Let's assume also that the following estimates, i.e. guesses made by us, apply to the six jobs. Each estimate is given as three numbers - effort in man-days (MD), schedule in elapsed time, number of people involved:

Write document	15.0 MD, 7.5 elapsed, 2 people
Circulate document	0.5 MD, 0.5 elapsed, 1 person
Review document	5.0 MD, 5.0 elapsed, 5 people
Revise and update document	4.0 MD, 2.0 elapsed, 2 people
Circulate document again	0.5 MD, 0.5 elapsed, 1 person
Review and sign off document	2.5 MD, 5.0 elapsed, 5 people

As always we document the basis for these estimates:

1. 'Write document' is 2 people working full time for a week and a half.
2. 'Circulate' is 1 person doing photocopying, faxing and mailing for half a day
3. 'Review' is 5 people each spending a day each reviewing the document and we give them a week to do it.
4. 'Revise' is the 2 people working full time, this time for 2 days.
5. 'Circulate again' is the same as the previous 'Circulate'
6. 'Review' is the same 5 people taking half a day each to review and sign off the document, and we give them another week in which to do it.

Thus:

Effort	27.5 MD
Schedule	20.5 elapsed
Critical Path	20.5 elapsed (Because the tasks must follow one another sequentially. This is not always the case. Also each activity is on the Critical Path.)
Milestones	The completion of each of the six tasks represents one possible set of milestones in the project. (The beginning of each task is an alternative set.)

Critical Path

Critical Path is important for a number of reasons:

- It tells you the shortest possible time in which the project will complete
- It identifies those jobs which, if they are delayed, will result in a delay or slip in the project as a whole
- It identifies those tasks which must be shortened if the project is to be shortened
- If a slip occurs on your project, the Critical Path identifies the jobs which must be worked on if the project is to be brought back on schedule
- The Critical Path is the reason why adding more people to a project may not necessarily make the kind of difference we would expect. To illustrate this let's see what happens if we add some people to our project above

Nearly 70% of the effort on this project is taken up with two tasks, 'Write document' and 'revise document'. If we were to add a person or even two people to these tasks our natural reaction would be to expect a substantial improvement on the schedule.

In practice, nothing could be further from the truth. Adding 1 person (i.e. increasing the team by 50%) reduces the schedule to

$$5 + 0.5 + 5 + 1.5 + 0.5 + 5 = 17.5, \text{ a saving of 15% on the original;}$$

while adding another person and increasing the team by 100% reduces the schedule to

$$4 + 0.5 + 5 + 1 + 0.5 + 5 = 16.0, \text{ a saving of only 21% on the original.}$$

And note that adding more people assumes that they can just slot in with no prior knowledge of the particular task, and be as productive as the people who were already there. Such an assumption is rarely the case in IT.

Indeed, there is an argument that says that in certain circumstances adding people to a project will not actually shorten the schedule at all. This argument is succinctly stated in Brook's Law [Ref.7].

Adding people to a late project makes it later.

Glossary of Terms

Change management   The process by which a Project Plan is modified in the course of the project.

Critical Path   The shortest elapsed time in which a job can be done.

Deadline   When a job must be complete by.

Deliverable   Something made, written, produced or created as a result of a job.

Dependency   A relationship between two jobs.

Effort   How much work is in a job.

Elapsed time   How long a job will take.

Estimating   Guessing. Trying to predict the future. Doing this based on some previous knowledge or experience.

Goal   Think of the project as a journey; the goal is your destination.

Job   Same as project or phase or activity or task.

Milestone   A milestone is any significant point in a project.

Objective   Think of the project as a journey; an objective is one of the points you have to pass on the way to your destination. To put it another way, each job has an objective.

PERT   Program Evaluation and Revue Technique.

PERT Chart   A network whose nodes represent project jobs and their durations, and whose links represent relationships between pairs of jobs.

Phase, Activity, Task	These are all terms used to describe sub-components into which a project can be broken down. In some organisations, these have specific meanings and relationships to one another. To avoid any conflict here, we use the term 'job' as being synonymous with any of these three terms.
Project	Any endeavour can be considered as a project. In our terminology 'project' and 'job' are synonymous.
(Project) budget	The cost of all or part of a project.
Project control	Trying to keep what actually happens on a project in line with the Project Plan.
(Project) costing	Working out what a project will cost.
Project monitoring	Checking how a project is proceeding against the Project Plan.
Project Plan	Your prediction of how you think the project will evolve. It is also the formal agreement between:
	➤ between the members of the team ➤ between the team and the project leader ➤ between the project team and its customer.
	Describes all aspects of the project identified during the planning process.
Resource allocation	Assigning people (or other resources) to jobs.
Risk analysis	Trying to predict what might go wrong on a project and allowing yourself some room for manoeuvre.
Work Breakdown Structure (WBS)	Structured list of jobs in a project.

Appendix 5

Additional forms

The Estimating Score Card

Estimating Score Card

Project

Author

Revision No.

Date

Phase	Estimated				Actual				Difference			
	Schedule (months)	%	Efffort (MM)	%	Schedule (months)	%	Effort (MM)	%	Schedule (months)	%	Effort (MM)	%

The Change Request Form

Change Request Form

Project Name _____   Project Number _____

_____   Chg. Req. Number _____

_____

Initiated by   Date _____

_____

Description of change request

_____

_____

_____

Reasons and perceived benefits

_____

_____

Priority: Essential to success of the project   ☐

              Required for implementation   ☐

              Can wait   ☐

Affected Tasks/Deliverables

_____

_____

Estimate of Cost and Time

_____

_____

Approved ☐   Rejected ☐   Date _____

Project Manager   Date _____

_____

Project Team Reviewed   Yes ☐   No ☐

Change Request Log

Change Request Log			
Log No.	Date Received	Date Reviewed	Rejected Y/N

Appendix 6

Learning Microsoft Project 4.1

Introduction

The purpose of this appendix is to present the minimum functionality of MS Project required by a project manager to assist in the running of a project. We will use MS Project to plan and schedule an exercise project.

The notes follow the standard steps required during the planning and execution of a project:

- Creating tasks
- Editing and moving tasks in the plan
- Setting task durations
- Setting dependencies between tasks
- Formatting and presenting the plan
- Assigning resources to tasks
- Saving the baseline

The user of these notes is assumed to have a basic understanding of how to use the MS Windows operating system.

Basics of project management

This module reviews some key project management topics and terminology. All of you are probably quite familiar with these topics so they will be dealt with very quickly.

Goal   Every individual working on a project, the project manager and the PM's manager MUST be able to succinctly state what is the goal of the project. Only then will everyone be working in tandem. Also, there should be only ONE goal.

Success factors

What is the definition of a successful project?

- Within agreed timescale

- To agreed budget

- Supplies required functionality and quality

Project Manager

Every project should have ONE and only ONE project manager who owns the project. This person is responsible for the project and will get the kudos when the project succeeds or will have his/her head chopped off when project fails.

On large projects there may be a number of project managers, each with responsibility for a certain part of the project. Each of these should be able to identify the boundaries of his/her project and the success factors associated with it.

Exercise 1.0   In your notepad and for your own private use only,
List the name of your project
List the goal of your project
List the project manager
List the success factors

Getting started with MS Project

This module introduces the major features of the MS Project product. The main thing to remember about MS Project is that it is just a fancy calculator, a tool to assist the Project Manager

It DOES NOT manage the project for you.

If you are a poor project manager, then using MS Project will probably make you worse. If you are a good project manager then using MS Project will give you greater control of your project and will increase your ability to communicate the project status.

Another point to note about MS Project is that it has been designed to cater for every possible project type and every possible Project Management style. It does not force you into doing things its way. You can develop and use your own PM style and MS Project will fit your way of managing projects. The down side of this however is that MS Project may at first seem rather complicated. There are at least 2 ways of doing everything in MS Project, and sometimes 6 or 7. In this course we shall normally use 1 or 2 ways and in your own projects you can choose whichever suits you best.

The standard MS Project screen contains a number of different areas

Title bar
This is the standard Windows title bar, with the control menu bar on the left and the minimise and maximise icons on the right.

Menu line
This is a standard Windows application menu. It allows access to all the underlying functionality of MS Project. The menu has the same eight standard commands as the other Microsoft Office products.

Standard Toolbar
This is a shorthand way of accessing frequently used menu options. The first 10 icons are identical for all the Office products. A feature, Tool Tips, is available which indicates the function of each icon. To activate this just pause the cursor on a icon.

Formatting Toolbar
This supplies additional icons to the toolbar to help outline your project and format your text.

Ribbon
When you are entering data in MS Project, the characters you are typing appear on this bar. You can also change or edit existing data on this bar.

Views
Views are a most powerful feature of MS Project. They provide many different ways of looking at the one underlying database in MS Project. Either a single view or a combination view (2 views on the one screen) can be displayed. Each view has a name and can be accessed from the view menu. Users can define their own views if required

The Gantt Chart view is the default view visible on start-up. This default can be changed if required.

The project database holds data on 3 areas of the project:-

- Tasks

- Resources

- Assignments of resources to tasks

Some of this data, e.g. task names and durations, is input by the user and the rest of this data, e.g. total project duration, is calculated by MS Project

Status bar   This line is displayed on the bottom of the screen.

You can control whether or not you wish the Tool bar, the Ribbon and the Status bar to be displayed. You do this using the Options or Customize commands within the Tools menu. We will not cover how this is done in this course.

Module 1.
Saving your project

In this module you learn how to save versions of your project to a disk file. You should save your work to disk at frequent intervals during any updating. You can do this using either the command in the File menu or the equivalent icon.

Project files should be saved in directories created specifically for that purpose, NOT in the WINPROJ directory. If you have an existing directory into which you wish to save your project files, ignore exercise 1.1 and continue with exercise 1.2. If you have not yet created a directory for your project files continue with exercise 1.1

Exercise 1.1.   Create new folder in which to save your project files

Click on the Start button at the bottom left of the screen

Select Programs

Select Windows Explorer and click

When the Exploring screen appears, select the folder (or drive)

in which you wish to create the new folder

Click the File Menu

Select the New command

Click on Folder command (a new folder is created)

Type in the name you wish to give to this folder

Return to MS Project by clicking the button on the bottom of the screen

Exercise 1.2.   Save using File menu

Click the File menu

Click the Save command (The File Save dialog box appears will appear)

(The default folder to save in will normally be the Winproj folder. You however, want to use the new folder you have just created.)

Click the Up one level button to navigate to the folder you need. The folder names are displayed as you navigate

In the File name box, type the name of your project. (You do not have to type the extension .MPP. MS Project will add this itself).

Click Save button (or use the Carriage Return (CR) key)

A shorter way of saving your project is to use the Save icon.

Exercise 1.3.   Save using the Save icon

Point the cursor at the Save icon and click

Module 2.
Creating tasks

This module shows how to create tasks in a project. When setting up a project we normally specify a project start date. This is usually the only date we specify and we let MS Project calculate the rest. We then identify each task in the project and how long it will take to complete. We then identify any relationships or dependencies between tasks.

The first thing we wish to do is to set up some general information about the project. We use the Project info dialog box to do this. Within the dialog box we use the TAB key to move from field to field. Use Shift+TAB to move backwards. Alternatively, use the mouse to click on the field you wish to enter.

Exercise 2.1.   Set up initial project information

Click the File menu

Click the Project Info command. (The Project Info dialog box appears.)

Select the Start Date field and enter the date on which you think the project will start (Don't worry about the accuracy of this date. You can easily change it later)

Click on the OK button to accept the input.

Click the File menu

Click the Properties command. (The Properties dialog box appears.)

Click the Summary tab

Select the Title field and enter a name for your project

Select the Manager field and enter your name

Click on the Project tab

Select the Comments field and enter a short description of the project.

Click on the OK button to accept the input.

Note that we enter only the start date. MS Project calculates the end date. There are many ways in MS Project to create task details but we will just use the Gantt Chart.

Exercise 2.2.   Enter the task names using Gantt Chart

Use mouse, or use the tab or arrow keys to select the task name cell of row 1

Type "Task A" and hit CR

Note that a bar has appeared on the Gantt Chart and the next row is selected. Automatically moving to the next row after entering a CR is an option that you can change if you wish.

Type "Task B" and hit CR

Type "Task C" and hit CR

The duration of each of these tasks is the default value of 1 day. We will change these values later.

Module 3.
Correcting errors

MS Project has a powerful undo feature if you make a mistake and wish to backtrack on something you have just done. In the last exercise we didn't really mean to enter Task A, so we shall delete it.

Exercise 3.1.   Clear an entry

Click in the Task Name column of Task A

Click the Edit menu

Click the Clear command and click All. (Note that this just clears the name of the task but leaves the rest of the entry untouched)

(We didn't mean to do that so we can undo what we have just done)

Click the Edit menu

Click the Undo Clear command

Exercise 3.2.   Delete a task

Click anywhere on the row for Task A

Click the Edit menu

Click the Delete Task command. (Note that this deletes the whole task entry)

(We didn't mean to do that so we can undo what we have just done)

Click on the Undo icon on the toolbar.

Exercise 3.3.   Delete a task using the keyboard

Click anywhere on the row for Task B

Press the Delete key on the keyboard. (Note that this also deletes the complete task entry)

(We didn't mean to do that so we can undo what we have just done)

Click on the Undo icon on the toolbar

Module 4.
Moving tasks

MS Project does not worry about the order of the tasks in the list but sometimes we want to move tasks to make the order more meaningful for ourselves. There are 2 main ways of doing this and you can use whichever is most comfortable for you.

Exercise 4.1.   Move a task

Select task "Task A" by pointing to the number 1 in the ID column and clicking

Click the Edit menu

Click the Cut (Task) command (Task A disappears from the list)

Point at the cell below "Task C" and click

Click the Edit menu

Click the Paste command (Task A reappears)

Exercise 4.2.   Move "Task A" back to its original position

Select task "Task A" by pointing to the number 3 in the ID column and clicking

Point to the number 3 in the ID column

Drag the row back to the top line. ("Task A" is now back in its original position)

Module 5.
Edit the contents of a cell

If we have made an error in an entry we have previously typed, we do not need to totally retype the entry. We can simply retype the section of the entry we need.

Exercise 5.1.   Edit the task name "Task C"

Select the Task Name field "Task C" by clicking on it (The text "Task C" appears in the entry bar)

Point between "Task" and "C" on the entry bar and click

Insert the word "number"

Click on the Enter box (the green tick mark), or hit CR (The task name is now "Task number C")

Module 6.
Entering task durations

This module introduces the various ways of specifying durations for a task. Duration is the working time needed to complete a task. A task's duration can be expressed in minutes(m), hours(h), days(d), or weeks(w). If no letter is specified, d is assumed. Non-working periods, for example weekends or public holidays, are not included in a task's duration.

Exercise 6.1.   Enter the durations for the current tasks

Select Duration field for "Task A" by clicking on it

Enter 4w and hit CR (Note the length of the Gantt bar changes)

Enter 3w in duration field for "Task B"

Enter 2w in duration field for "Task number C"

A milestone is an important checkpoint in the schedule. The project manager can use milestones to highlight when certain tasks or events should either start or complete. Milestones are most useful for providing clear reports to management on important dates in the project. You specify a milestone by setting the task duration to zero.

Exercise 6.2.   Insert a milestone task

Select the top task, "Task A", by clicking on it

Click the Insert menu

Click the Insert Task command (Note that you can achieve the same result by hitting the Ins key on the keyboard)

Enter "Start of Project" as the Task Name

Select the Duration field of "Start of Project"

Enter 0 and hit CR (Note that the bar on the Gantt Chart changes to a symbol and the date is displayed).

Module 7.
Using HELP

This module introduces the various HELP features available in MS Project.

MS Project uses a type of Help known as Hypertext. It has an extremely large volume of on-line reference information which can be accessed in a variety of ways depending on your need. The Help is displayed in a separate window and will usually contain some text underlined in green. These words or phrases are indices into further Help text. You click on these to display the further Help text.

Exercise 7.1.   Display Help on inserting tasks

Click the Help menu

Click the Answer Wizard command (The Help Topics window will appear)

Type "insert a task"

Click the Search button (A list of topics pertaining to this general area will be displayed. Most are not relevant to us but one appears to be what we want.)

Select the topic "Add a task between existing tasks"

Click the Display button

(Note also that at the bottom of each Help window there is frequently a section headed "See also". This is very useful for indicating other areas that you may wish to examine)

(When you have finished reading about the inserting)
Click either the Minimise or the Close icon on the top right of the window to hide it, or the Help Topics button to return to Help.)

A common way into the Help system if you know the subject on which you wish to get Help is to use the Help command on the menu and to use the Index command.

Exercise 7.2.   Display Help on "Creating task durations"

                    Click the Help menu

                    Click the Microsoft Project Help Topics command

                    Click the Index tab

                    Type "cr" (The topics on creating are displayed)

                    Select "creating durations"

                    Click the Display button

                    (When you have read the first 3 items)
                    Click each of the greater than buttons in turn

The index is extremely large and you may sometimes find it difficult to find the exact topic you are looking for. Another way of looking at the Help is to imagine you are looking at a large set of books. This is the way the contents are organised. Assume for example that you want to find out more about how task durations.

Exercise 7.3.   Find out about task durations

                    (If you are not already in the Help window)
                    Click the Help menu and click the Microsoft Project Help Topics command

                    Click the Contents tab

                    Select the Project Planning Process book and click the Open button

                    Select the Creating a Schedule book and click the Open button

                    Select the Tell Me About... book and click the Open button

                    Select Using Durations and click the Display button

                    (When you have finished reading the topic) click the Done button

The index is one method of navigating the Help system. An alternative method of navigating is by using cue cards. A cue card is a step-by-step procedure that you can follow when you need to undertake a certain task. You can display a cue card while you work in MS Project and it stays on the screen until you minimise or close it.

Exercise 7.4.   Use cue card to learn how to change task duration

(If you are not already in the Help window)
Click the Help menu and click the Microsoft Project Help Topics command

Click the Contents tab

Select the Project Planning Process book and click the Open button

Select the Creating a Schedule book and click the Open button

Select the How do I... book and click the Open button

Select Changing a task duration and click the Display button

(When you have read the first 3 items)
Click each of the greater than buttons in turn

MS Project provides a nicely structured tutorial that covers the basics of using MS Project. This Quick Preview is accessed from the Help menu.

A final point to note about Help. To get further information concerning a warning or error message, press the F1 key while the message is displayed.

Module 8.
Using views

This module discusses how views are used by MS Project to provide the power and flexibility. It also reviews the use of tables and forms.

Views are a most powerful feature of MS Project. The View is the means of entering, changing and displaying the contents of the underlying database in MS Project. By using a variety of Views, you can look at the same project information in different ways as you organise your project. There are 2 types of view; Single pane and Combination.

MS Project binds together the data in the 2 combination views. When you move from one row to another in the top view (using either the arrow keys or selecting with the mouse), the data displayed in the bottom view will reflect the change.

You use the View menu to change from one view to another.

Exercise 8.1.   Change to a different view

Click the View menu

Click the Calendar command (This shows tasks on a day-to-day basis)

Click the View menu

Click the PERT command (This shows the dependencies, if any, between tasks. On the current project we have not yet set any dependencies)

Pick View menu

Pick Gantt (The Gantt is the default view in MS Project. It shows the list of tasks on the left hand side and a calendar of when they are happening on the right hand side)

You change to a combination view by using the Window menu. Note that only one view of a combination view is current at one time. This is indicated by the blue border down the left hand side.

Exercise 8.2.   Change to a combination view

Click the Window menu

Click the Split command

Exercise 8.3.   Change back to a single view

Click the Window menu

Click the Remove Split command

An alternative method of moving between single and combination views is to use the mouse. You can change to a combination view by dragging in the small square in the bottom right hand corner of the window.

Exercise 8.4.   Change to a combination view

Move the cursor to the square box in the bottom right corner just below the scroll arrow (the shape of the cursor will change to a double arrow)

When the cursor changes hold down the mouse button and drag up (A horizontal divider line will appear with another view under it).

You change from a combination to a single view by dragging the horizontal divider line to the bottom of the screen.

Views are primarily of two types, table views and form views (the Calendar and PERT views are the 2 exceptions). Tables are spreadsheets used in views to display information on either tasks or resources. The rows are either task or resource names and the columns are fields of information about the task or resource. The left hand side of the Gantt Chart view is an example of a spreadsheet. We will return to tables in later exercises.

Forms display information in a field format. The information pertains to a single task or resource.

There are 2 main forms, one for tasks and one for resources. These can be formatted in detail and the Format menu provides some standard forms. Forms are most useful when displayed in the bottom view. An example of a form view is the Task Form that is displayed in the bottom view when you Split the Gantt Chart view. We will return to forms in future exercises.

The Gantt Chart Wizard is an interactive assistant to help format the Gantt Chart view to the way we want it.

Exercise 8.5.   Learn what the various icons are

Point at the leftmost icon on the top toolbar and leave the pointer on it for a few seconds (A little cue card will pop up giving the name of the icon)

Point at each icon in turn

Exercise 8.6.   Change Gantt Chart to highlight Critical Path

(Ensure that you are displaying the Gantt Chart view)

Click the Gantt Chart Wizard icon (The 3rd from the right on the top toolbar)

Read the directions and Click the Next button

Select Critical Path in Step 2 window as the information to be displayed

Click the Finish button

Click Format it button

Click Exit Wizard (The longest task on the Critical Path is highlighted in red)

Module 9.
Setting task dependencies

This module shows how to set task dependencies (called relationships in MS Project) using a number of different methods. We will also practise at using different views.

The most common relationship between tasks is when one task cannot start until another task finishes. This is known as a Finish-Start (FS) relationship or dependency. An obvious example of this type of relationship is during the building of a house when the foundations must be dug before the concrete can be poured, and the concrete must harden before the walls can be built. MS Project assumes we want this type of relationship unless we tell it otherwise.

Exercise 9.1.   Set dependency using Gantt view and menu

Use the cursor to select Tasks A, B and C

Click the Edit menu

Click the Link Tasks command (MS Project automatically changes the start date of Task B to start when Task A is finished and changes the start date of Task C to start when Task B has finished. This is reflected on the Gantt Chart.

Exercise 9.2.   Unset dependency using Gantt view and menu

Use the cursor to select Tasks A, B and C

Click the Edit menu

Click the Unlink Tasks command

Exercise 9.3.   Set dependency using the toolbar

Use the cursor to select Tasks A, B, C

Click the Link Tasks icon on the Toolbar

Module 10.
Using calendars

This module discusses how calendars are used by MS Project.

Calendars are used by the scheduler to map task and project durations onto an actual set of dates. The calendar allows public holidays, company holidays, weekends, and working hours to be accounted for by the scheduler.

MS Project provides a Standard Calendar which can then be amended as required by the user.

MS Project also provides resource calendars. There can be one per resource type and you can use either the Standard or a project calendar as the base for it. This is very useful for scheduling holidays or for scheduling resource types with different working hours.

Exercise 10.1.   Update Standard calendar to include Public holidays

Click the Tools menu

Click the Change Working Time command (The Calendar will appear)

Click the vertical scroll arrow to move to May. Click on 1st. Select Nonworking

Repeat for December 25th, December 26th, New Year's Day

and any other public holidays

Click the OK button

The workhours are used by the scheduler to understand how many hours of work are available in each day to complete the amount of work which has been calculated for each task. For the next exercise we will change to a 4-day week, 10 hours per day. We will not work on Fridays.

Exercise 10.2.   Create a Project calendar and amend it

Click the Tools menu

Click the Change Working Time command

Click the New button

Type "Test" as name of new calendar

Click the OK button

Select the M, T, W, Th by dragging the mouse (Every Monday, Tuesday, Wednesday and Thursday in the calendar is selected)

In the Working Time section amend finishing hours to 19:00

Click the F (Every Friday in the calendar is selected)

Select Nonworking

Click the OK button (This amends these days for every month in the calendar)

Having created a special project calendar we must now get the project plan to use it. We do this by amending some of the basic project information.

Exercise 10.3.   Reset Project calendar

Click the File menu

Click the Project Info command

Click the arrow to the right of the Calendar field and select

"Test"

Click the OK button (MS Project will now schedule this project using the new Test calendar)

Exercise 10.4.   Amend Timescale display to show the new Nonworking times

Click the Format menu

Click the Timescale command

Click the Nonworking tab

Select the "Test" Calendar

Click the OK button (The Fridays are now displayed as Nonworking time using the Test calendar)

Module 11.
Outlining tasks

This module introduces the concept of outlining of tasks. For the purpose of this exercise we need some further tasks in our project plan.

Exercise 11.1.   Enter further tasks

Enter tasks D through K onto the plan

Set duration of each to 1 week

Set a standard Finish-Start dependency between each one (A to K)

We have reached the stage in our planning when we need to examine the overall plan and report to our manager on it. We currently have just a list of tasks so the first step is to organise these a little better.
We will identify 3 major sections in our project:

- Initial section, Tasks A to D
- Middle section, Tasks E to G
- Final section Tasks H to K

We will insert these as outline tasks in our project.

Exercise 11.2.   Insert summary tasks

Select "Task A" (by clicking on the Task Name field)

Click the Insert menu

Click the Insert Task command

Type "Initial section"

Select "Task A"

Click the Indent button on the formatting toolbar (the right pointing arrow) (For "Initial section" note the change in duration and the change in bar format)

Select tasks B, C, D and click Indent button

Repeat for "Middle section" before "Task E" ("Middle section" will have the same indentation as Task D. This is not correct as it is not a subtask of "Initial section". You will need to Outdent it prior to indenting the tasks E, F, G underneath it)

Repeat for "Final section", above "Task H"

Exercise 11.3.   Hide and show subtasks

Click on the "Task Name" text in the column header (This selects all the tasks in the project)

Click the Hide Subtasks button on the Format toolbar (only the 3 summary task bars are now displayed)

Select "Initial section" task

Click on Show Subtasks button on Format toolbar (This displays only the subtasks of the selected summary task)

To show all subtasks, click on the Show All Tasks button on the Format toolbar

We sometimes want to schedule a task to occur on a regular basis, for example, a status meeting. We can easily do this with MS Project.

Exercise 11.4.   Enter a recurring task

Select an empty task row e.g.16

Click the Insert menu

Click the Insert Recurring Task command

Set Name = Status meeting

Set Duration = 1h

Set This Occurs = Monthly, The First Monday

Set Length = For 6 Occurrences

Click OK (6 subtasks are created under the summary task "Status meeting")

Module 12.
Printing views

At this point in our project planning we want to print the plan in order for others to be able to examine it. We will print this information in 2 different ways. First, we will print the Gantt Chart and second, we will print a list of the tasks with their start and finish dates.

MS Project provides 2 printing features, print views and print reports. We will use the print views in this section. As the name implies, this prints the view currently displayed on the screen.

For each type of view and report we can define the header, footer, margins, fonts, colours, etc. We will use the defaults initially.

The preview functionality allows us to view on the screen the appearance of the report prior to us sending it to the printer. Note that you should ALWAYS preview before you print in order to check how many pages you will have. Note also that the Print functionality allows you to print information between certain dates.

Exercise 12.1.   Print Gantt Chart view

Click the File menu

Click the Print command (the Print dialog box appears)

Click the Print Preview button

Note that the cursor changes to a magnifying glass

Click the mouse to examine the output in more detail

Click on the One page and Multiple page icons on the toolbar

(If ready to print) Click the Print button, else click the Close button

Before we print the table of dates we need to amend the layout. We will create a new table to suit our own requirements. The information we need is similar to that in the task sheet table but we don't need the resource details.

Exercise 12.2.   Create a new table called "Task List"

Click the View menu

Click the Table command

Click the More Tables command

Select Entry

Click the Copy button (The Table Definition dialog box appears)

Set Name = "Task List"

Select Width column of Predecessors entry

Set = 8

(Title of Name entry is currently "Task Name". We will change it to "My tasks")

Select Title column of Name entry, set to "My tasks"

Select Title column of Duration entry, set to "effort"

Select Name entry

Select Insert Row button (A blank row appears above the Name row)

Select the Option button (The down arrow on the right hand side of the (blank) entry bar) to display the allowable field entries

Use the vertical scroll arrow and select WBS (A new field, WBS, is inserted before the Name field)

Select Resource Names entry

Click Delete Row button

Click OK button

Click Close button

Now that we have created our new table, Task List, we will display it in the Task Sheet view.

Exercise 12.3.   Display new table

Click the View menu

Click the More Views command

Select Task Sheet

Click the Apply button

Click the View menu

Click the Table command

Select Task List (The new table format is displayed)

Exercise 12.4.   Format and Print new table

Click the File menu

Click the Page Setup command

Click the Header tab

Click on the Font button (the button with the A)

Set Item to Change = Header Centre (line1)

Set Font = Times New Roman

Set Size = 14

Set Font Style = Bold

Click OK button (If no title is displayed you have omitted to set the Title on the Properties dialog box)

(Insert a 2nd header line showing the table name)
Move cursor after &(Project Title) on the first header line and Enter CR

Enter "Task List"

Click the Print Preview button

(If OK), click Print button

Module 13.
Assigning resources

This module discusses how to assign a resource to a task. Resources are the people, equipment and supplies used to complete tasks in a project. A resource is considered by MS Project to be a resource type and there can be one or many units of each type. For example, you can have 5 painters available to your project and 2 ladders, and you can also have Joe Smith and Ann Kelly. In MS Project terms you have 5 units of resource "Painters", 2 units of resource "Ladders", 1 unit of resource "Joe Smith" and 1 unit of resource "Ann Kelly".

The resource pool is the total of all resources in an MS Project project plan. The resource pool for a project can be maintained with the project plan or can be maintained in a totally separate project plan and thus shared by a number of projects. In a later module we shall show how to share a resource pool across a number of projects.

There are 2 separate steps to be undertaken when assigning a resource to a task. First the resource must be created (defined). Then the resource must be assigned to work on the task or tasks required

Note that a resource is assigned to a task. MS Project then calculates, from the duration of the task, the amount of work the resource is doing on this task. When you assign a resource MS Project assumes you need one unit of the resource to work full time for the duration of a task.

There are many different methods of creating and assigning resources. The following exercises will use some of them. We will first create a new project and display a useful combination of views for assigning resources.

Exercise 13.1.   Set up views for assigning resources

Click the File menu

Click the New command

(If the Project Info dialog box appears click the OK button)

Click the File menu

Click the Properties command

Set Title = Resource project

Click the OK button

Click the Window menu

Click the Split command (this gives a useful combination of views to use when assigning resources, the Gantt Chart on top and the Task Form on bottom)

Exercise 13.2.   Create the resources

Click the View menu

Click the Resource Sheet command

In row 1 of Resource Name column type "Anne" and hit CR

Type "Brian" and hit CR

Type "Consultant" and hit CR

Click the View menu

Click the Gantt Chart command

Exercise 13.3. Assign a single resource to a task (Method 1)

Create "Task 1" with duration = 2 w

Click on "Task 1" to select it

Click anywhere on the bottom view (This selects the Task Form as the current view)

Type "Anne" in the Resource name column

Click the OK button ("Anne" will appear at the right hand end of the task bar on the Gantt Chart. Note also that 1 unit of "Anne" is assigned to Task 1 and there is 80 hours of work to complete.)

Exercise 13.4. Assign a single resource to a task (Method 2)

Create "Task 2" with duration = 2w

Click on "Task 2" to select it

Click the Insert menu

Click the Resource Assignment command (the Resource Assignment window is displayed)

Click on "Brian" in Resource Assignment window to select him

Click the Assign button (We have now achieved exactly the same result as we did in method 1)

Click the Close button

Exercise 13.5.   Assign a single resource to a task (Method 1a)

Create "Task 3" with duration = 2w

Click on "Task 3" to select it

Click in the Resource Name column on bottom view (This selects the Task Form as the current view)

Select the Option button (The down arrow on the right hand side of the (blank) entry bar above the Gantt Chart) to display the available resource names
Select "Consultant" (Consultant appears in Resource Name column)

Type 0.8 in Units column

Click the OK button ("Consultant" has now been assigned for only 80% of her time (0.8 units) to Task 3. Note that the work she has to do in the 2 weeks is 64 hours)

Exercise 13.6.   Assign a single resource to a task (Method 2a)

Create "Task 4" with duration = 2w

Click on "Task 4" to select it

Click the Resource Assignment Icon on the toolbar (the Resource Assignment window is displayed)

Select "Consultant" in Resource Assignment window

Type 0.8 in units column

Click the Assign button (We have now achieved exactly the same result as we did in method 1a)

Having assigned the Consultant to these tasks we have the problem that, since the tasks are scheduled for the same time, the Consultant is scheduled for more hours in the day than we have specified in the workhours section of the calendar. MS Project has many ways to display overallocation. The main idea is to display a resource view. An overallocated resource will be highlighted in RED. First, let us look at the resource pool.

Exercise 13.7.   View Resource pool

Click anywhere on the top view to select it

Click the View menu

Click the Resource Sheet command (Note that the entry "Consultant" is displayed in red to indicate an overallocation)

Exercise 13.8.   View Resource Graph

Click anywhere on the top view to select it

Click the View menu

Click the Gantt Chart command

Click "Task 3" to select it

Click anywhere on the bottom view to select it

Click the View menu

Click the Resource Graph command (The resources (Consultant) assigned to "Task 3" are displayed. Note that 1.6 units of Consultant are required for the duration of this task and the overallocation is displayed in red on the histogram. Note also that the resource name "Consultant" is displayed in red, indicating an overallocation somewhere)

Click "Task 1" to select it (The peak units for "Anne" are displayed. Note that Anne is not overallocated)

Exercise 13.9.   View Resource usage in hours

Ensure bottom view (Resource Graph) is selected

Click the Format menu

Click the Details command

Click the Work option (The histogram now displays in units of work)

Select different tasks to see the work details change on the bottom view

Exercise 13.10. View Resource usage

Ensure bottom view (Resource Graph) is selected

Click the View menu

Click the Resource Usage command (This gives the hours worked per day for a resource)

If you wish you can display resource information on a full view

Exercise 13.11. View Resource usage on full view

Click the Window menu

Click the Remove split command

Click the View menu

Click the Resource graph command

Click the View menu

Click the Resource usage command

Module 14.
Resource levelling

This module discusses what we can do to eliminate the overallocation of resources.

Resource Levelling is the elimination of the overallocation of resources on tasks. The project manager can/should do this manually or MS Project can do it automatically. In the previous example Joe is overallocated because he is simultaneously working on 2 tasks full time and on a third task for half his time. Thus 2.5 units of Joe are required but we have set the max. units of Joe to 1.

A project manager should try to manually eliminate the overallocation before letting MS Project automatic level. Try one or more of the following to eliminate an overallocated resource:-

- Increase the max. units of a resource available
- Assign different resource to task
- Delay the start of a task by entering a delay value
- Change relationships between tasks
- Specify overtime
- Extend working hours

Before we start to examine the overallocations we need to have a suitable timescale displayed on the Gantt Chart. We will display months and weeks.

Exercise 14.1.   Change Gantt Chart format

Click the View menu

Click the Gantt Chart command

Click the Format menu

Click the Timescale command

Under Major Scale select units = months

Under Minor Scale select units = weeks (Note the example of the new format is displayed at the bottom of the window)

Set Count = 1

(You have numerous choices for the format of the date label)
Set Label = (your own choice)

Click OK

Now we will add the resource toolbar to the screen.

Exercise 14.2.   Adding the resource toolbar

        Click the View menu

        Click the Toolbars command

        Select Resource Management toolbar

        Click the Show button

        Click the Close button (We now have an extra toolbar displayed)

Next we will change the bottom view to a more appropriate one

Exercise 14.3.   Finding the overallocation

        (If you are displaying only a single view)
        Click the Window menu and the Split command

        Select bottom view

        Click the View menu

        Click the Resource Graph command

        Click the Format menu

        Click the Details command

        Select Work

        Select Task 1 on the Gantt Chart view

        Click the Goto Overallocation icon (On the Gantt Chart the next task with an overallocated resource is highlighted and the Gantt Chart has scrolled to display this task)

        Click the Goto Overallocation icon again. (The next task with an overallocated resource is highlighted)

We will solve the overallocation by assuming we have 2 Consultants to do the tasks.

Exercise 14.4.   Solving the overallocation

Select bottom view

Click on Information button (The resource information dialog box for resource "Consultant" is displayed)

Set Max Units = 2

Click OK (The red overallocation disappears)

Module 15.
Using the baseline

This module discusses the concept of saving a copy of the project plan at the end of the planning period.

When you have completed the planning you can take a copy of the start and end dates of each task. This is called the baseline. These can be used in future comparisons to check the progress of the project against the original plan. The Baseline is a record of the task dates, duration, work, and costs, as originally planned.

There are 3 sets of dates identified by MS Project when using the baseline:

Current   The currently scheduled start and end dates of each task. These may change with each amendment you make to the plan.

Baseline   The original start and end dates of each task as saved in the Baseline

Actual   The start and end dates of tasks that have been completed or are in progress.

Exercise 15.1.   Setting the baseline

Click anywhere on the top view to select it

Click the Tools menu

Click the Tracking command

Click the Save Baseline command

Select For Entire Project

Click the OK button (A copy of your current plan has now been saved. We can see an overview of this.)

Click the File menu

Click the Project Info command

Click the Statistics button
(This window gives a single page overview of the status of the project. The start and finish dates, the duration, the work and the cost, together with the percentage complete, are given. Note that at this point in time the current and the baseline figures are identical)

Click the Close button

We have now completed the planning stage of the project using MS Project.

Appendix 7

Learning Timeline 6.0

Introduction

The purpose of this Appendix is to identify and present the minimum functionality of Timeline required by a Project Manager when running a project. To demonstrate this we will use Timeline to plan and schedule an exercise project.

The Appendix is laid out as a sequence of exercises which take the reader through the standard steps required during the planning and execution of a project:

- Creating tasks
- Editing and moving tasks in the plan
- Setting task durations
- Setting dependencies between tasks
- Formatting and presenting the plan
- Assigning resources to tasks
- Saving the baseline
- Updating project status
- Tracking and reporting progress against plan

The exercises which follow assume that you have a basic understanding of how to use the MS Windows operating system.

The exercises are identified with a number and a title line and have a shaded background. The subsequent lines are indented and are the instructions to be followed by the reader. Lines contained within brackets are comment lines. The terminology used follows standard MS Windows practice. For example, the phrase 'Click the XXX menu' means 'Point the cursor at the XXX item on the menu line and press the mouse button'.

Module 1.
Getting started with Timeline

In this module we will learn how to start the Timeline application, and look at the main functions available to the user.

Timeline uses the term database rather than the term file to describe the area on disk where it maintains the users project information. In the first exercise we will create a new database in which to maintain our project information. When you run Timeline for the second and subsequent times, you will normally wish to open an existing database rather than to create a new one.

Exercise 1.1.   Starting Timeline

                       Double click the Time Line 6 program icon
                       (After a standard Install, this is found in the Time Line 6
                       program group)

                       Click the Cancel button on the Open Database dialog
                       screen

                       Click the File menu

                       Click the New Database command

The initial window in Timeline is the OverView window. The OverView window contains 6 categories of information. The first 3 categories refer to project specific information while the second 3 categories refer to Timeline specific information. The vertical scroll bar on the right hand side of the window allows you to scroll through the categories. As we shall see later, a plus sign (+) to the right of the category icon indicates that there are further levels of information available.

Projects   This category shows the projects in the current
                       database, together with their associated views. In a
                       new database, an empty project, called Untitled1, is
                       automatically created.

Calendars   This contains the master calendar for the database,
                       resource calendars for any resources created and any
                       other calendars defined.

Resource Views   This contains the standard views to display resource
                       information.

Layouts	This category contains all the predefined view formats supported by Timeline. We will examine these in more detail in Module 9.
Conditions	This category contains pre-defined filters and highlights.
Custom Columns	This category holds the column definitions that you set up to display data in your own terminology or with your own algorithms.

The standard Timeline screen contains a number of different areas:

Title bar	Called Time Line, this is the standard Windows title bar, with the control menu bar on the left and the minimise and maximise icons on the right.
Menu line	This is a standard Windows application menu. It allows access to all the underlying functionality of Timeline.
Toolbar	This is simply a shorthand way of accessing frequently used menu options. The toolbar can be displayed in this position or as a floating toolbar on the screen. A feature, Tool Tips, is available which indicates the function of each button. To activate this just pause the cursor on a button and the description is displayed on the status bar at the bottom of the screen.
Views	Views are a most powerful feature of Timeline. They provide many different ways of looking at the one underlying database in Timeline. Each view has a name and view can be defined by the user.
	The Gantt chart view is the default view visible on start-up. This default can be changed if required.
Status bar	This line is displayed on the bottom of the screen.

You can control whether or not you wish the Toolbar and the Status bar to be displayed. You do this using the Tools or the Options Menus. We will not cover how this is done in this Appendix.

Module 2.
Saving your project

In this module you learn how to save versions of your project to the database on disk.

You should save your work to disk at frequent intervals during any updating. You can do this using either the command in the File menu or the equivalent icon.

Project databases should be saved in directories created specifically for that purpose, NOT in the TL6 directory. If you have an existing directory into which you wish to save your project data, ignore Exercise 2.1. and continue with Exercise 2.2. If you have not yet created a directory for your project data continue with Exercise 2.1.

Exercise 2.1.   Create directory to save files

Click on the control menu (the bar in the very top-left corner of the screen

Click on the Switch To option

Select Program Manager by clicking on the text and then click on the Switch To button

When the Program manager screen appears, double click on the icon for Main

When the Main window appears, double click on the File Manager icon

When the File Manager window appears, click on the File menu

Click on the Create Directory command and create a directory for your project data

Return to Timeline by using the control menu again

Exercise 2.2.   Save using File menu

Click on the File menu

Click on the Save Database command. If this is the first time you have saved this project, the Save as dialog box appears.

In the directory area of the box, double click on the directory required (the directory you created in Exercise 2.1). This will cause the filenames of any databases to be displayed.

In the database name box, type the name you want to give to your database. (This is a filename and must therefore be a maximum of 8 characters long. You do not have to type the extension .TDB. Timeline will add this itself).

Click on OK button (or use the Carriage Return (CR) key)

A shorter way of saving your project is to use the Save icon.

Exercise 2.3.   Save using the Save icon

Point the cursor at the Save Current Database icon and click

Module 3.
Creating tasks

This module shows how to create tasks in a project.

When setting up a project we normally specify a project start date. This is usually the only date we specify and we let Timeline calculate the rest. We then identify each task in the project and how long it will take to complete. We then identify any relationships or dependencies between tasks.

The first step we do is to create a project in the database.

Exercise 3.1.   Create a new project

Click on the File menu

Click on the New Project command

Enter 'Testing' as project name

Click on the OK button to accept the input. (A window displaying the standard Gantt chart appears)

The next thing we wish to do is to set up some general information about the project. We use the project information dialog box to do this. Within the dialog box we use the TAB key to move from field to field. Hold down SHIFT and press TAB to move backwards. Alternatively, use the mouse to click on the field you wish to enter.

Exercise 3.2.   Set up initial project information

Click on the Options menu

Click on the Project Information command. (The Project Information dialog box appears)

Select the Manager field and enter your name

Select the Project Start Date field and enter the date on which you think the project will start (Don't worry about the accuracy of this date. You can easily change it later)

Click on the OK button to accept the input.

Note that we enter only the start date. Timeline calculates the end date.

At this stage we also wish to set the recalculation option to manual. This means that Timeline will NOT automatically recalculate schedule dates every time we make a change in the project. We will learn later in the document how to force Timeline to recalculate the schedule.

Exercise 3.3.   Set the Recalculate option to manual

Click the Options menu

Click the Calculations Settings command

Ensure the Do Automatic Recalculation checkbox is unchecked

Click the OK button

There are many ways in Timeline to create task details but we will just use the Gantt chart. The Gantt chart consists of 2 parts, the spreadsheet on the left and the timing information on the right. We will use the spreadsheet part to enter the task information and Timeline will calculate and display the timing information on the right.

Exercise 3.4.   Enter the task names using Gantt chart

Click on the Window menu

Click on the View entitled Testing-Standard-Gantt
(The window changes to a Gantt Chart)

If not already selected, use the mouse, or use the tab or arrow keys to select the task name cell of row 1

Type "Task A" and hit CR

Note that the next row is selected

Type "Task B' and hit CR

Type 'Task C' and hit CR

The effort of each of these tasks is the default value of 5 days. We will change these values later.

Module 4.
Correcting errors

Timeline has a powerful undo feature if you make a mistake and wish to backtrack on something you have just done. In the last exercise we didn't really mean to enter task C, so we shall delete it.

Exercise 4.1.   Delete a task

Click anywhere on the row for Task C

Click the Edit menu

Click the Delete Task command. (Note that this deletes the whole task entry)

(We didn't mean to do that so we can undo what we have just done)

Click the Edit menu

Click the Undo Task Delete command

Exercise 4.2.   Delete a task using the keyboard

Click anywhere on the row for Task C

Press the Delete key on the keyboard. (Note that this also deletes the complete task entry)

(We didn't mean to do that so we can undo what we have just done)

Click the Edit menu

Click the Undo Task Delete command

Module 5.
Moving tasks

Timeline does not worry about the order of the tasks in the list but sometimes we want to move tasks to make the order more meaningful for ourselves. There are 2 main ways of doing this; you can use whichever is most comfortable for you.

Exercise 5.1.   Move a task

Select task "Task A" by pointing anywhere on the row and clicking

Click the Edit menu

Click the Cut command (Task A disappears from the list)

Select the row below "Task C" by pointing at it and clicking

Click the Edit menu

Click the Paste command (Task A reappears)

Up until this point in the exercises the cursor we have been using was the Select Tool. We will now change the cursor to the Move Tool.

Exercise 5.2.   Move "Task A" back to its original position

Click the Tools menu

Click the Move Tool command

Select task "Task A" by pointing anywhere on the row and clicking

Point to the 'Task A' row and the cursor changes shape to a small square with 4 arrows on it

Drag the row back to the top line. (Task "A" is now back in its original position)

Exercise 5.3.   Move "Task A" again

Point to the Activate Move Tool icon on the toolbar and click

Point to the 'Task A' row and the cursor changes shape to a small square with 4 arrows on it

Drag the Task "A" row to another position

Point to the Activate Select Tool icon on the toolbar and click

Module 6.
Edit the contents of a cell

If we have made an error in an entry we have previously typed, we do not need to totally retype the entry. We can simply retype the section of the entry we need.

Exercise 6.1.   Edit the task name "Task C"

Select the task name field "Task C" by clicking on it

Point between "Task" and "C" and click

Insert the word "number"

Click anywhere on the window or hit CR (the task name is now "Task number C")

Module 7.
Entering task effort

This module introduces the various ways of specifying effort for a task.

Effort   is the amount of work needed to complete a task. A task's effort can be expressed in seconds (s) minutes (m), hours (h), days (d), weeks (w), months (m) or years (y) . If no letter is specified, d is assumed.

Duration   is the amount of time needed to complete a task. Non-working periods, for example weekends or public holidays, are not normally included in a task's duration. If one resource is working full time on a task, the values for duration and effort are equal.

The spreadsheet on the standard Gantt chart has a column for effort and a column for duration. These columns are normally hidden behind the timesheet part of the Gantt view. To display them, point the cursor at the thick vertical line dividing the spreadsheet from the timescale and drag to the right.

Exercise 7.1.   Enter the effort for the current tasks

Select Effort field for "Task A" by clicking on it

Enter 4w and hit CR (note the length of the Gantt bar changing)

Enter 3w in effort field for "Task B"

Enter 2w in effort field for "Task number C"

The spreadsheet is an efficient method of displaying at the same time information concerning a number of tasks. Another method of displaying information is to use a form. A form only displays information about one task at a time.

In Timeline, forms are called info boxes and the Task Info Box is a window which allows us to view and edit more advanced information of a task. This window can be left on the screen if preferred.

Exercise 7.2.   Access the Task Info Box (using 2 different methods)

Method 1

Click the Tools menu

Click the Task Info Box command (A window displaying the Task Info Box appears)

When you want to close the window double click the control menu bar

Method 2

Click on Show Task Info Box icon on Toolbar

When you want to close the dialog box double-click the Control menu bar

A milestone is an important checkpoint in the schedule. The project manager can use milestones to highlight when certain tasks or events should either start or complete. Milestones are most useful for providing clear reports to management on important dates in the project. You specify a milestone by setting the task duration to zero. However, you have another step to take before you can enter a duration for a task.

Timeline recognises 2 types of task, an effort driven task and a fixed duration task.

Effort Driven   The duration of this task varies according to the number of resources assigned to it. For example, painting the walls of a house will have a shorter duration if 2 painters are doing it rather than just 1.

Fixed Duration   The duration of this task is not effected by the number of resources assigned to it. An example would be a week's training course, the duration of which does not change regardless of the number of attendees.

Exercise 7.3.   Insert a milestone task

Select the top task by clicking on it

Click the Edit menu

Click the Insert Task command (note that you can achieve the same result by hitting the Ins key on the keyboard)

Enter "Start of Project" as the task name

Move this task to the top of the list

Click the Show Task Info Box Icon

Select 'Start of Project' by clicking on the row

Click the Fixed Duration option button on the Task Info Dialog Box. (Note that the Effort field becomes greyed and the duration field becomes available).

Enter 0 in duration field and hit CR

Click on the Gantt chart to select it. (Note that the bar on the Gantt chart changes to a diamond symbol to indicate a milestone).

Module 8.
Using HELP

This module introduces the various HELP features available in Timeline.

Timeline uses a type of Help known as Hypertext. It has an extremely large volume of on-line reference information which can be accessed in a variety of ways depending on your need. The Help is displayed in a separate window and will usually contain some text underlined in green. These words or phrases are indices into further Help text. You click on these to display the further Help text.

The quickest method of getting Help is to use the context sensitive Help. At any point in the application you can hit the F1 function key and context sensitive help information will be displayed.

Exercise 8.1.   Use the F1 key to display Help on creating (inserting) tasks

Click the Edit menu

Press the F1 function key
(the Timeline Help window will appear displaying information

on the Undo command. This command is the first in the list on
the Edit menu and is selected by default when you enter the
menu)

Click the See Also button

Click on the green underlined text "The Edit Menu"
(a further window is displayed giving details of all the
commands on this menu. Note that there is frequently a
vertical scroll bar on the right hand side of the window to
allow you to look at text past the bottom of the window.)

(When you have finished reading about the Insert <item type>
command)
Click either the minimise icon on the top right corner of the
Help window or click the File menu at the top of the window,
and click the Exit command

A common way into the Help system if you know the subject on which you
wish to get Help is to use the Help command on the menu and to use the
Contents command.

Exercise 8.2.   Display Help on "Creating task durations"

Click the Help menu

Click the Contents command

Click on 'Working with Tasks, Dependencies...'

Click on 'Setting Task Duration and Dates'

Click on 'Setting Duration for a Fixed-Duration Task'

It is easy to progress through the Help system from topic to topic. If you
click on an underlined topic, help information on that topic is displayed.

Exercise 8.3.   Investigate durations further

Point at "duration" and click

Point at 'elapsed time' and click

Point at 'time units' and click

The Help system keeps a record of where you have looked.

Exercise 8.4.   Navigate the Help system

Point at the Back button and click

Point at the History button and click

The Help system is extremely large and you may sometimes find it difficult to find the exact topic you are looking for. There is a search feature available in Help to assist with this problem. Assume, for example, that you want to find out about how to save a database.

Exercise 8.5.   Find out how to save a database

(If you are not already in the Help window)
Click the Help menu and click the Search for command

On the Help window, click the Search button

Type "save" (and note the context sensitive topics appear, at this stage 'Saving' is selected)

Click the Show Topics button (at this stage 'Save As' is selected)

Click the Go To button

Help is managed by a separate application, Timeline Help, and the information is displayed in a separate window. You can therefore make it larger or smaller as you wish or you can arrange it tiled or cascaded with other windows. You may sometimes find it useful to display the Help window on the screen at the same time as the project window.

Exercise 8.6.   Display Help window alongside Timeline

Click the Control menu button (in top left hand corner of active window)

Click the Switch To command

Click the Tile button (All active windows are displayed on the screen together)

> Minimise unwanted programs (everything other that Timeline and Timeline Help) by clicking on the Minimise icon on the top right corner of the window.

The index is one method of navigating the Help system. An alternative method of navigating is by using How To. This is a set of step-by-step procedures that you can follow to carry out some common operations in Timeline. They are most useful when the Help window is tiled with Timeline..

Exercise 8.7.   Use How To learn how to create a new project

Click the Help menu

Click the How To command

Click on 'Working with Projects and Sub-projects'

Click on 'Creating a New Project'

Timeline provides a nicely structured tutorial that covers the basics of using Timeline. This is accessed from the Tutorial command in the Help menu.

A final point to note about Help. To get further information concerning a warning or error message, press the F1 key while the message is displayed.

Module 9.
Using views

This module discusses how views are used by Timeline to provide the power and flexibility. It also reviews the use of tables and forms.

Views are a most powerful feature of Timeline. The View is the means of entering, changing and displaying the contents of the underlying database in Timeline. By using a variety of Views, you can look at the same project information in different ways as you organise your project. There are 6 view types in Timeline.

OverView   This gives a view of the database and the projects. The other 5 views refer to the project.

Gantt chart   The Gantt view is the primary view in Timeline, and consists of 3 sections.

➤ The spreadsheet pane is the left hand side of the screen and displays information in tabular format.

➤ The timescale pane is the right hand side of the screen and graphically displays information about the start and end dates of tasks.

➤ The graph pane is at the bottom of the screen and displays information concerning resources assigned to the tasks.

PERT	The PERT view graphically displays dependency information
Timescaled PERT	This is really a Gantt view with additional lines showing dependency detail
Crosstab	This is essentially a Gantt chart but showing resource rather than task information in the timescale pane.
Resource	The resource view displays information about resources in a spreadsheet format.

You use the View menu to change from one view to another.

Exercise 9.1.   Change to a different view

Click the View menu
Click the New Time-Scaled PERT View command

Click the View menu
Click the New PERT View command

Click the View menu
Click the New Crosstab View command

Click the Window Menu
Click the Testing - Standard Gantt view

Spreadsheets are used in views to display information on either tasks or resources. The rows are either task or resource names and the columns are fields of information about the task or resource. We will return to spreadsheets in a later exercise.

Forms are also used in views to display information, in a field by field format, on a single task or resource. There are 4 main forms, the 4 Info boxes.

An important concept for the Project Manager to be aware of is the Critical Path of the project. The Critical Path is the sequence of tasks linked by dependencies that determines the shortest possible duration of the project. These tasks are calculated and identified by the Critical Path Method algorithm, which is the scheduling algorithm used by Timeline. If any one of this sequence of tasks is delayed, then the finish date of the project is delayed. The Project Manager must therefore monitor these tasks even more carefully than any of the other tasks in the project. Timeline provides the functionality to highlight this sequence of tasks.

Exercise 9.2.   Change Gantt chart to highlight Critical Path

        Click on the Options Menu

        Click on the Highlights command

        Click on the Option button for Condition 1 (the down pointing arrow to the right of the field)

        Select Critical Task condition

        Click the OK button.
        (The tasks on the Critical Path are highlighted in red)

Module 10.
Setting the recalculation preferences

This module shows how to recalculate the project either manually or automatically.

    Before we continue further with our project planning we will examine the way Timeline recalculates the project schedule. Whenever we change any data in the project, (for example, changing the duration of a task) the project dates should be recalculated. We can manually do this at any time or we can request that Timeline does it automatically whenever we change data.

Exercise 10.1.   Recalculate the schedule using the menu

        Click the Options menu

        Click the Calculations Settings command

Ensure the Do Automatic Recalculation checkbox is unchecked

Click the OK button

Click the Options menu. (Note that there is a recalculate message on the status line)

Click the Recalculate Now command. (Note that the message has disappeared)

Exercise 10.2.   Recalculate the schedule using the function key

Press the F9 key

For the remainder of the exercises we will set the recalculation option to automatic so that we will immediately see any change to the project schedule.

Exercise 10.3.   Set Calculation to automatic

Click the Options menu

Click the Calculations Settings command

Check the Do Automatic Recalculation checkbox

Click the OK button

(If the Co-Pilot dialog box appears, leave automatic recalculation on and click the OK button)

Module 11.
Setting task dependencies

This module shows how to set task dependencies using a number of different methods. We will also practise at using different views.

The most common relationship between tasks is when one task cannot start until another task finishes. This is known as a Finish-Start (FS) relationship or dependency. An obvious example of this type of relationship is during the building of a house when the foundations must be dug before the concrete can be poured, and the concrete must harden before the walls can be built. Timeline assumes we want this type of relationship unless we tell it otherwise.

Exercise 11.1.   Set dependency using Gantt view and menu

(Ensure you are using the Select Tool)
Use the cursor to select Tasks A, B and C

Click the Task menu

Click the Set Dependencies command (Timeline automatically changes the start date of Task B to start when Task A is finished and changes the start date of Task C to start when Task B has finished. This is reflected on the Gantt chart.)

Exercise 11.2.   Unset dependency using Gantt view and menu

Use the cursor to select Tasks A, B and C

Click the Task menu

Click the Remove Dependencies command

Click the OK button if the Remove Dependencies dialog box appears

Exercise 11.3.   Set dependency using the function keys

Use the cursor to select Tasks A, B, C

Press the F3 function key on the keyboard

Redo Exercise 11.2 to remove the dependencies.

Exercise 11.4.   Set dependency using the Connect Tool

Click the Tools menu

Click the Connect Tool command

Select Task A

Point to the 'Task A' task (the cursor shape changes to a chain link shape)
(You can point to either the task row on the Spreadsheet or to the task bar on the Timescale)

Hold down the mouse button and drag to 'Task C'

Release mouse

Note on selecting multiple items (e.g. tasks) in a windows environment.

If items are beside one another, point to first item, hold down mouse button and drag to last, or click on first item, point to last item, hold down shift key and click.

If items are separated, click on first item, point to next item, hold down CTRL key and click.

Module 12.
Using calendars

This module discusses how calendars are used by Timeline.

Calendars are used by the scheduler to map task and project durations onto an actual set of dates. The calendar allows *public holidays, company holidays, weekends,* and *working hours* to be accounted for by the scheduler.

Timeline provides a Master Calendar which can then be amended as required by the user.

Timeline also provides resource calendars. There can be one per resource type and this is very useful for scheduling holidays or for scheduling resource types with different working hours.

Exercise 12.1.   Update Master calendar to include public holidays

Click on Options Menu

Click on Holidays command

Select Country = United Kingdom

Click on Good Friday to deselect it

Click the OK button

Click the Window menu

Click the OverView view

Click on Calendars

Double click on Master Calendar

Click on scroll arrow to display May

Select May 1st by clicking on the square.

Click the Set Exception button

Click the Off All Day box

Click the OK button

Repeat for the remaining public holidays

Click the OK button

The workhours are used by the scheduler to understand how many hours of work are available in each day to complete the amount of work which has been calculated for each task. For this project we will set workhours for all Thursdays finishing at 18:00 and workhours for all Fridays finishing at 16:00.

Exercise 12.2.   Create a Project calendar and amend it

Click the Options menu

Click the Master Calendar command

Click the Edit Shift Button.

Click on Thu and change finishing hours to 18:00

Click on Fri and change finishing hours to 16:00

Click the OK button

Click the OK button

Module 13.
Outlining tasks

This module introduces the concept of outlining of tasks.

For the purpose of this exercise we need some further tasks in our project plan.

Exercise 13.1.   Enter further tasks

Enter tasks D through K onto the plan

Set effort of each to 1 week

Set a standard Finish-Start dependency between each one (A to K)

We have reached the stage in our planning when we need to examine the overall plan and report to our manager on it. We currently have just a list of tasks so the first step is to organise these a little better.

We will identify 3 major sections in our project:

➤ Initial section, Tasks A to D
➤ Middle section, Tasks E to G
➤ Final section Tasks H to K

We will insert these as outline tasks in our project.

Exercise 13.2.   Insert summary tasks

Select "Task A" (by clicking on the task name field)

Click the Edit menu

Click the Insert Task command

Type "Initial section" (ensure this task is in front of Task A)

Select "Task A"

Click the Outline menu

Click the Indent command (For "Initial section" note the change in duration and the change in bar format)

Select tasks B, C, D

Click the Outline menu

Click the indent command

Repeat for "Middle section" before "Task E"

Repeat for "Final section", before "Task H"

Exercise 13.3.   Hide and show subtasks

Click the Outline Menu

Click the Collapse All command (only the 3 summary task bars are now displayed)

Select 'Initial section' task

Click the Outline Menu

Click the Hoist command (This displays only the subtasks of the selected summary task)

(To show all,) click the Outline menu

Click Dehoist All

Module 14.
Printing views

At this point in our project planning we want to print the plan in order for others to be able to examine it. We will print this information in 2 different ways. First, we will print the Gantt chart and second, we will print a list of the tasks with their start and finish dates.

Timeline provides 2 printing features, print views and print reports. We will use the print views in this section. As the name implies, this prints the view currently displayed on the screen.

For each type of view and report we can define the header, footer, margins, fonts, colours, etc. We will use the defaults initially.

The preview functionality allows us to view on the screen the appearance of the report prior to us sending it to the printer. Note that you should ALWAYS preview before you print in order to check how many pages you will have. Note also that the Print functionality allows you to print information between certain dates and to print a certain layout of pages.

Exercise 14.1.   Print Gantt chart view

Click the File menu

Click the Print command

Click the Preview button

(We want the Gantt chart to print in Landscape mode)
Click the Page Setup button

In the Page Orientation group click the Landscape option button

Click the OK button. (Note that the cursor changes to a magnifying glass when you move it over the print area).

Click the mouse to examine the output in more detail

Click on the arrow icons to show other pages if necessary

(If ready to print) Click the Print button, else click the Cancel button

Before we print the table of dates we need to amend the layout. We will create a new spreadsheet to suit our own requirements. The information we need is similar to that in the standard spreadsheet but we don't need the resource details.

Exercise 14.2.   Create new table

Click the View menu

Click the Format Gantt Layout command

Click the New button, change name to Task List and click the

OK button

Select Resources in the Column Name column and click
Delete button

Select Total Cost, click Delete button

Select Task Name

Click the Insert button to insert another column

Select top Task Name

Click Option button (on the right hand side of the cell to
display the allowable field entries)

Select WBS (A new field, WBS, is inserted before the Name
field)

Click on Time Scale tab

Unset Show Time Scale checkbox

Click the OK button

Now that we have created our new table, Task List, we need to
automatically display the WBS codes.

Exercise 14.3.   Display WBS codes

Click the Tools menu

Click the WBS Manager command

Click Number Blank Tasks

Click All Tasks

Click the OK Button

Exercise 14.4.   Print new table

Click File menu

Click Page Setup

Click Edit button in Title and Legends group box

Click in Header Text box, Press F1 Key

Click the 'expansion symbols' text. (These are symbols we can insert in the print output and Timeline will automatically fill in the values at print time)

Insert &m on second header line (to display the manager name on the print output)

Click OK button

Click the 'Fonts & Colors' button.

Font = Times New Roman, Size = 14, Bold,

Click the OK button

Click the OK button

Click the File menu

Click the Print Preview command

If OK, click the Print button

Module 15.
Assigning resources

This module discusses how to assign a resource to a task.

Resources are the people, equipment and supplies used to complete tasks in a project. A resource is considered by Timeline to be one of four cost types and there can be one or many units of each type. The 4 cost types are:

Fixed Cost   This is a one-time expense applied to a task

Time Cost	This is an expense assigned for the length of a task. For example, the cost of renting equipment or the cost of an external contractor
Unit Cost	This is an expense based on quantity and is used to cost materials
Resource	This is similar to Time Cost but has the additional concept of limited availability. This is normally used for the people on the project.

For example, you can have 5 painters available to your project as time costs and 2 ladders as fixed costs, and you can also have Joe Smith and Ann Kelly as resources.

The resource pool is the total of all resources in a Timeline database. The resource pool for a project can thus shared by a number of projects in the one database.

There are 2 separate steps to be undertaken when assigning a resource to a task:

1. The resource must be created (defined)
2. The resource must be assigned to work on the task or tasks required

Note that a resource is assigned to a task. Timeline then calculates, from the duration of the task, the amount of work the resource is doing on this task and the associated cost. When you first assign a resource Timeline assumes you need one unit of the resource to work full time for the duration of a task. You can subsequently change this if necessary.

There are many different methods of creating and assigning resources. The following exercises will use some of them. In your own projects you need only use one method of assigning resources.

Exercise 15.1.   Create a single resource

Click the Window menu

Click OverView view

Double click the view Standard Resource

Set the following values

Name = JCB, press the TAB key
Resource type = resource
Cost = 200/d

Press CR

Exercise 15.2.   Assign a single resource to a task (Method 1)

Click the File menu

Click the New Project command
 Name = Resource Test

Create Task1, 2 weeks' effort

Click the Task menu

Click the Assign Resources command

Select JCB

Click the OK button

Exercise 15.3.   Assign a single resource to a task (Method 2)

Create Task2, 2 weeks' effort

Select Task2,

Click the Tools menu

Click the Assignment Info Box command

Click the Add button

Select JCB, click the OK button
(The Edit Resource Assignment box appears which allows you
to further edit the assignment)

Set Requested Quantity = 0.5

Click the OK button

Note that the JCB is only assigned for 50% of its time to this task. The effort is still 2 weeks, therefore the duration is now 4 weeks.

Exercise 15.4.   Assign a single resource to a task (Method 3)

Create Task3, 2 weeks' effort

Click the Window menu

Click the Tile command

Close all windows except the Gantt view and the Resource view

Click the Tools menu

Click the Connect Tool

Point to JCB in the Standard Resource spreadsheet and drag to Resource column of Task3 on the Gantt spreadsheet

Having assigned the JCB to these 3 tasks we have the problem that, since the tasks are scheduled for the same time, the JCB is scheduled for more hours in the day than we have specified in the workhours section of the calendar. Timeline has many ways to display overallocation. The main idea is to display a histogram.

Exercise 15.5.   View Resource usage

Click on the Gantt view to select it

Press F6 to display the Format Gantt dialog box

Click the Edit button

Click on the Graphs tab

Click the Graphs checkbox in Show group

Click the Insert button

On the second line select Resource Name = JCB

On the second line select Graph Type = Histogram

Click the OK button

Maximise the Gantt view

(Recalculate if necessary)

The graphs show both cost and effort. The dashed line on the histogram shows the JCB availability (1 unit). However the dark shading indicates the JCB effort on the project (2.5 units). The JCB is overallocated by 1.5 units.

The Resource Calendar is another level of sophistication in scheduling. For each resource type we can specify a different set of working days and/or hours. Timeline will then take these into account when scheduling tasks.

Exercise 15.6.   Resource Calendar

Click the Window menu

Click the Resource window

Click the Resource menu

Click the Calendar for JCB

Select 2 days next week

Click the Set Exception button

Click the Off All Day checkbox

Click the OK button

Click the OK button

Display the Gantt view and note change of end dates

Module 16.
Resource levelling

This module discusses what we can do to eliminate the overallocation of resources.

Resource Levelling is the elimination of the overallocation of resources on tasks by moving the start and end dates of tasks. The Project Manager can/should do this manually or Timeline can do it automatically. In the previous example the JCB is overallocated because it is simultaneously working on 2 tasks full time and on a third task for half the time. Thus 2.5 units of the JCB are required but we have set the maximum availability of the JCB to 1.

A project manager should try to eliminate manually the overallocation before letting Timeline automatic level. Try one or more of the following to eliminate an overallocated resource:

> Increase the maximum units of a resource available
> Assign different resource to task
> Delay the start of a task by entering a delay value
> Change relationships between tasks
> Specify overtime
> Extend working hours

Before we start to examine the overallocations we need to have a suitable format displayed on the Gantt chart. We will display weeks.

Exercise 16.1.   Change Gantt chart format to show weeks and graphs
                  .
                  Click the Window menu

                  Click the Standard Gantt view

                  Click the View menu

                  Click the Format Gantt command

                  Click the Edit button

                  Click the Timescale tab

                  Set Time Units = Weeks

                  Click the Graphs tab

Select all checkboxes

Click the OK button

Exercise 16.2.   Solving the overallocation (1)

Point the cursor at the bar for Task 3

Drag the bar to the right until the start is after the end of Task 1

(If Co-Pilot appears, click the OK button)

The JCB is now assigned for 1.5 units over the project.

Exercise 16.3.   Solving the overallocation (2)

Select Task 3

Click the Window menu

Click the Standard-Resource View

Set Availability of JCB = 2

Click the Window menu

Click the Standard Gantt view

We can let Timeline solve the overallocation itself:

Exercise 16.4.   Solving the overallocation (3)

Click the Options menu

Click Calculations settings command

Set :
   Quick Levelling
   No Automatic recalculation

Create 4 tasks, A, B, C, D, 5 days' effort each

Assign Joe to each task

Click the View menu

Click the Format Gantt command

Click the Edit button

Click the graph tab

Click the Insert button

Set Resource Name = Joe
Set Graph Type = Histogram

Click the OK button

Press F9 function key to recalculate and level

Module 17.
Using the baseline

This module discusses the concept of saving a copy of the project plan at the end of the planning period.

When you have completed the planning you can take a copy of the start and end dates of each task. This is called the baseline. These can be used in future comparisons to check the progress of the project against the original plan. The Baseline is a record of the task dates, duration, work, and costs, as originally planned.

There are 3 sets of dates identified by Timeline when using the baseline:

Current   The currently scheduled start and end dates of each task. These may change with each amendment you make to the plan.

Baseline The original start and end dates of each task as saved in the Baseline

Actual   The start and end dates of tasks that have been completed or are in progress.

Exercise 17.1.   Setting the baseline

Click the Options menu

Click the Project Information command

Project Start Date = 1/2/96

Click the OK button

Click the Task menu

Click the Set Baseline command

Click the All Tasks option button

Click the OK button. (A copy of your current plan has now been saved. We can see an overview of this.)

Click the Options menu

Click the Project Information command

(This window gives a single page overview of the status of the project. The number of tasks, the start and finish dates, the duration, the work and the cost are given. Note that at this point in time the current and the baseline figures are identical)

We have now completed the planning stage of the project using Timeline.

Module 18.
Updating to reflect actual progress

This module discusses how to track the project using task status.
   There are 2 approaches to monitoring project status as work progresses:

1. Update on a task by task basis using task status
2. Update on a resource by resource basis using resource work

In Timeline either method may be used. Regardless of which method is used a basic project administration system is required in order to gather the data needed.

Status information you will need at each update time includes:

> ➤ the dates each task actually started or finished
> ➤ how long the task took
> ➤ how much work remains to be completed at the time of your status check

You can update all dates manually or let Timeline automatically update for you.

Exercise 18.1.   Update using tables (assume we are 2 weeks into the project)

Click the Window menu

Click the Standard Gantt view

Click the Options menu

Click the Preferences command

Set Detailed Tracking = No

Click the OK button

Click the Options menu

Click the Calculation Settings command

Set As Of Date = 15/2/96

Click the OK button

Click the View menu

Click the Format command

Click the option button to the right of Layout Name field

Layout name = Updating

Click the OK button

Exercise 18.2.   Update and view the progress

Set % Complete for Task 1 = 100

Set % Complete for Task 2 = 50

Set % Complete for Task A = 100

Set % Complete for Task B = 50

Press the F9 function key to recalculate

Exercise 18.3.   Update using percentage complete (assume we are 3 weeks into the project)

Click the Options menu

Click the Calculation Settings command

Set As-Of-Date = 22/2/96

Click the OK Button

Click the Window menu

Click the Standard Gantt view

Select the tasks you want to update (Task2,3,B,C) by clicking on the left arrow of each row

Click the Task menu

Click the Update % Complete command

Set Calculate Based on As-of-Date option

Click the OK button

Bibliography

1. Roald Amundsen, *The South Pole*, John Murray, 1912
2. Dr. Robert Ballard, *The Discovery of the Titanic*, Hodder and Stoughton, 1987
3. Barry Boehm, *Software Engineering Economics*, Prentice Hall, 1981
4. John Boorman, *Money Into Light*, Faber and Faber 1985
5. Ken Bradley, *PRINCE: A Practical Handbook*, Butterworth-Heinemann 1993
6. F.P. Brooks, *No Silver Bullet: Essence and Accidents in Software Engineering*, IEEE Computer, April 1987.
7. F.P. Brooks, *The Mythical Man-Month*, Addison-Wesley, 1975
8. Phillip Bruce and Sam M. Peterson, *The Software Development Project*, Wiley-Interscience, 1982
9. Bruce Catton, *Pictorial History of the Civil War*, American Heritage Publishing Co., 1960
10. Bruce Catton, *The Coming Fury*, Washington Square Press, 1961
11. Bruce Catton, *Terrible Swift Sword*, Washington Square Press, 1963
12. Bruce Catton, *Never Call Retreat*, Washington Square Press, 1965
13. Apsley Cherry-Garrard, *The Worst Journey in the World*, Penguin Books, 1983
14. Clausewitz, *On War*, Penguin Classics, 1984
15. Joseph Conrad, Recollections on the loss of the Titanic, *New English Review*, May 1912
16. Phillip Crosby, *Quality is Free*, McGraw-Hill, 1979
17. Michael Davie, *The Titanic*, The Bodley Head, 1986
18. Tom DeMarco, *Structured Analysis and Systems Specification*, Prentice Hall, 1978
19. Tom DeMarco, *Controlling Software Projects*, Yourdon Press, 1982

20. Tom DeMarco and Timothy Lister, *PeopleWare*, Dorset House Publishing, 1987
21. Jake Eberts and Terry Ilott, *My Indecision is Final*, Faber and Faber 1990
22. Roger Fisher and William Ury, *Getting to Yes*, Hutchinson Business, 1981
23. James N. Frey, *How to Write a Damn Good Novel*, St. Martin's Press, 1987
24. Paul Fussell, *The Great War and Modern Memory,* Oxford University Press, 1975
25. John Giles, *The Somme Then And Now*, Bailey Brothers and Swinfen, 1977
26. Gerald Gliddon, *When the Barrage Lifts*, Gliddon Books, 1987
27. Colonel Archibald Gracie, *Titanic*, The Blackstaff Press, 1991
28. Trevor Griffiths, *Judgement Over the Dead*, Verso, 1986
29. Henry Hampton and Steve Frayer, *Voices of Freedom*, Bantam, 1990
30. Roland Huntford, *Scott and Amundsen*, Wiedenfeld and Nicholson, 1993
31. Roland Huntford, *Shackleton*, Hodder and Stoughton, 1985
32. Roland Huntford, *The Last Place on Earth*, Pan Books, 1985
33. Roland Huntford, *The Amundsen Photographs*, Hodder and Stoughton, 1987
34. International Organisation for Standardisation, *ISO9001 - Quality Systems - Model for Quality Assurance in Design, Development, Production, Installation and Servicing*, First Edition, 1987
35. Sue Limb and Patrick Cordingley, *Captain Oates - Soldier and Explorer*, Batsford, 1982
36. Walter Lord, *A Night To Remember*, Penguin Books, 1981
37. John Macdonald, *Great Battlefields of the World*, Michael Joseph, 1984
38. Lyn Macdonald, *They Called It Passchendaele*, Macmillan, 1978
39. Lyn Macdonald, *Somme*, Michael Joseph, 1983
40. Larry McMurtry, *Lonesome Dove*, Pan Books, 1990
41. Geoffrey Marcus, *The Maiden Voyage*, Allen and Unwin, 1969
42. Roger Mear and Robert Swan, *In The Footsteps of Scott*, Jonathan Cape, 1987
43. Martin Middlebrook, *The First Day on the Somme*, Allen Lane, 1971
44. A.A. Milne, *The House at Pooh Corner*, Methuen, 1923
45. Philip Orr, *The Road to the Somme*, The Blackstaff Press, 1987
46. Herbert Ponting, *The Great White South*, Duckworth, 1921
47. Laurence H. Puttnam and Ware Myers, *Measures for Excellence*, Yourdon Press, 1992

48. Christopher Ralling, *Shackleton*, BBC, 1983
49. Brian Rothery, *ISO9000*, Gower, 1991
50. Ann Savours, *Scott's Last Voyage - Through the Antarctic Camera of Herbert Ponting*, Sidgwick and Jackson, 1974
51. Robert Falcon Scott, *Scott's Last Expedition (2 vols)*, Smith, Elder & Co., 1914
52. Robert Falcon Scott, *Scott's Last Expedition*, Methuen, 1983
53. William Seymour, *Yours to Reason Why - Decision in Battle*, Sidgwick and Jackson, 1982
54. John Terraine, *The Road To Passchendaele*, Leo Cooper, 1977
55. *The Times History of the War*
56. J.R.R. Tolkien, *The Lord of the Rings*, Allen & Unwin, 1968
57. Wyn Craig Wade, *The Titanic - End Of A Dream*, Penguin Books, 1980
58. Geoffrey C. Ward, Ric Burns and Ken Burns, *The Civil War*, American Documentaries, 1990
59. Arnold and Betty Watson, *Roster of Valor - The Titanic Halifax Legacy*, 7 C'S Press, 1984
60. Gerald M. Weinberg, *An Introduction to General Systems Thinking*, John Wiley & Sons, 1975
61. Lauren Ruth Wiener, *Digital Woes - Why We Should Not Depend on Software*, Addison-Wesley 1993
62. John Winkler, *Winning Sales and Marketing Tactics*, Butterworth Heinemann 1989
63. Andrew Yule, *David Puttnam: The Story So Far*, Mainstream Publishing Co., 1988

Index

We'd like to hear from you ...

Only that way, will we know whether any of the material in this book has made a difference *to you*.

Write and tell us whether you tried any of the stuff, what you did, and what happened. Were you happy with the result? Did it change the way you work? Should there have been *other* things included in the book that might have made things easier for you?

You can call, fax, email or write to us. The addresses and numbers are shown below.

You may also be interested to know about ...

Project Management Briefing - the journal of Structured Project Management

Published by ETP, the Structured Project Management company. For a complimentary copy, call, fax, email or write to us. The addresses and numbers are shown below.

Silver Bullet - the complete system to run successful projects.

Is a software product for Windows which implements the approach detailed in this book. For more information, call, fax, email or write to us. The addresses and numbers are shown below.

ETP
The Structured Project Management Company
Moatstown House,
Athy,
Co. Kildare,
Ireland.

Tel.   +353 507 31989
Fax.   +353 507 31092
e-mail   taffy@gpo.iol.ie